Palgrave Studies in Cross-disciplinary Business Research, In Association with EuroMed Academy of Business

Reflecting the growing appetite for cross-disciplinary business research, this series aims to explore the prospects of bringing different business disciplines together in order to guide the exploration and exploitation of scholarly and executive knowledge. Each book in the series will examine a current and pressing theme and consist of a range of perspectives such as management, entrepreneurship, strategy and marketing in order to enhance and move our thinking forward on a particular topic.

Contextually the series reflects the increasing need for businesses to move past silo thinking and implement cross-functional and cross-disciplinary strategies. It acts to highlight and utilize the emergence of cross-disciplinary business knowledge and its strategic implications across economic sectors, geographic regions and organizational types.

Published in conjunction with the EuroMed Academy of Business, books will be published annually and incorporate new scientific research works developed specifically for the book or based on the best papers from their conferences. Over the last decade EuroMed have developed a cross-disciplinary academic community which comprises more than 30,000 students and scholars from all over the world.

Each submission is subject to a proposal review and a double blind peer review. For further information on Palgrave's peer review policy please visit this website: https://www.palgrave.com/gp/book-authors/your-career/early-career-researcher-hub/peer-review-process. For information on how to submit a proposal for inclusion in this series please contact Liz Barlow: liz.barlow@palgrave.com.

For information on the book proposal process please visit this website: https://www.palgrave.com/gp/book-authors/publishing-guidelines/submit-a-proposal

More information about this series at
http://www.palgrave.com/gp/series/15956

Demetris Vrontis
Alkis Thrassou • Yaakov Weber
S. M. Riad Shams
Evangelos Tsoukatos
Leonidas Efthymiou
Editors

Business Under Crisis Volume I

Contextual Transformations

palgrave
macmillan

Editors
Demetris Vrontis
School of Business
Univesrity of Nicosia
Nicosia, Cyprus

Alkis Thrassou
School of Business
University of Nicosia
Nicosia, Cyprus

Yaakov Weber
School of Business Administration
College of Management
Rishon Lezion, Israel

S. M. Riad Shams
Newcastle Business School
Northumbria University
Newcastle upon Tyne, UK

Evangelos Tsoukatos
Department of Accounting and Finance
Hellenic Mediterranean University
Heraklion, Greece

Leonidas Efthymiou
School of Business
University of Nicosia
Nicosia, Cyprus

ISSN 2523-8167 ISSN 2523-8175 (electronic)
Palgrave Studies in Cross-disciplinary Business Research, In Association with EuroMed Academy of Business
ISBN 978-3-030-76566-8 ISBN 978-3-030-76567-5 (eBook)
https://doi.org/10.1007/978-3-030-76567-5

Cover illustration: Daniele Levis Pelusi via Unsplash.com

This Palgrave Macmillan imprint is published by the registered company Springer Nature Switzerland AG.
The registered company address is: Gewerbestrasse 11, 6330 Cham, Switzerland

Contents

Notes on Contributors

Xanthippe Adamoglou is an adjunct lecturer at the University of Macedonia, Thessaloniki, Greece, where she teaches international business management, international business relations, and analysis of the international business environment. She holds a PhD from the Department of Balkan, Slavic and Oriental Studies, University of Macedonia. She is simultaneously a postdoctoral researcher in the Department of Business Administration at the University of Macedonia. She has worked as a research analyst in the Ministry of Macedonia and Thrace, Thessaloniki, Greece.Adamoglou is the author of many academic papers published in top international refereed journals. Moreover, her academic work is in the proceedings of numerous international scientific conferences, such as EIBA and EBEEC. Her academic interests include a wide range of subjects such as foreign direct investments, entry mode strategies, institutional theory, and coevolution theory. Adamoglou besides her academic background has also worked as an accountant assistant and as a finance liaison officer in the private sector.

Alessandro Augurio is a research fellow in management at the Department of Economics of the University of Campania "Luigi Vanvitelli" in Capua. He achieved a PhD in entrepreneurship and innovation at the Second University of Naples, during which he began to face the phenomenon of servitization in the manufacturing industries. He was a visiting PhD in 2015 at the University of Bedfordshire in Luton. He collaborates with the chairs of management and firm-market relationships at the Department. His main research areas are servitization, digitalization, and e-mobility.

Asha Bhatia is the director of research at Universal Business School. She has 23 years of work experience. She holds a PhD in management studies and has served as a strategist and policy maker in the social sector. She is a keen researcher, over 22 of her research papers have appeared in leading peer-reviewed international journals of repute, and she has authored a book chapter, "Universal Brotherhood Through Yoga", which was released by the Hon. Vice President of India and completed four funded research projects. She is the only professor selected from India to the 15-member board of the ENACTUS Global Faculty Research Network, where she represents Asia. She has won numerous accolades—Distinguished woman in the field of management—Global women summit India—2019 and Education excellence award for Social and Economic Development, Azerbaijan, 2019. She has conducted numerous MDPs for Mumbai Police and the Indian Navy.

Ravi Teja Boddapati holds a bachelor's degree in the field of engineering and is pursuing his MBA in marketing from the Universal Business School. His interests lie in entrepreneurship. He has work experience in logistics industry.

Diego Campagnolo is Associate Professor of Business Organization at the University of Padua. He is also a research fellow of the NCMM of Ohio State University and Affiliate ICRIOS of the Bocconi University of Milan. He is the scientific director of the MBA for entrepreneurs of CUOA Business School. He obtained a PhD in economics and management at the University of Padua. He has been visiting at the Ohio State University, the Guangzhou University, and the Boston University. His research interests include organizational design, organizational resilience, organizational modularity, innovation in knowledge-intensive business services, and internationalization processes of SMEs. He has been the Italian principal investigator of the European research project sponsored by JP Morgan Chase Foundation "Business Resilience Among

Disadvantaged Groups: A European Study" in cooperation with the Enterprise Research Centre, UK. His work has been published in *International Journal of Management Reviews, Industry & Innovation, Journal of Organization Design, The IMP Journal, Global Business and Management Research: An International Journal* and other international journals and books with international editors.

Laura Castaldi is Assistant Professor of Business Economics and Management at the Department of Economics of University of Campania "Luigi Vanvitelli". She received her PhD in entrepreneurship and innovation from the Second University of Naples. She was a visiting scholar in 2004 and a visiting research scholar in 2015 at the Snider Entrepreneurial Research Center, the Wharton School. She teaches innovation management and coordinates the technology transfer activities at the Department of Economics, University of Campania "Luigi Vanvitelli". Her main research areas are knowledge management, inter-organizational collaborations, growth dynamics of firms operating in innovative industries, entrepreneurship and firm creation, entrepreneurship education, digitalization, and servitization.

Teresa Cerchiello is a PhD student in Entrepreneurship and Innovation in the Department of Economics of the University of Campania "Luigi Vanvitelli". Since 2018 she has been collaborating with the chairs of economics and business management and business-market relations of Prof. Clelia Mazzoni and with the chair of economics and innovation management of Prof. Laura Castaldi at the Department of Economics of the University of Campania "Luigi Vanvitelli". She is an appreciator of the subject in economics and business management and economics and innovation management. Her main research fields are "digital technology entrepreneurship" and "e-mobility". She is the author of several papers on these issues presented at different conferences in Europe, including Italy.

Panagiotis E. Dimitropoulos is a faculty member of the Department of Sport Organization and Management, University of Peloponnese. He has a PhD in Economics from Hellenic Open University, and an MA in Banking and Finance from Bangor University. He has taught sport financial management and investments for several years at undergraduate and graduate levels. His research interests include sport finance and corporate accounting and financial analysis. His articles have appeared in international academic journals such as *European Sport Management Quarterly*, *International Journal of Sport Finance*, *International Journal of Sport Management and Marketing*, *British Accounting Review*, *Corporate Governance: An International Review*, *Journal of Economic Behavior and Organization*, and *R&D Management*.

Leonidas Efthymiou is Assistant Professor in Organisation, Tourism and Hospitality Studies at the University of Nicosia. He previously worked at Unicaf University, Intercollege, Pearson Education, and the University of Leicester. He has also taught online for Universities in Europe, Africa, and the United States. He also travels frequently to Africa, in his capacity as instructional designer. He has co-edited and published several books, articles, media reports, policy papers, and encyclopaedia articles. His research output lies at the intersection of employment, digitization, and education. He has received a number of awards, including the best PhD Thesis award, by the Academy of Management in 2011, Boston Massachusetts. Prior to this, he trained at the University of Leicester (PhD, MSc), Derby (BA), and the Higher Hotel Institute Cyprus (Dip. Hons).

Mara Franco holds a PhD in Business and Management Studies from the School of Economics and Management of the University of Porto. She is an assistant professor lecturing curricular units in the Marketing and Strategy fields and an integrated researcher of CiTUR-UMa. She coordinates research in carrying capacity in tourism, consumer behaviour in tourism and digital marketing applied to tourism services. She is an author of scientific papers published in indexed international journals and of publications presented in peer-reviewed conferences. In 2020, she won a Literati Award for Excellence, supported by Emerald Publishing, with a Highly Commended Paper. Also, she is co-editor-in-chief of the *European Journal of Tourism, Hospitality and Recreation*.

Martina Gianecchini holds a PhD from the University of Udine and is Associate Professor of Human Resource Management at the University of Padova, Italy. She is the scientific director of the Executive Master in

Human Resource Management at CUOA Business School (Italy). She has been a visiting scholar at Université de Montréal (Canada), Katholieke Universiteit of Leuven (Belgium), and Liaoning University of Shenyang (China). She is HR Ambassador for the Academy of Management, and she is a member of the European Academy of Management and European Group of Organization Studies. Her main research interests are on career management, labour market dynamics, and entrepreneurship especially in cross-cultural contexts. She is a member of the international research group 5C (Cross-Cultural Collaboration on Contemporary Careers—https://5c.careers/), which involves more than 30 countries and aims at understanding meanings, determinants, and outcomes of careers around the world. Her work has been published in *Organization Studies*, *Journal of Organizational Behavior*, *International Journal of Human Resource Management*, *Human Resource Management Journal*, *Human Resource Management Review*, *European Management Journal*, and other journals.

Prashant Goyal holds a bachelor's degree in the field of commerce and is pursuing his MBA in marketing from the Universal Business School. His research interests lie in entrepreneurship. He has written and published in a Scopus indexed international journal of repute. He works at Enactus UBS.

Paolo Gubitta, PhD from the Ca' Foscari University of Venice, is Full Professor of Business Organization and Entrepreneurship at the University of Padova, Italy. He is scientific director of the Digital and Hybrid Jobs Lab at the University of Padova and of the Center for Entrepreneurship and Family Business at CUOA Business School (Italy). He has been an adjunct professor at the College of Business of University of Michigan Dearborn (US) (2006–2015). He held visiting professor positions at L. Recanati Business School Tel Aviv University (2014), University of Lugano (2013–2014), Guangzhou University (2012), and Sun Wah International Business School of Liaoning University (2011). His main research topics are entrepreneurship, organization of family firms, science- and technology-based new ventures and KIBS, digital transformation of jobs (hybrid jobs). He is the author and co-author of several books contributions. His works have been published in *Family Business Review*,

Entrepreneurship and Regional Development, *Journal of Technology Transfer*, and *International Journal of Entrepreneurship and Innovation Management*.

Komal Jain holds a master's and a bachelor's degree in the field of Commerce and is pursuing her MBA in Finance from the Universal Business School. Her research interests lie in entrepreneurship and financial modelling. She is a part of the Research Department at Enactus UBS.

Hans Rüdiger Kaufmann, after many international academic engagements, was officially ranked Full Professor Marketing at the University of Nicosia (February 2013). Since the beginning of 2016 he is also affiliated with the University of Applied Management Studies Mannheim. He has been a launching member and president (2007–2009) of the international research network on consumer behaviour, CIRCLE. Furthermore, he is a launching member, vice-president and previous research coordinator of the EuroMed Research Business Institute (EMBRI), and member of the editorial board of the network's Emerald journal, the *EuroMed Journal of Business*. From 2012 to 2016, Rudi was a member of the Board of the AMA Global Marketing SIG as vice chair communications. He is a member of the editorial board of a variety of other journals and author/editor of 15 books (mainly in the field of consumer behaviour, marketing and entrepreneurship) and 6 e-books (Thompson Reuters accredited conference proceedings). In addition, he is an associate editor of the ABS-ranked *World Review of Entrepreneurship, Management and Sustainable Development*, a visiting professor of John Moores University Liverpool, the International Business School of Vilnius University, and a visiting professor of the University of Vitez (Chair of Entrepreneurship). He co-initiated and participated in a variety of EU-supported research projects and participates as invited speaker on several global occasions.

Vasiliki Kounnou is a PhD student in the University of Macedonia, Thessaloniki, Greece. She holds a Master of Science degree from Erasmus University, Rotterdam, the Netherlands, with specialization in Health Economics. As a PhD student, she provided assistant teaching in the Department of Balkan, Slavic and Oriental studies in the University of Macedonia, Thessaloniki, Greece, where she is enrolled. Her research interests focus on industrial economics and health economics, and her dissertation explores the determinants of firm profitability in the Greek pharmaceutical industry.She is the author of academic papers published in international journals, and she has attended international academic conferences. She has worked as an administrative officer in health care sector and as a project management assistant in a consultancy firm in Thessaloniki. She works in the Department of Master's Programs in Medical School in Aristotle University in Thessaloniki, Greece.

Dimitris Kyrkilis is Vice Rector of Administrative, Academic and Student Affairs, University of Macedonia, Greece, since August 2018. He is a professor in the Department of Balkan, Slavic and Oriental Studies, University of Macedonia, Thessaloniki, Greece, where he teaches international business and regional integration in Eastern and Southeastern Europe, and international development and global South. He received a PhD in Economics from the University of Manchester, and his academic interests include a wide range of subjects such as economic development and investments in Eastern Europe and Balkans, international business and foreign direct investment, international economics, and economic development and growth. He has a great experience in management in academic and student affairs as a director of the graduate programme "MA in Politics and Economics of Eastern and South-eastern Europe" Department of Balkan, Slavic, and Oriental Studies, University of Macedonia, Thessaloniki, Greece, and head of the Department of Balkan, Slavic and Oriental Studies in the University of Macedonia, Thessaloniki, Greece. He is the author of over 300 articles, and half of them are published in top international refereed journals. He wrote seven scientific books and attended more than 50 top international conferences. He has supervised more than five research projects and has more than 100 citations.

Simona Leonelli is a research fellow at the University of Padova (Italy). Previously, she was a postdoctoral research fellow at the University G. d'Annunzio Chieti-Pescara (Italy), where she received her PhD in Accounting, Management and Finance in 2017. She was visiting at Skema Business School (Nice, France). Her main research interest lies in the area of entrepreneurship (i.e., personality traits, individual resilience, start-ups' innovation, and entrepreneurial orientation), and business organization (i.e., organizational resilience and ambidexterity). Her articles have appeared in numerous journals including *Journal of Small Business and Entrepreneurship* and *Journal of Entrepreneurship and Small Business*. She is the author of two books: *Entrepreneurial Personality and Small Business Management*, and *Sustainable Entrepreneurship*. She is an adjunct professor of business organization, behaviour in organization, and organization design and governance of human capital at the University of Padova.

Clelia Mazzoni is Full Professor of Management in the Department of Economics at the University of Campania "Luigi Vanvitelli". Her previously held posts at the same university include head of department and dean of the economics faculty. She has been a co-ordinator of the PhD Program in Entrepreneurship and Innovation, and a member of the Senate House and the Board of Administration at the same university. She has also been a member of the Assessment Unit of the University of Naples "L'Orientale". She is the author of several monographic studies, and many articles are published in scientific journals both in Italy and abroad. She is head of the Economics Division of the review Diritto ed Economia dei Mezzi di Comunicazione (Law and Economics of the Means of Communication), of which she is a co-founder. Her main research fields include the communication industry (from media publishing to mobile communication) and e-mobility sector, the market segmentation models, the market and competition analysis, the systemic analysis of enterprises and relations between firms and the macro-environment, and the economics of complexity.

Larisa Mihoreanu is a medical doctor and economist holding a Magna Cum Laude PhD in Medical Business Administration and Management next to postdoctoral qualifications in Neuropharmacology acquired in prestigious universities of Romania, France, and the UK. As Associate Professor at Bucharest University of Economic Studies, she focuses her research on health policies. Her academic competences and robust expertise nurture the passion for results, and the high commitment for excellence empowers a multicultural professional experience and global awareness in the field. Dr. Mihoreanu represented Romania as the Health Technologies Assessment expert, member of Pharmaceutical Products and Medical Devices WP, during Romania's Presidency of the Council of the European Union. She founded KCL Guy's Researchers Society, chaired Young Researchers' Committee within European Society for Complex Systems and set up Alternative Sciences Association. She has won the 2009 CRS Jorge Heller Journal of Controlled Release Outstanding Paper Award and the 2017 MEDICS International Conference Award. Her publications include a book, four chapters, and over 40 articles highly cited in outstanding journals.

Rita Mura is Lecturer in Management at Foro Italico University, Rome (Italy). She received her PhD in Economics and Finance at the University of Rome "Sapienza". Her main research interests are focused on sustainability, corporate social responsibility, and social accountability in sport organizations.

Mario Nicoliello is a researcher in Business Administration at University of Genoa, Italy, where he teaches management accounting and business administration. His research interests are in accounting education, accounting history, sport management, and performance measurement in public sector. In particular, in sport sector his research regards the management of big sport events.

Giorgio Portaluri is a PhD student in Sport Management and Economics at "Foro Italico" University, Rome (Italy). His main research interests lie on climate change effects on sport business as well as on environmental sustainability practice and innovation in sport management.

Ursula Schinzel, an online tutor at Unicaf University, has a Doctorate in Business Administration and teaches online and delivers Webinars: Doctoral Supervision, Strategic Leadership (in English and French), Theories of Management (in English and French), Research, MBA Dissertation, Professional Development, Organizational Strategy and Planning, Innovation, Management, and Social Psychology. She also teaches German, French, and Luxembourgish languages with CapLangues Luxembourg, and Sports with Ville de Luxembourg. She studied international business, management, and human resources in London, Paris, and Saarbrücken (Germany) with internships in the United States. Her areas of research interest include responsible leadership, cross-cultural management, e-HRM, digital recruitment, multicultural and multilingual environments, language and cultural dimensions following Hofstede and Schein, innovation and change. She delivers lectures and keynote speeches at international conferences (Academic OASIS, AIB, ANZIBA, BAM, EIASM, EIBA, EURAM, EUROMED, Organization Management, the Learner) in German, English, French, Italian, Spanish and Luxembourgish. She publishes in *Journal of Strategic and International Studies* (*JSIS*), *Journal of Customer Behaviour* (*JCB*), *Journal of Business and Economics* (*JBE*), and *World Review of Entrepreneurship, Management and Sustainable Development* (*WREMSD*). She is the book author with Frieling-Verlag Berlin, and a member of the editorial board of *Journal of Academic Oasis* (*JOASIS*), *JSIS* and *International Journal of Organizational Analysis* (IJOA; Emerald).

S. M. Riad Shams is a lecturer at the Newcastle Business School, Northumbria University, UK. He has published eleven books, contributed articles to top-tier international journals, and guest-edited for various reputable journals, including the *Journal of Business Research*, *Journal of International Management*, *International Marketing Review*, and *Technological Forecasting and Social Change*. He is the founder and co-editor of book series *The Annals of Business Research* and *The Palgrave Studies in Cross-disciplinary Business Research*. His research interests are in the areas of organizational identity, brand and reputation management; strategic management and sustainable development; and stakeholder relationship management focusing on people, planet and profit, strategic agility in international business, and pedagogic management. He obtained a second place in the Cambridge-Kent-Czinkota Competition for Excellence in International Business Research—2019 and is entered into the Kent Business School's Book of Honour. He received the Emerald Literati Award (Outstanding Paper) in 2019, the Emerald Literati Award (Outstanding Reviewer) in 2018, and the EuroMed Research Award in 2014.

Alkis Thrassou is a professor at the School of Business, University of Nicosia (UNic, Cyprus, EU). He holds a PhD in Strategic Marketing Management from the University of Leeds (LU, UK), as well as a B.Eng. (LU) and an MSc (UNic) in engineering. He is also a chartered marketer

(FCIM), a chartered construction manager (FCIOB), a chartered management consultancy surveyor (MRICS), and a senior research fellow of the EuroMed Academy of Business (SFEMAB/EMRBI). He is an associate editor of the *EuroMed Journal of Business* and the managing editor of book series *The Palgrave Studies in Cross-disciplinary Business Research*. He has extensive academic and professional/industry experience, has published over 160 works in the fields of Strategic Marketing and Management, and retains strong ties with industry, acting also as a consultant.

Alessandra Tognazzo is an assistant professor at the Department of Economics and Management at the University of Padova, where she received her PhD in 2012. She teaches a master course of family business and an undergraduate course of organization design. In 2010 she was visiting PhD at the Master of Research in Management, IESE Business School, Barcelona. She has received a "Best Ph.D. Proposal" Award from the Family Business Network-IFERA. In 2012 she co-authored a work which won the ASFOR-EMERALD Teaching Case Study-Competition. She is the author and co-author of several book contributions, and some of her management and entrepreneurship articles have appeared in international journals (*Family Business Review*, *Entrepreneurship and Regional Development*, *Journal of Technology Transfer*, *International Journal of Entrepreneurship and Innovation Management*, and *International Review of Entrepreneurship*). Her research interests include family business, SMEs, entrepreneurship, and leadership.

Evangelos Tsoukatos is Associate Professor of Management at the Hellenic Mediterranean University and an adjunct faculty at the University of Nicosia, Cyprus, and the Hellenic Open University. He holds a PhD in Management Science from the Lancaster University Management School (LUMS), UK, a BSc in Mathematics from the Aristotelion University of Thessaloniki, Greece, a postgraduate diploma and MSc in Operational Research from LUMS, UK. Dr Tsoukatos holds the position of vice president—operations and development at the EuroMed Research Business Institute. He has authored and edited books and journal special issues and has heavily published internationally in scholarly journals and presented in academic conferences. For his published research, he has gained wide recognition from his peers. He is an associate editor of the *EuroMed Journal of Business* (*EMJB*) and editorial board member in a number of international scholarly journals.

Francesca Vicentini is Associate Professor in Corporate Strategy at "Foro Italico" University, Rome (Italy). Her main research interests are focused on business models and team dynamics and, recently, on the role of circular economy.

Laura Mariana Vlăducă is a business lawyer, awarded with PhD in Business Administration and Law. She holds a lecturer position at Hyperion University of Bucharest, where she teaches international financial and commercial laws and informal economics. Vlăducă worked as the Board of Directors' adviser of the Alternative Sciences Association aimed to develop and implement a new conception and vision in the field of scientific research of excellence through real-time applications in education, market and society.Vlăducă is highly involved in promoting women and young people as scientists of international value. More than 40 papers of her work have appeared as books and articles in international outstanding reviews and journals.

Demetris Vrontis is a professor and vice rector for Faculty and Research and Professor of Strategic Marketing Management at the University of Nicosia, Cyprus. He is the founder and editor-in-Chief of the *EuroMed Journal of Business*, an associate editor of the *International Marketing Review*, an associate editor of the *Journal of Business Research*, and a consulting editor of the *Journal of International Management*. He has wide editorial experience and has successfully edited over 60 guest editions in top-tier journals. He is the president of the EuroMed Academy of Business, which serves as an important and influential regional academy in the area of business and management, and the managing director of Gnosis: Mediterranean Institute for Management Science. His work has widely appeared in about 300 refereed journals, 45 books, and 60 chapters in books, and he has presented papers to over 80 conferences around the globe. He is a fellow member and certified Chartered Marketer of the Chartered Institute of Marketing and a Chartered Business Consultant.

He is also serving as a consultant and is a member of the Board of Directors to several international companies.

Janhavee Ravindra Walvadkar is an Indian native who is a "Senior Specialist Human Resources" in the headquarters of an international organization in Germany. She holds her bachelor's degree in Commerce. After graduation, she moved to Germany in 2018 to pursue her master's degree. Walvadkar has graduated with a master's degree in Business Management with specialization in Human Resource Management at the University of Applied Management Studies in Mannheim, Germany; her master thesis explored the digital transformation of processes in an international organization, mainly focusing on learning and development.

Yaakov Weber is a professor and teaches courses on strategic management, mergers and acquisitions management, strategic alliances, corporate strategy, cross-cultural management, and global strategic management. He has lectured in various universities in United States (e.g. NYU), Western and Eastern Europe, and China, in graduate schools of business administration as well as executive programmes, in private and public organizations, as well as industrial associations for CEOs and directors. He also participates in, and conducts, international PhD seminars and PhD committees, and is a referee in international PhD exams. Weber's studies were published in top leading international academic journals, such as *Strategic Management Journal*, *Journal of Management*, *Management Science*, *Journal of Business Research*, *California Management Review*, and *Human Relations*. His papers have received more than 7000 citations in leading journals and books. Many of his papers were selected by various academic collections and were described as representing "the most significant new material" and "most important works published in Sociology" (in 1996). Other papers are "2nd most cited in last 5 years" (2010–2015) and "most read" (2011–2015), or "most downloaded" in 2017, in leading journals. He has served as an associate editor and in editorial boards of several journals and acts as a referee for numerous leading journals. He is a guest editor for special issues in leading journals, such as *California Management Review*, *Human Resource Management*, and *Journal of World Business*. Weber is the winner of the Outstanding Author Contribution Award. His book *A Comprehensive Guide for Mergers and Acquisitions*

(2014) was invited by *Financial Times*. This and his other books are available on AMAZON. Also, co-editor of three book series at EMERALD, Rutledge, and Palgrave Macmillan, Weber is co-founder and co-president (for the past ten years) of the EuroMed Business Research Institute (www.emrbi.org), the EuroMed Academy of Business, and the EuroMed Research Centre. Weber has been a senior consultant to CEOs, top executives, and directors in leading domestic and international companies—such as Coca-Cola, Dead-Sea Works, and Society of Israel Plastics & Rubber Manufacturers, largest international Engineering company in Israel, health-care organizations, the USA-Israel Chamber of Commerce, large and small organizations in the chemical industry, high-tech industry, and many others in various industries as well as to the largest international consulting firm in Israel. His large project of international consulting was to an international merger in Moscow, Russia. Weber has conducted numerous workshops to top executives in many countries. Recently he conducted workshop to the senior executives of one of the four largest investment companies in China.

List of Figures

List of Tables

1

Editorial Introduction: Crisis in Context

Alkis Thrassou, Leonidas Efthymiou, Demetris Vrontis, Yaakov Weber, S. M. Riad Shams, and Evangelos Tsoukatos

1.1 Book Context and Theoretical Foundations

Business under crisis is not an exemption. Crises, in fact, are often the driving force of change, be it technological, social, economic or other. And it is the most adaptive, reflexive, resilient and innovative companies that survive such conditions, in some cases even using them as springboards for development and growth at the product or market levels (Vrontis et al., 2012). And while crises range in nature, geography and

A. Thrassou • L. Efthymiou (✉) • D. Vrontis
School of Business, University of Nicosia, Nicosia, Cyprus
e-mail: thrassou.a@unic.ac.cy; efthymiou.l@unic.ac.cy; vrontis.d@unic.ac.cy

Y. Weber
School of Business Administration, College of Management, Rishon Lezion, Israel
e-mail: yweber@bezeqint.net

D. Vrontis et al. (eds.), *Business Under Crisis Volume I*, Palgrave Studies in Cross-disciplinary Business Research, In Association with EuroMed Academy of Business, https://doi.org/10.1007/978-3-030-76567-5_1

duration, and are often contextually unique, they also share commonalities in terms of their conditions, demands and challenges on businesses.

Even while writing these lines, several critical events have occurred around the world within a timeframe of a few hours. A military coup in Myanmar put billions worth of business investments at risk (Liu, 2021); a series of volcanic eruptions in the Hawaiian Islands stranded commercial airliners and caused damages to local businesses (Hawaiian Volcano Observatory, 2021); the world's biggest free-trade agreement came into force among Japan, China, South Korea, Australia, New Zealand and another ten Asian countries—which covers 2.2 billion people, with a combined GDP of $26.2 trillion (Errol, 2021). At the same time, thousands of businesses around the world remained temporarily closed due to COVID-19 (Sraders & Lance, 2020). At the more extreme end of the spectrum, other businesses, varying from small enterprises to multinational corporations, such as the 'beauty' firm L'Occitane and the car-rental company 'Hertz', filed bankruptcies and went permanently out of business (Ventura, 2020). And to add to these events, 40 active wars are currently taking place around the world, destroying communities and disrupting the economic and business activities of the nations involved. For many, this is 'business as usual' (Gewirtz, 2020). The non-linear nature of the external environment entails that crisis is unavoidable and should be accepted as an embedded business characteristic. Critical events stem from external forces, relating to political, environmental, social, technological, economic and legal changes, and hence the widespread use of 'PEST/LE' tool, coined by Francis Aguilar in 1964 (Rastofi & Trivedi, 2016).

In spite of its common and repetitive pattern, business under crisis can be contingent upon the uniqueness of its milieu, in combination with the

S. M. R. Shams
Newcastle Business School, Northumbria University,
Newcastle upon Tyne, UK
e-mail: riad.shams@northumbria.ac.uk

E. Tsoukatos
Department of Accounting and Finance, Hellenic Mediterranean University,
Heraklion, Greece
e-mail: tsoukat@staff.teicrete.gr

actions and choices made by individual businesses in its vein. This book aims to further our knowledge and understanding of these environmental conditions and identify the accords and dissonances of the context of business under crises, and how this might affect its content. The collection of chapters, herein, retains a macroscopic view of the topic and allows a comprehensive perspective on and holistic comprehension of the direct and peripheral forces shaping business under crisis.

1.2 Business Crisis at the Intersection of Technology and Human Behaviour

Existing and new technologies within an industry can be seen as opportunities or threats to businesses. Technological applications may offer solutions to business problems, or lay the groundwork for a crisis (Thrassou et al., 2020). This is because technology refers not to a single force, but rather to the processes through which people at the workplace act, function, plan and institutionalise. In this part of the book, we explore technology as a complex phenomenon that influences, and is influenced by human behaviour, often resulting to business crisis. To support this argument, we present below a few examples:

(a) **Impact on Employment**. Considerable business investments have been made in the field of technology, including robots, block chain, analytics and artificial intelligence, aiming to enhance workplace productivity and efficiencies (Efthymiou et al., 2019). However, while many of the activities carried out by workers today become automated, questions are raised about the future of work, and whether enough jobs will be available to employ everyone (Manyika, 2017).

(b) **Human Error**: The 1984 gas leak in Bhopal, India, killed thousands, whereas the radiation accident at Chernobyl two years later killed thousands more (Crandall et al., 2014). Technology failed due to human error. In both cases, contamination forced hundreds of businesses to close, limitations were imposed on agricultural production, and costs were added on manufacturing, among others.

(c) **Technology Coordination**. While technology offers ways out of the crisis, for some businesses, it is the crisis itself. Iconic organisations, which appeared to be slow in adopting, coordinating and adapting to new technologies, vanished. Some of the examples include Kodak and Blockbuster Video (Gershon, 2013).
(d) **Impact on Culture.** Although some cultures have a natural tendency towards digital payments and cashless technologies (e.g. the Swedish), other societies, such as the Greek, have a material attachment to cash (Batiz-Lazo & Efthymiou, 2016a). So when the Greek government imposed digital payments in an attempt to reduce its shadow economy and unrecorded transactions, some Greek businesses resisted. This is not the first time that governments have attempted to limit the growth of informal economy through cashless technologies—not necessarily in a successful manner (Batiz-Lazo & Efthymiou, 2016b).
(e) **Crisis in Work-Life Balance.** Technological improvements have an impact on our lives, both inside and outside the workplace. Also, digitisation has accelerated further, due to the COVID-19 crisis, which occurred in 2020. The correlation between technology and crisis, transformed our lives to a point where the environments inside and around the workplace have been interpenetrated. Online conferencing, online ordering, online learning, digital supply chains and distributed work, among others, made us do 'two years of digital transformation in two months' (Sparato, 2020). Technology is no longer restricted to the workplace. Rather, work as a social process, and aspects of our private life, have been entrapped within an interconnected socio-technical realm.

These examples, are indicative of the impact that technology has on businesses, and how its complex nature often results to crisis. Technology, nevertheless, is not a stand-alone factor. As we discuss later, a business crisis is often attributed to environmental events.

1.3 Environmental Crisis

The critical events occurring by environmental phenomena couldn't be absent from this book. At least one chapter focuses solely on environmental crisis, whereas other chapters refer to environmental factors as they relate to other subject matters. Environmental crisis can take many forms. It may appear as a single catastrophic event, or a prolonged emergency, whose outcome is likely to make a decisive difference. For instance, the Indian-Ocean earthquake and tsunami in 2004, was a single event. It killed an estimated 227,000 people. Several industries paralysed in 14 different countries for almost a year (Fenn, 2014).

The climate crisis, on the other hand, is a prolonged, critical condition, comprised by different events, which potentially impacts every country. The first, historic report warning of the imminent global warming appeared in a report by the US National Academy of Sciences in 1979 (Archer & Rahmstorf, 2012). Ever since, climate crisis has had a great influence on research and practice, with more than 10,000 scientific articles being published on an annual basis (with one of their keywords being 'climate').

Furthermore, the climate crisis is costly for businesses, as it increases the need for governance and comprehensive climate strategies. Also, there is an increasing pressure on businesses by stakeholder-groups, who advocate environmental risks and concerns (Coppola et al., 2019). However, while climate crisis is challenging and costly to some businesses, it offers great commercial opportunities to others. More specifically, opportunities created by the climate crisis, include 'improvement of environmental, financial and operational performance; improvement of relations with stakeholders; [and] the generation of opportunities for new business' (Seles et al., 2018, p. 771).

1.4 Business Under Crisis: Motion and Reprise

In the absence of institutional harmonisation, crisis becomes habitual and repetitive (Bresciani et al., 2013). To explain this further, let us consider the example of the eurozone. In 2010, Portugal faced the hardest and most challenging crisis of the past two decades (Pereira et al., 2020). A year later, in 2011, crisis became prevalent in Ireland. The collapsing construction market, which was financed by banks, forced Ireland to request recapitalisation by the European Union and the International Monetary Fund (Walker, 2018). For identical reasons, Spain requested a full bailout in 2012 (Veld et al., 2014). A year later, in 2013, crisis forced Cyprus to shut its banking systems for almost two weeks. In the end, recapitalisation was achieved by funding the banks with depositors' money—also known as a bail-in (Efthymiou & Michael, 2013, 2016). Two years later, in 2015, it was Greece's turn to shut down its banking system. A decline of the Greek GDP by 25% led the country to its third bailout programme (Galbraith, 2015). In all countries, the extent of the crisis, and its manifold manifestations, left a scar on businesses, entrepreneurship, employment and the society as a whole. These are just a few contextual examples, among many, revealing that in the absence of harmonised control mechanisms, crisis could be in motion within a certain economic block.

In addition, crisis demonstrates repetition patterns. It has a yesterday, today and tomorrow (not necessarily in that order). For argument's sake, let us re-consider the repetition patterns of the examples we discussed in the chapter's first paragraph.

- *'While these lines were written … A military coup in Myanmar, put billions worth of business investment at risk'* (Liu, 2021). However, a simple search on the net reveals that about 70 alleged coups took place around the world within two decades—on most occasions, with enormous effect on markets and businesses (Westerman, 2021).
- *'A series of volcanic eruptions… stranded commercial airliners, and caused damages in local businesses'* (Hawaiian Volcano Observatory, 2021). As a matter of fact, five days later, another set of volcanic eruptions occurred in Italy and Guatemala, disrupting airliners' and other business activities (Ramsay, 2021; Volcano Discovery, 2021).
- *'[T]housands of businesses around the world are temporarily closed* [or] *permanently out of business'* (Ventura, 2020). Since the 1700s, economic crises came to be known as re-occurring global events, often attributed to the capitalistic system itself (Koselleck & Richter, 2006).

The concept is associated with bankruptcies, trade, the stock market, debt, and even the insolvency of entire countries.

- *'These critical events, moreover, take place while 40 active wars around the world... disrupt the economic and business activities of the nations involved'.* While these lines were written, an interesting statement was issued by the UK government, calling world leaders for a temporary ceasefire to be implemented in all wars around the world, so that local populations can be vaccinated against coronavirus (Sabbagh, 2021). This 'temporary' call is also revealing of the repetitive nature of crisis, and its recurring impact on businesses and the society in general.

What such examples tell us is that the nature of a crisis often remains the same, whereas what changes is the context. Also, as we explain further, a crisis is not always about opposite dramatic events. Rather, as we explain further, business stability and crisis may have more elements in common than what many theorists and practitioners believe.

1.5 Conceptual Dualisms

Due to its perpetual and repetitive nature, business crisis has been a core concept for organisational literature for many decades. Most scholars have largely attempted to examine and explain critical events through dualistic approaches. Examples of dualisms include 'crisis-response', 'change-stability' and 'change-resistance' forms of analysis. By adopting such approaches, certain concepts are defined as opposites (Poole & Van de Ven, 1989).

Recent accounts, nevertheless, offer alternative ways of dealing with critical events. They reject traditional dualistic classifications, on the basis that they miss important elements surrounding the complexity of the subject matter (Santoro et al., 2018). One such approach suggests that organisations are not necessarily independent from crisis. On the contrary, they could be seen as being productive of, and generating crisis. In other words, organisations, along with crisis and stability, interpenetrate rather than mechanistically producing one another (Lewin, 1999). Within this dynamic, crisis and change can be explored as embedded characteristics of organisations. Mitleton-Kelly (2003), for instance, suggests that change becomes part of the organisation's culture rather than something that is seen as a reaction to events. Crisis and change are accepted elements, though not necessarily fully controlled—such as current trends and wider changes in society (e.g. Efthymiou, 2018; Efthymiou et al., 2020). Being more attuned to this idea, means that organisations are more likely to be thinking what the forces of crisis may be, and examine how they shape them in their favour (Lewin, 1999). Likewise, Farjoun (2017) maintains that stability and change are fundamentally interdependent. While being contradictory and conceptually distinct, they are also complementary, mutually enabling and a constituent of one another. Within this framework, several accounts in the field of strategic management prescribe how organisations can prepare for, survive and manage critical events, before, during and after they occur (e.g. Crandall et al., 2014; Koronis & Ponis, 2018).

This chapter, of course, does not aim at presenting an exhaustive list of crisis' characteristics and triggers. Given the variations of critical events, and how they manifest themselves in different contexts, such an attempt would be an impossible task. What we are mostly interested in is to emphasise the importance of 'context' and its complexities. For crisis, as a concept and notion, the context is crucial to any understanding of the meaning that should or could be attached to it. As the chapters of this book convey, crisis can be multi-layered, ambiguous and poly-dimensional, manifesting itself in different ways, depending on the context. Therefore, the current book adds to the existing literature, through a composition of contextual accounts, individual yet interconnected.

1.6 Book Content and Structure

Based on the foregoing analysis, this book presents another 11 chapters, aiming to advance our understanding on the specifics and complexities of businesses under crisis. The careful selection of chapters in the book serves multiple purposes, whereas, the value is both contemporary and historical. First, the chapters contextualise the latest critical events in companies, industries and sectors around the world. They inform us on the nature of the crisis and its impact, along with implications for practitioners and scholars. Second, the book serves as a time-capsule, encompassing original, contemporary accounts, while offering lessons for future consideration. So that future readers (managers, theorists or students) can return to the book, evaluate individual cases and think of the things that can/could be done to either respond to or prepare for a crisis.

Moreover, the first two chapters can be located in the broader field of finance. Chapter 2, titled 'US Foreign Direct Investments in the Eurozone: A Distance Analysis in View of Global Crisis—Evidence from the Manufacturing Sector', examines how multinational enterprises (MNEs) respond to the forces of the post-crisis environment in conjunction with distance. Drawing on a sample of 85 US foreign expansion cases to five eurozone countries, the authors (Kyrkilis Dimitris, Adamoglou Xanthippe and Vasiliki Kounnou) hypothesise that, under crisis conditions, institutional distance has a negative impact, whereas economic distance has a positive one on the FDI attraction of countries hit by crisis. The countries involved are Greece, Ireland, Italy, Spain and Portugal. The model hypotheses are tested through the random effect model, applied to the panel data set. The chapter's results reveal that economic distance has a statistically significant negative effect on US outflows to eurozone economies. In addition, institutional distance also has a negative effect on such outflows. The chapter contributes to our understanding of foreign investments under crisis conditions through a set of managerial implications and recommendations for future research.

Then, Chap. 3 provides empirical evidence regarding the impact of litigation risk on audit and non-audit fees during and after the 2008 financial crisis. The author Panagiotis Dimitropoulos adopts a panel cross-sectional regression model in order to analyse the fees' cost-structure. The sample is comprised by 93 non-financial companies listed on the London Stock Exchange (LSE). The empirical results of this research suggest that the litigation risk during the FC period do not influence the level of both auditing and non-auditing fees in the UK. After the FC period, nonetheless, clients have exerted the fee pressure on their auditors to limit the non-auditing service fee payments.

Subsequently, Chap. 4 explores the impact of crisis on SMEs. More specifically, the authors (Diego Campagnolo, Martina Gianecchini, Paolo

Gubitta, Simona Leonelli and Alessandra Tognazzo) are interested in SMEs' resilience to crisis. Using a descriptive approach on a sample of Italian SMEs, the chapter investigates the causes undermining their survival and the actions undertaken to counter the effects of a crisis. While proactive actions are limited due to their reduced resources, their fast decision-making processes can facilitate the identification of effective concurrent actions. Findings contribute to the debate in the field of resilience and crisis management by advancing current understanding of the relationship between sources of threats and response actions in SMEs.

The following two chapters look into customers' changing consumption patterns. Chapter 5, titled 'Changes in Consumption Patterns of Tourists After the COVID-19 Pandemic', communicates the transformation of the tourism experience. More specifically, the author (Mara Franco) explains how the crisis conditions transform and redefine tourists' preferences and the market as a whole. Changes concern a shift from authentic experiences guided by native people, to experiences confined to 'home', made possible by advances in technology. Changes in consumption patterns of tourists are uncovered, through a systematic literature review based on previous outbreaks, as well as the ongoing COVID-19. Amidst crisis, the chapter explores the opportunity to learn more about the consumer and their attitudes towards organisations. The analysis contributes to theory through a number of practical and managerial implications.

Also in the field of consumption, Chap. 6 (by Mazzoni Clelia, Castaldi Laura and Augurio Alessandro) explores the impact of COVID-19 on e-mobility. The analysis departs with the identification that COVID-19 drove sales in several industries to sharp decline. Supply chains have been interrupted, whereby some of the industries have to go through industrial reconversions. Also, consumers' consumption behaviour has changed the context in which e-mobility has been developing, raising questions about its worldwide evolution. Within this fluid economic context, the aim of the chapter is to depict changes in e-mobility, along with changing consumption patterns, by focusing on the elements influencing the diffusion of electric under COVID-19.

Moreover, the next two chapters explore businesses under crisis in two unique sport contexts. Chapter 7, by Rita Mura, Francesca Vicentini and

Giorgio Portaluri, explore the impact of climate crisis on the sport sector, along with challenges and opportunities for sports organisations. The analysis adopts a qualitative approach to investigate the climate adaptation and the dependence on climate crisis of the Italian Sports Federations. The results were analysed through the Natural Resources Dependent Theory (NRDT) and enabled four main issues to emerge: infrastructures, human resources, financial stability, networks and partnership. Even if the sport alone cannot turn back the flow of climate change, it represents an essential player, able to reach great audiences and solutions.

Chapter 8, titled 'The Impact of COVID-19 on the Mega Sport Events: The Case of the Postponement of Olympic Games "Tokyo 2020"', analyses the impact of the crisis on the business model of Olympic Games. Using the Stakeholder Theory framework, the chapter illustrates the consequences of the postponement on the different groups involved in the games. The research demonstrates how the crisis, initially considered a negative event, can instead prove to be an opportunity to formulate a new and more inclusive business model. Within this spirit, the author (Mario Nicoliello) explores how the crisis has enabled us to rethink about the Olympics in a more sustainable way.

Furthermore, two of the book's chapters can be located at the intersections of crisis, technology and Human Resources. Chapter 9, titled 'Business Under Crisis: Digital Transformation of Learning and Development', is authored by Janhavee Ravindra Walvadkar and Hans Rüdiger Kaufmann. The authors explore technology-led changes in the human resource department, and more specifically, the function of learning and development (L&D) in an international organisation. The study explores the assessment and transformation of manual processes into digitalised methods. The emphasis is on digital synchronisation of L&D. The main aim is to comprehend the bottlenecks of digital transformation and propose possible solutions to mitigate the challenges. The analysis draws on empirical data, collected through interviews and qualitative case studies. The chapter contributes to the field of digital transformation with suggested guidelines for organisations and practitioners.

Also in the field of human resources, Chap. 10 is titled 'Business Under Crisis Talent Management and Responsible Leadership in Luxembourg in Pandemic Times'. The author (Schinzel Ursula) looks into the link between talent management and responsible leadership in Luxembourg, before and during the COVID-19 crisis. The first part of the study was conducted prior to the pandemic outbreak (2019) through 26 semi-structured interviews. Then another 15 semi-structured interviews were conducted during the lockdown of 2020. The analysis identifies the acceleration of digitalisation as the primary impact on talent management. The chapter concludes with a set of questions for future research.

Reporting from the healthcare sector, Chap. 11 (titled, 'The Revealing Shades of the Pandemic Crisis in Romania', by Larisa Mihoreanu and Laura Mariana Vlăducă) deals with the impact of SARS-CoV2 pandemic. More specifically, it breaks into procurement, unauthorised operations with medical and pharmaceutical products, subjective interpretations of laws and the impact on the medical sector. Drawing on real examples, the analysis presents positive examples, as well as wrongdoings in the healthcare sector. As a way forward, the chapter suggests a versatile healthcare system, centred around patients and digital technologies.

Last but not least, Chap. 12, titled 'Transforming India's Logistics Industry During COVID-19 Crisis', tackles head on the challenges faced by the logistics industry in India. Drawing on interviews with business leaders, the authors (Asha Bhatia, Komal Jain, Ravi Teja Boddapati, and Prashant Goyal) identify a considerable reduction in the overall imports and exports during the lockdown period, whereas many small logistic-service providers have gone out of business. On the other hand, it was also interesting to note that some entrepreneurs have managed not only to survive but also to expand their business. The chapter adds to a body of literature, suggesting that crisis is often an opportunity for innovation and positive change.

Finally, in the foregoing analysis, we intentionally refrained from offering a definition for 'crisis'. Rather, we seek to add to the established ways of understanding critical events in businesses through a selection of contextual accounts. Based on their interest, readers may select particular cases, read from cover to cover or, simply, utilise the index to navigate the book.

References

Archer, D., & Rahmstorf, S. (2012). *The climate crisis*. Cambridge University Press.

Batiz-Lazo, B., & Efthymiou, L. (2016a). Introduction: The 360 degrees of cashlessness. In B. Batiz-Lazo & L. Efthymiou (Eds.), *The book of payments: Historical and contemporary views on the cashless economy* (pp. 1–10). Palgrave Macmillan.

Batiz-Lazo, B., & Efthymiou, L. (2016b). *The book of payments: Historical and contemporary views on the cashless economy*. Palgrave Macmillan.

Bresciani, S., Thrassou, A., & Vrontis, D. (2013). Change through innovation in family businesses: Evidence from an Italian sample. *World Review of Entrepreneurship, Management and Sustainable Development, 9*(2), 195–215.

Bruno Michel Roman Pais Seles, Ana Beatriz Lopes de Sousa Jabbour, Charbel José Chiappetta Jabbour, Paula de Camargo Fiorini, Yusliza Mohd-Yusoff, Antônio Márcio Tavares Thomé. (2018). Business opportunities and challenges as the two sides of the climate change: Corporate responses and potential implications for big data management towards a low carbon society. *Journal of Cleaner Production, 189*, 763–774. ISSN 0959-6526, https://doi.org/10.1016/j.jclepro.2018.04.113

Coppola, M., Krick, T., & Blohmke, J. (2019). Feeling the heat?: Companies are under pressure on climate change and need to do more. *Deloitte Insights*. Available at https://chapterzero.mx/wp-content/uploads/2021/05/Deloitte_Feeling-the-heat.pdf. Accessed 07 October 2021.

Crandall, W. R., Parnell, J. A., & Spillan, J. E. (2014). *Crisis management: Leading in the new strategy landscape* (2nd ed.). Sage.

Efthymiou, L. (2018). Worker body-art in upper-market hotels: Neither accepted, nor prohibited. *International Journal of Hospitality Management, 74*, 99–108.

Efthymiou, L., & Michael, S. (2013). When cards and ATM's are the only choice: A fortnight in Cyprus with no banking system, nor trust. MPRA Paper. Retrieved June 20, 2019, from https://mpra.ub.uni-muenchen.de/50646/

Efthymiou, L., & Michael, S. (2016). The Cyprus cash crash: A case of collective punishment. In B. Batiz-Lazo & L. Efthymiou (Eds.), *The book of payments: Historical and contemporary views on the cashless economy* (pp. 131–140). Palgrave Macmillan.

Efthymiou, L., Orphanidou, Y., & Panayiotou, G. (2019). The latest from the tourism front: Technology, innovation and disruption. *The European Financial Review, 4*(5), 39–43.

Efthymiou, L., Orphanidou, Y., & Panayiotou, G. (2020). Delineating the changing frontstage and backstage segregation in high-end and luxury hotels. *Hospitality & Society, 10*(3), 287–312. https://doi.org/10.1386/hosp_00025_1

Errol, O. (2021). Mega trade pact delivers. [online] Abmagazine.accaglobal.com. Retrieved February 9, 2021, from https://abmagazine.accaglobal.com/global/articles/2021/jan/business/mega-trade-pact-delivers.html

Farjoun, M. (2017). Beyond dualism: Stability and change as a duality. *Academy of Management Review, 35*(2), 202–225. https://doi.org/10.5465/amr.35.2.zok202

Fenn, C. (2014). The human and financial cost of the Indian Ocean tsunami – interactive. [online] *The Guardian*. Retrieved February 13, 2021, from https://www.theguardian.com/global-development/ng-interactive/2014/dec/25/human-financial-cost-indian-ocean-tsunami-interactive

Galbraith, J. (2015). The IMF's "Tough Choices" on Greece. In the 'Project Syndicate', published 16/06/2015. Retrieved June 20, 2015, from http://www.project-syndicate.org/commentary/imf-greece-debt-restructuring-by-james-k-galbraith-2015-06

Gewirtz, D. (2020). 2021: Now that disruption is business as usual, we must rise above crisis mode. *ZDNet*. Available at https://www.zdnet.com/article/2021-now-that-disruption-is-business-as-usual-we-must-rise-above-crisis-mode/. Accessed 07 October 2021.

Gershon, R. (2013). Innovation failure. Chapter 3. In A. B. Albarran (Ed.), *Media management and economic research in a transmedia environment*. Routledge.

Hawaiian Volcano Observatory. (2021). Kīlauea – Volcano updates. Usgs.gov. Retrieved February 7, 2021, from https://www.usgs.gov/volcanoes/kilauea/volcano-updates

Koronis, E., & Ponis, S. (2018). A strategic approach to crisis management and organizational resilience. *Journal of Business Strategy, 39*(1), 32–42.

Koselleck, R., & Richter, M. (2006). Crisis. *Journal of the History of Ideas, 67*(2), 357–400. Subject to https://about.jstor.org/subject to https://about.jstor.org/.

Lewin, A. (1999). *Complexity: Life at the edge of chaos* (2nd ed.). University of Chicago Press.

Liu, N. (2021). EU-China investment deal threatens US-Europe Relations. VOA News. Retrieved February 7, 2021, from https://www.voanews.com/east-asia-pacific/voa-news-china/eu-china-investment-deal-threatens-us-europe-relations

Manyika, J. (2017). Technology, jobs, and the future of work. *McKinsey Global Institute*. Available at https://www.mckinsey.com/featured-insights/employment-and-growth/technology-jobs-and-the-future-of-work. Accessed 07 October 2021.

Mitleton-Kelly, E. (2003). *Complex systems and evolutionary perspectives on organisations: The application of complexity theory to organisations*. Pergamon.

Pereira, J. M., Ribeiro, H., Ribeiro, B., Silva, A., & Alves, S. R. (2020). The impact of economic austerity measures on corporate performance: The case of an SME-dominated construction industry. In A. Thrassou, D. Vrontis, Y. Weber, S. M. R. Shams, & E. Tsoukatos (Eds.), *The changing role of SMEs in global business*. Palgrave Studies in Cross-disciplinary Business Research, In Association with EuroMed Academy of Business. Palgrave Macmillan. https://doi.org/10.1007/978-3-030-45831-7_6

Poole, M. S., & Van de Ven, A. H. (1989). Using paradox to build management and organizational theories. *Academy of Management Review, 14*, 562–578.

Ramsay, S. (2021). Guatemala: There's nowhere to hide – hundreds of thousands live in the shadow of three erupting volcanoes. [online] Sky News. Retrieved February 21, 2021, from https://news.sky.com/story/guatemala-three-active-volcanoes-are-erupting-at-the-same-time-and-if-things-get-bad-theres-nowhere-to-hide-12222334

Rastofi, N., & Trivedi, M. K. (2016). PESTLE technique: A tool to identify external risks in construction projects. *International Research Journal of Engineering and Technology (IRJET), 3*(1), 384–388. e-ISSN: 2395-0056.

Sabbagh, D. (2021). Dominic Raab calls for ceasefires to enable Covid vaccinations. [online] *The Guardian*. Published 17 February, 2021. Retrieved February 18, 2021, from https://www.theguardian.com/politics/2021/feb/17/dominic-raab-calls-for-ceasefires-to-enable-covid-vaccinations

Santoro, G., Vrontis, D., Thrassou, A., & Dezi, L. (2018). The internet of things: Building a knowledge management system for open innovation and knowledge management capacity. *Technological Forecasting and Social Change, 136*, 347–354.

Sparato, J. (2020). Two years of digital transformation in two months. Vice President for Microsoft 365. Retrieved February 9, 2021, from https://www.microsoft.com/en-us/microsoft-365/blog/2020/04/30/2-years-digital-transformation-2-months/

Sraders, A., & Lance, L. (2020). Nearly 100,000 establishments that temporarily shutdown are now out of business. [online] Fortune. Retrieved February 7, 2021, from https://fortune.com/2020/09/28/covid-buisnesses-shut-down-closed/

Thrassou, A., Uzunboylu, N., Vrontis, D., & Christofi, M. (2020). Digitalization of SMEs: A review of opportunities and challenges. In A. Thrassou, D. Vrontis, Y. Weber, S. M. R. Shams, & E. Tsoukatos (Eds.), *The changing role of SMEs in global business* (pp. 179–200). Palgrave Studies in Cross-disciplinary Business Research, in Association with EuroMed Academy of Business. Palgrave Macmillan. https://doi.org/10.1007/978-3-030-45835-5_9

Veld, J., Kollmann, R., Pataracchia, B., Ratto, M., & Roeger, W. (2014). International capital flows and the boom-bust cycle in Spain. *SSRN Electronic Journal.* Retrieved December 12, 2020, from https://ec.europa.eu/economy_finance/publications/economic_paper/2014/pdf/ecp519_en.pdf

Ventura, L. (2020). Global Finance Magazine – The World's Biggest Bankruptcies 2020. [online] *Global Finance Magazine.* Retrieved February 7, 2021, from https://www.gfmag.com/global-data/economic-data/worlds-biggest-bankruptcies

Volcano Discovery. (2021). Etna Volcano: Second spectacular eruption within 48 hours lights the night sky. Retrieved February 18, 2021, from https://www.volcanodiscovery.com/etna/current-activity.html

Vrontis, D., Thrassou, A., Chebbi, H., & Yahiaoui, D. (2012). Transcending innovativeness towards strategic reflexivity. *Qualitative Market Research, 15*(4), 420–437.

Walker, A. (2018). Eurozone bailout programme is finally over. [online] *BBC News.* Retrieved February 6, 2021, from https://www.bbc.com/news/business-45186511

Westerman, A. (2021). Myanmar's coup will be 'Painful' for already struggling economy, analysts warn. Published 5 February, 2021. [online] Npr.org. Retrieved February 18, 2021, from https://www.npr.org/2021/02/05/964405285/myanmars-coup-will-be-painful-for-already-struggling-economy-analysts-warn?t=1613651785135

2

US Foreign Direct Investments in the Eurozone: A Distance Analysis in View of Global Crisis. Evidence from the Manufacturing Sector

Xanthippe Adamoglou, Vasiliki Kounnou, and Dimitris Kyrkilis

2.1 Introduction

Given the mounting importance of distance in the international business (IB) domain, researchers have convincingly argued that "essentially, international management is management of distance" (Kostova et al., 2019, p. 467). Despite its importance, this emphasis revolved around mature and stable environments, circumventing the significance of rapidly turbulent and changing ones, that is environments in crisis (Powell, 1991; Scott, 1995; Wright et al., 2005). However, economic crisis is a condition that signals the destruction of an existing condition and leads to the creation of a new one. It brings about a new equilibrium that is mainly characterized by a new economic and "institutional contract" or by new rules of economic activity.

X. Adamoglou (✉) • V. Kounnou • D. Kyrkilis
University of Macedonia, Thessaloniki, Greece
e-mail: adamoglou@uom.edu.gr; kyrkilis@uom.edu.gr

D. Vrontis et al. (eds.), *Business Under Crisis Volume I*, Palgrave Studies in Cross-disciplinary Business Research, In Association with EuroMed Academy of Business, https://doi.org/10.1007/978-3-030-76567-5_2

In this direction, researchers (Courvisanos, 2009; Filippetti & Archibugi, 2011; Williams & Martinez, 2012) have demonstrated that foreign direct investment (FDI) patterns tend to change in crisis periods, meaning, in many cases, severe declines in FDI inflows and outflows. Other scholars have underlined that multinational enterprises (MNEs) are likely to exhibit a complex pattern of responses in times of crisis (Alfaro & Chen, 2010; Williams & Martinez, 2012). However, no research work, to the best of the authors' knowledge, has addressed the notion of distance under crisis conditions, which indicates the need for this research to fill the gap in relevant literature.

The aim of this research is to investigate the relationship between distance and FDI flow patterns in crisis conditions. More specifically, the chapter examines how multinational enterprises (MNEs) effectively respond to the unfavourable forces of the post-crisis environment in conjunction with the notion of distance.

In order to highlight the above, we follow the next two steps: First, we incorporate institutions under crisis conditions into the OLI paradigm (Dunning & Lundan, 2008), adopting the argument that "institutional distance between two countries is not a binary concept. Instead, institutional distance emerges as a process that depends on whether or not an organisational field is stable or in crisis" (Phillips et al., 2009, p. 340). Second, we adopt the argument by Phillips et al. (2009) that institutional and economic distance may and in fact should incorporate the conceptualization of institutional uncertainty, arguing that when uncertainty because of crisis increases, institutional and economic distances increase, as well. In this context, it is hypothesized that (a) in post-crisis conditions, institutional distance negatively influences the FDI attraction of countries hit by crisis. On the contrary, (b) economic distance positively influences the FDI attraction of such countries.

The paradigm of the recent financial and economic crisis in the context of United States (US)-European Union (EU) FDI flows emerges as a useful and under-examined setting for two reasons. First, US and the EU have extensive investment ties, the magnitude of which is clearly reflected by the continuous collaboration of their global supply chains, trade in services and mutual cross-border investments (Congressional Research Service, 2020). Second, the 2008 financial crisis clearly stresses that, despite the EU members having shared a Customs Union (CU), different countries experienced the global crisis at a different scale. This implies that institutional and economic distance are present, even within the same cluster of countries.

Bearing all these considerations in mind, the chapter contributes to the literature on the recent global financial and economic crisis and FDI flows in different and simultaneous aspects: First, it provides innovative insights into the way the notion of distance is conceptualized under unconventional circumstances, that is a global crisis. Second, it addresses the call of Chung and Beamish (2005) for a deeper understanding of the complex dynamics taking place in economies at times of crisis. Third, and in contrast to the mainstream and ad hoc selection of countries, the research emphasizes a cluster of economies that, despite their seemingly institutional similarity, still present heterogeneous institutional configurations, which implies that MNEs investing in them experience the notion of distance to a different extent. Last, by revealing a statistically significant effect of distance at times of crisis, we contend that the OLI paradigm may and should be extended into the context of MNEs market internationalization to include crisis conditions.

The sample consists of 85 foreign expansion cases concluded by US investors in five Eurozone countries, namely, Greece, Ireland, Italy, Spain and Portugal. The dataset is sourced from the US Bureau of Economic Analysis (BEA) and extends between the years 2009 and 2018. A random effect model has been applied to the panel data set to test hypotheses. The rest of the chapter is structured as follows: A literature review is presented, underlining that the conceptualization of distance has not been examined thus far in the light of crisis conditions. The section of US-EU FDI flows justifies why distance between the United States and the EU matters. The conceptual framework and hypotheses development are based on analysis. The econometric methodology has been employed in order to test the validity of the research hypotheses, to describe the sample data utilized when applying the econometric testing, and ultimately, to construct the model. Hypothesis testing presents the results produced by the empirical application of the model. Discussion analytically elaborates on empirical results and managerial implications before, finally, presenting suggestions for future research.

2.2 Literature Review

Before literature review takes place two things have to be emphasized. First, although there is abundant literature on FDI determinants, literature related to the latest global financial crisis and FDI flow patterns is scarce. Second, literature related to distance and the recent financial crisis is even more scarce. Given these conditions, such research proceeds with the delineation of the relationship between the recent global economic crisis and the different FDI patterns employing two paths: micro- and macro-level analysis.

In macro accounts, Ucal et al. (2010) have underlined that the recent global financial and economic crisis had a powerful impact on FDI. This takes place because, after recording an upturn in the years before the crisis, FDI decreased in the consequent years. In a similar manner, Poulsen and Hufbauer (2011), comparing the current FDI recession in response to prior FDI crisis, demonstrate that the 2008 financial crisis was the biggest one, thus far, leading to one of the greatest changes in FDI patterns. In their turn, Dorneana et al. (2012), integrating the relationship described earlier within the region of Central and Eastern European countries, produce two findings: First, economic growth has a significantly positive influence on FDI levels. Second, the global economic crisis is closely related to the effectiveness of the host country's regulatory institutions.

Focusing on the relationship between the economic crisis and the entry mode strategy domain before and after the Asian economic crisis, Chung and Beamish (2005) concentrate on the impact of policy reforms on the entry characteristics and MNEs survival in emerging economies. They demonstrate that MNEs take the form of wholly owned subsidiaries versus joint ventures (JVs), majority JVs versus minority JVs, and trading operations versus manufacturing operations in the post-crisis institutional environment. Similarly, Williams and Martinez (2012), through the reconciliation of Transaction and Institutional theory, empirically document the impact of the recent global crisis on MNEs entry mode choices, revealing a statistically significant interaction between the national-level governance and a temporal financial crisis.

In terms of MNEs performance, Alfaro and Chen (2010) reflected a complicated and heterogenous relationship between global crisis and FDI performance. More specifically, they have demonstrated that the effects of MNEs expanding into countries with a sharper crisis display a greater advantage over local firms. On the contrary, MNEs expanding into countries with a greater crisis incidence display less satisfactory performance in such countries.

In micro accounts, Alvarez and Görg (2007), comparing the reaction of MNEs and local firms to an economic downturn in Chile, support that MNEs behave much more differently than local firms in times of economic crisis. Tong and Wei (2009), emphasizing the FDI composition in emerging economies, illustrate that "the volume of capital flows *per se* has no significant effect on the severity of the credit crunch" (p. 1).

Considering all the aforementioned contexts, the research at hand proceeds and examines how MNEs effectively respond to the unfavourable forces of the post-crisis environment in conjunction with the notion of distance.

The US-EU FDI Flows

US expansion into EU economies provides an important research setting for the study of reconciliation between the recent global economic crisis and FDI flows for two reasons. First, the EU (EU-27) has been one of the most dynamic regions in terms of FDI activity worldwide and one of the largest recipients of FDI in the world (Villaverde & Maza, 2015). In 2015, the then EU-28 recorded the highest share of both inward and outward FDI stocks, that is 25.3% and 30.7% of worldwide FDI stock, respectively (UNCTAD, 2017). Similarly, in 2018, the EU economy comprised 21.8% (or $18.8 trillion)—excluding the UK, the amount comes to 18.5% (or $15.9 trillion)—of the global economy with Germany being the EU's largest economy followed by France with 15% and Italy with 11% (shares based on GDP values expressed in US dollars).

In this framework, the US has emerged as the largest investor in the EU, accounting for 25% of the total number of FDI projects in EU Member States during this period (23% of the total deal value). This close relationship is attributed to the extensive and globally significant trade and investment ties that have evolved since World War II, positively enhanced by the growth of global supply chains, trade in services and cross-border investment between the two continents.

The magnitude of FDI interaction between the US and the EU is also reflected in the activity structure of US FDI in the EU, which is dominated by manufacturing, banking and the financial sector (Congressional Research Service, 2020). In 2018, the most significant US country destinations in the EU were the Netherlands ($883.2 billion), the UK ($757.8 billion), Luxembourg ($713.8 billion) and Ireland ($442.2 billion). Moreover, in 2017, affiliates of US majority-owned MNEs in EU-28 had sales of $2.4 trillion and employed 4.4 million workers (Congressional Research Service, 2020).

Besides the close FDI activity between the two continents, the second reason justifying the choice of US expansion into the EU, and, more particularly, Greece, Italy, Portugal and Ireland, is that the EU depicts a unique and characteristic paradigm of multilevel governance (Nugent, 2010). The EU includes economies mainly categorized in the same cluster, that is market-based economies, each one of which, from a comparative institutionalism perspective, articulates "a unique national business system, i.e., a configuration of different socio-economic institutions interconnected in a coherent manner" (Konzelmann & Fovargue-Davie, 2012, p. 650). The 2008 financial and economic crisis clearly stressed such differences in the single currency zone.

In particular, EU members, despite sharing the euro common monetary union, experienced the financial and economic crisis to different scales, elucidating major concerns about the sustainability of the European edifice. In institutional terms, according to Ferrera (1996), this disparity is mainly attributed to institutional differences between North and South EU countries. The latter, in contrast to the former, are characterized by "a highly fragmented and 'corporatist' income maintenance system dominated by dualism and polarization in terms of income maintenance and pensions, in health care welfare mix (state/family/church/charity), in extensive clientelism and 'patronage machines', which distribute cash subsidies to political client groups" (Rhodes, 1996, p. 6).

Similarly, in economic terms, the disparity is attributed to structural differences between "exporting countries with current account surpluses (Austria, Belgium, Finland, Germany, the Netherlands, and, to a lesser extent, France) and domestic demand-led countries with current account deficits (Italy, Spain, Greece, Portugal, and, occasionally, Ireland)" (Johnston & Regan, 2014, p. iii). The outcome of this disparity was that the latter countries experienced different levels of both private and public debt that rendered them particularly vulnerable to different changes in confidence levels in international capital markets, and, subsequently, to different levels of fiscal problems (Johnston & Regan, 2014). In this framework, the apparent EU cohesion is still characterized by institutional and economic differences which emphasize the concept of distance even within a single edifice.

Conceptual Framework and Development of Hypotheses

Following Dunning and Lundan's argument (2008) that formal institutions (North, 1990) are important components for interpreting the determinants and outcomes of MNEs activity under unstable conditions, the research develops its conceptual framework based on formal institutions. This takes place because, in crisis times, formal institutions play a greater role than informal ones in foreign firms' FDI decisions, since host governments can change FDI policies rather quickly, while informal policies may need several years to change (Delios & Beamish, 1999).

In this setting, in Dunning's (1980, 1988) OLI paradigm a main location variable is institutional distance, which allows for the interdependence between the firm and national institutions at both micro- and macro-levels (Dunning & Lundan, 2008a). Thus, the specific ownership assets possessed by MNEs can be characterized in terms of particular assets, the ability of the firm to effectively coordinate the utilization of such assets and institutionally related assets, that is structural upheavals (McGuiness & Demirbag, 2012).

However, according to Phillips et al. (2009) institutional distance may also include institutional uncertainties, that is severe structural upheavals, such as strong knowledge voids, which "move" beyond the contemporary institutional distance conceptualization, or Liability of Foreignness (LoF). This argument is grounded on reasoning that, when MNEs internationalize, their activities abroad may encounter not only institutional contexts, where key institutions differ, but also contexts composed of institutions that are not well institutionalized.

These uncertainties are particularly important when considered in the light of economies in crisis conditions (Cantwell et al., 2010). In the long term, such economies in order to address institutional uncertainties implement drastic policy reforms. However, in short term, these reforms initiate a chaos in the way business environments operate. Drastic reforms shake the existing order of institutional setting and apply a new version of it. So, MNEs suffer a complicated institutional environment, which, in turn, makes it difficult for them to "interpret policy signals coming to them" (Chung & Beamish, 2005, p. 38).

In this direction, researchers (Mody, 1999; Newman, 2000) have argued that in pre-crisis conditions, there are sectors mainly affected by such changes. One of them, the manufacturing sector, which in pre-crisis conditions tends to be government protected, in post-crisis conditions is characterized by the implementation of neoliberal (IMF imposed) transformations that signal the "opening" of previously "closed" sectors. However, this "opening" leads MNEs to suffering institutional uncertainty, during and after a crisis, such as nationwide demonstrations and strikes, which disrupt labour forces, supply chains, raise the cost of capital, and subsequently, increase the costs of maintaining the personnel (Henisz & Delios, 2004). This condition forces MNEs subsidiaries to abstain from investing in such economies, and subsequently, negatively affect the capabilities of economies in crisis to attract FDI inflows (Persson & Tabellini, 2003; Acemoglu & Robinson, 2006). The outcome of this double-edged condition is that MNEs face a high degree of ambiguity and complexity, and, therefore, a greater degree of institutional uncertainty, which, in turn, increases the risk for international business, and subsequently, the institutional distance between home and host countries (Phillips et al., 2009). In this framework, and considering that institutional distance encapsulates the conceptualization of institutional uncertainty borne by crisis conditions, it is hypothesized that

Hypothesis 1 *In the post-crisis institutional environment of countries severely hit by the global economic and financial crisis, institutional distance negatively affects the ability of such countries to attract FDI flows.*

Considering that economic distance refers to the economic development between two markets (Ghemawat, 2001; Tsang & Yip, 2007), this, subsequently, leads us to reconcile economic distance with the institutional perspective of it, which refers to a wide range of market institutional, socio-economic and demographic factors that outperform the narrow conceptualization of economic growth (Dunning & Fortanier, 2007; Håkanson & Ambos, 2010). Such institutional perspective of economic distance, however, allows us to proceed by articulating two additional arguments: First, to extend and integrate the reasoning of Phillips et al. (2009) into economic distance, arguing that economic distance may also involve institutional uncertainty related to market institutions inefficiencies borne by crisis conditions in the country. Second, to integrate economic distance into the locational advantages of the OLI paradigm, arguing that ownership advantages are also translated into particular assets, the ability of the firm to effectively coordinate ownership advantages in relation to host markets' institutions inefficiencies.

In this context, the main argumentation considering economic distance is developed along two main strands: resource exploitation and resource exploration arguments. The latter argues that MNEs explore opportunities for new resources in countries more developed than their home country, in order to obtain strategic assets, including technology and management, and making expertise available in the host country.

Whereas, the former argues that MNEs invest in host countries that are less developed than their home country, in order to exploit and maintain their firm's specific ownership advantages. Such argument is particularly important concerning host countries that experience a crisis (Tsang & Yip, 2007), since the crisis leads to a transition phase, which, in turn, introduces the transformation from a "relationship-based, personalized transaction structure to a rule-based, impersonal exchange structure" (Peng, 2003, p. 275). Such a transition, however, invites a two-fold interpretation: On the one hand, a number of economic inefficiencies are underlined in crisis-facing economies, which must be addressed. On the other hand, MNEs derived from sound-structured institutions facing such inefficiencies, perceive them as opportunities to expand into countries-in-crisis and continue exploiting their own core competencies. This takes place because local firms, as opposed to MNEs which derive from well-institutionalized environments, are considered to be lagging behind in terms of technological, managerial and marketing expertise and less familiarized with liberal and open market-based economic systems (Child & Markuczy, 1993), especially those related with the manufacturing sector (Chung & Beamish, 2005), as presented in Hypothesis 1.

This comparison derives from Dunning's (1993) argument that it is not the absolute level of ownership advantages that determines the ability of a country's firms to penetrate a particular market, but the strength of these advantages vis-a-vis those of another country's firms. In this sense, host countries that are less economically developed, and subsequently, present economic distance from more developed ones, emerge as attractors of FDI activity. So, considering economic distance as a location variable that includes the institutional uncertainty borne by crisis conditions, it is hypothesized that

Hypothesis 2 *In the post-crisis institutional environment of countries severely hit by the global economic and financial crisis, economic distance positively affects the ability of such countries to attract FDI flows.*

2.3 Methodology

Data Collection and Sample

In order to test the hypotheses presented earlier, secondary data were collected by the US Bureau of Economic Analysis (BEA), the official agency of the American Department of Commerce (https://www.bea.gov/data/intl-trade-investment) for the time period 2009 until 2018. The data consist of the annual US FDI flows to five EU countries (Greece, Ireland, Spain, Italy and Portugal), listed in the following sectors: food, chemicals, primary and fabricated metals, machinery, computers and electronic products, electrical equipment, appliances and components, transportation equipment and other manufacturing. As of 2009, the American Department of Commerce has included 85 foreign equity investments, of which 50 are included in this research. The rest have been excluded because of incomplete data.

Dependent Variable

As mentioned earlier, the dependent variable of the model is the US FDI outflows from the manufacturing sector towards five EU countries from 2009 to 2018. The US FDI flows are expressed in million dollars and log transformation has been used to improve the performance of the model.

Independent Variables

Economic Crisis

Considering that the aim of the research is to investigate the behaviour of US FDI flows into five EU countries, in conjunction with the notion of distance framework in post-crisis conditions, two steps are followed in relation to crisis conditions: First, the construction of a time dummy variable to embody the effect of the economic crisis during and after the crisis. Such a dummy variable takes the value of 1 for the years of the financial crisis and the value of 0 for the years which were not affected by it. Second, the construction of two interaction terms, namely, economic distance and institutional distance. This takes place because interaction terms depict the marginal effect of including the dimension of crisis into the independent variables of economic and institutional distances. So, the institutional interaction term results from multiplying the institutional distance with the time dummy variable and the economic distance interaction term results from multiplying the economic distance with the time dummy variable.

Institutional Distance

The research approaches institutions as formal institutions, defining institutional distance as the extent of dissimilarity in relation to the formal institutions of two countries (Xu & Shenkar, 2002). The components chosen for constructing the index for formal distances relied on prior research (Wan & Hoskisson, 2003; Chao & Kumar, 2006; Gaur et al., 2007; Lee et al., 2014). In particular, three formal indicators were incorporated into the analysis: government effectiveness, political stability and absence of violence and rule of law. The formula for the calculation of this index is the modified formula for cultural distance based on the Kogut and Singh (1988) research:

$$\mathrm{ID} = \Sigma\left[\left(I_{ij} - I_{ik}\right)^2 / V_i\right] / n \tag{1}$$

where,

- ID is the aggregate institutional distance.
- I_{ij} is the index value for formal institution dimension between i (US) and j country (Greece, Ireland, Italy, Spain and Portugal).
- V_i is the variance of the index for dimension i.
- I_{ik} represents the index value for formal institution dimension between i (US) and j country (Greece, Ireland, Italy, Spain and Portugal).
- n is the total number of dimensions (regulative) used in institutional distance (government effectiveness, political stability, absence of violence and rule of law).

Economic Distance

The research approaches economic distance as GDP per capita differences, and more particularly, as the extent of GDP dissimilarities between two countries. The dataset is sourced from the World Development Indicators database of the World Bank (https://data.worldbank.org). GDP differences are expressed in constant prices of 2017. The formula for the calculation of economic distance is based on Kogut and Singh (1988) formula for cultural distance modified for economic distance. In this sense, the economic distance index is as follows:

$$ED = \Sigma\left[\left(GDP_{ij} - GDP_{ik}\right)^2 / V_i\right] / n \tag{2}$$

- GDP_{ij} is the gross domestic product in PPP between i (US) and j country (Greece, Ireland, Italy, Spain and Portugal)
- GDP_{ik} is the gross domestic product in PPP between i (US) and j country (Greece, Ireland, Italy, Spain and Portugal)
- V_i is the variance of the index for the dimension i
- n is the total number of the GDP dimension

The Model

In order to test the aforementioned hypotheses, the study was conducted using a random effect model with the least square method, since random effect models have at least two major advantages: first, it offers the possibility of estimating shrunken residuals. Shrunken residuals have been proposed to allow for uncertainty in estimates for small samples (Aitkin & Longford, 1986). This means that effect estimates, based on very few enterprises, are not given undue weight. Second, it accounts for differential enterprise effectiveness, meaning that the unobserved characteristics that influence US FDI flows are not correlated with institutional and economic distances. So, taking into consideration the aforementioned context, the variation across entities is assumed to be random and uncorrelated with the predictor or independent variables included in the model (Wooldridge, 2015). In this framework, the algebraic form of the function set to econometric testing is as follows:

$$\begin{aligned}\log FDI_{i,t} = a_0 + a_1 \log ED + a_2 \log FI + a_3\, ED * Dummy_{i,t} \\ + a_4\, FI * Dummy_{i,t} + v_{i,t}\end{aligned} \tag{3}$$

where US $FDI_{i,t}$ is the dependent variable of US FDI flows into the five EU countries (Greece, Italy, Spain, Portugal and Ireland) for the years from 2009 to 2018. The term a_0 is the constant term, log*Ed* and log*ID* are the independent variables of economic distances and institutional distances, respectively. $ED*Dummy_{i,t}$ and $ID*Dummy_{i,t}$ are the interaction terms of economic distances and institutional distances, respectively, multiplied by the dummy variable of the financial crisis. a_1 and a_2, a_3 and a_4 are independent variable coefficients, which would be calculated, and v_{it} is the composite error term.

2.4 Results and Testing of Hypotheses

Prior results are presented, and a number of tests have been applied. The first group of tests applies two panel unit root tests and examines the preciseness of the results, or else whether the results lack economic significance (Wooldridge, 2015). The first test refers to a panel unit root test, which examines whether the series of the model are stationary or contain a unit root (Wooldridge, 2015). The second form of tests refers to the Levin-Lin and Chu (LLC) and Pesaran and Shin panel unit root test (IPS), which test whether the null hypothesis has a unit root. Interpreted together these two tests can be summarized as follows: the *p*-value is less than 0.05 at the significance level of 5%, underlining that the null hypothesis is rejected and the alternative one for stationarity is accepted (see Table 2.1). Next, autocorrelation issues are addressed. In this setting, the Durbin-Watson statistic test has indicated the value of 1.72 (Table 2.2), implying that there is a slightly positive autocorrelation not sufficient to negatively affect the reliability of the present model.

Proceeding with the results of regression, first, the fit of the model is examined (Table 2.2). R^2 equals 0.56, implying that 56% of the variation of the output variables is explained by the independent variables and the model is statistically significant (Prob> $F = 0.000$) at the 5% level. So, the model at hand has a good explanatory power. In this framework, the results of the model indicate that both independent variables are statistically significant. In particular, the sign of the economic distance is negative and statistically significant, indicating that economic distance

Table 2.1 Panel unit root test results

Test	Variables	LLC	IPS
	Logfdi	-8.77840 (0.0000)*	-3.31133 (0.0000)*
	Loged	-8.08585 (0.0000)*	-2.51946 (0.0059)*
	Logfi	-7.68251 (0.0000)*	-2.80757 (0.0000)*

Authors' Design, 2020
*$p<0.05$; Eviews 9

Table 2.2 Results of panel linear regression–random effect specification

Variables	Y_{it} = logFDI
logED	-0.63 (0.00)*
logFI	0.45 (0.00)*
$ED\_D_{i,t}$	-0.56 (0.04)*
$FI\_D_{i,t}$	-0.089 (0.00)*
Constant	13.6
Numb.Observ	50
Adj R^2	0.56
Prob>F	0.000*
Durbin-Watson	172,364

Authors' Design 2020
*$p<0.05$; EVIEWs 9

negatively affects the ability of European countries to attract FDI flows. Furthermore, the sign of institutional distance is positive and statistically significant, indicating that institutional distance positively affects the ability of the EU countries to attract FDI flows.

However, in order to present a holistic approach of the effect of each independent variable on the dependent one, it is important to examine not only the effect of the main independent variables (economic and institutional distances) on the dependent one but also the effect of interaction terms on the dependent variable. This allows us to precisely compare and depict how the inclusion of the crisis dimension into the model affects the dependent variable.

With this aim in view, the results show that the effect of the interaction term of economic distance continues to be negative and statistically significant, stressing that the marginal effect of the crisis has not changed the impact of economic distance on the dependent variable. Concerning the effect of institutional distance, it is indicated that the effect of the main variable of institutional distance on the dependent variable is statistically significant and positive. Whereas the effect of the interaction term of institutional distance changes, documenting a negative and statistically significant effect on the dependent variable.

Testing the Hypotheses

Taking into consideration all mentioned earlier, it is indicated that the overall marginal effect of institutional distance (the intercept term) shows, *ceteris paribus*, a negative impact on US FDI flows into the five EU countries. On the contrary, economic distance, *ceteris paribus*, shows a positive effect on US FDI flows into the EU countries, for the period analysed. In particular, Hypothesis 1 suggested that institutional distance negatively affects the ability of European countries to attract FDI flows; this is strongly supported by the regression results indicating that formal institutions reduce the volume of US FDI into those countries. Furthermore, Hypothesis 2 suggested that economic distance positively affects the ability of European countries to attract FDI flows; it is indicated that, in the post-crisis framework, economic distance does not function as an incentive for the EU countries to attract US FDI flows.

2.5 Discussion, Managerial Implications and Avenues for Future Research

Discussion

Despite the progress made in distance literature, little is known about how the conceptualization of distance behaves under crisis conditions. This study focuses on the need to investigate how MNEs effectively respond to the unfavourable forces of the post-crisis environment in conjunction with the notion of distance. The context of the present analysis is the US-EU FDI flows. To this end, the study makes the following contributions: It provides innovative insights into the way the notion of distance is conceptualized under global crisis circumstances. It addresses the call made by Chung and Beamish (2005) for deeper understanding of the complex dynamics that take place in economies in times of crisis. It emphasizes a cluster of economies that, despite their seemingly institutional similarity, still delineate heterogeneous institutional configurations as they experience the notion of distance to different extents. Last, it suggests that the OLI paradigm may and should be extended so as to include crisis conditions in the context of MNE market internationalization.

Overall, it is indicated that in the post-crisis institutional environment of countries severely hit by the global economic crisis, institutional and economic distances negatively affect the ability of such countries to attract FDI flows. Such realizations lead us to the following:

US investors in crisis conditions not only consider the notion of distance but also perceive distance as a broader notion that encapsulates the uncertainty borne by the crisis. So, in line with our argument, institutional and economic distances, incorporating the conceptualization of institutional uncertainty, do matter in crisis conditions. More particularly, considering the institutional distance hypothesis, two main conclusions can be drawn:

First, the opening of previously closed sectors, such as manufacturing, signals an unfavourable transition phase mainly accommodated by institutional uncertainty, and therefore, a greater degree of institutional distance. Second, US investors in the post-crisis environment are concerned about transformed formal institutions, and more specifically, government effectiveness, regulatory quality and the rule of law (Bevan & Estrin, 2004); these are perceived as significant obstacles when considering expanding into Greece, Ireland, Italy, Spain and Portugal. Especially the latter contrasts with the trend of most empirical studies supporting that transformations in host countries' institutional environments lead to an increase in FDI inflows in these host countries (Choi et al., 2016). This variation is explained by the argument that Greece, Italy, Portugal, Spain and Ireland, and Greece and Portugal in particular, which are included into the largest reformers between 2008 and 2013, according to the OECD Product Market Regulation indicator (European Economy Series, 2014), are still facing persistent inefficiencies in the post-crisis era. Such inefficiencies are what motivate US investors to redirect their investment attention to other Member States that may respond more effectively, as opposed to the countries hit by crisis, to the needs of US investors (European Economy Series, 2014).

Turning to the economic distance hypothesis, another two points are also underlined. First, the negative influence of economic distance on the ability of EU countries to attract FDI flows, in relation to the positively expected relationship between them. This pattern of behaviour is attributed to the difficult economic position of the EU countries studied, which significantly widened the US-EU economic distance, making US investors express doubts both about the time of recovery of such economies and about US investors' capacity to manipulate or control such economic differences (Tsang & Yip, 2007). As a result, US MNEs avoid investing in such countries. The second point underlined is that the exploitation argument does not seem to work in the current context. One possible explanation is that MNEs, evaluating the location advantage of internationalization, tend to first internalize into countries with similar market conditions before expanding into business landscapes with larger economic distances. This strategy is consistent with the classic internationalization model.

Managerial Implications

The findings derived from the sample point to a number of guidelines for MNEs operating in environments under crisis conditions. First, formal institutions affect the attractiveness of a given host country (Dunning & Lundan, 2008). In particular, it is stressed that there is a close relationship between economic activity and institutions, which signals that the effectiveness of institutions in the post-crisis environment conditions the capability of host countries to facilitate or not their key economic goals, such as the attraction of FDI. Second, the relatively new aspect of MNEs' agentic activity, that is institutional entrepreneurship, which addresses the paradox of embedded agency articulated by the Institutional theory (Hotho & Pedersen, 2012) has to be underlined. In this direction, the study emphasizes that MNEs do not merely respond to their institutional context but may, in certain circumstances, act to manage this context (Phillips et al., 2009). Last but not least, the use of the eclectic "tripod"

(Dunning, 2000, p. 164) herein underlines another two points: first, the configuration of the OLI paradigm, facing any firm, and the response to that configuration are strongly contextual, since the OLI paradigm can offer explanations even in unstable conditions. Second, OLI can effectively accommodate and interpret both the conceptualizations of institutional uncertainty and institutional distance, providing a holistic approach of the relationship between FDI activity and crisis conditions.

Future Research

All of the above also provide a sound basis for further research, particularly under conditions before and after a crisis. This aspect would enhance the understanding of how MNEs effectively respond to the unfavourable forces of a post-crisis environment in conjunction with the notion of distance. Furthermore, the inclusion of control variables, such as country- and international trade-related ones, which take into account other than FDI policies would provide an in-depth insight into the role of institutional environment factors in the way MNEs react to post-crisis conditions. Last, the replication of our analysis into different data samples and various contexts of analysis, such as the Asian crisis, would enhance the validity of the present results.

References

Acemoglu, D., & Robinson, J. A. (2006). *Economic origins of dictatorship and democracy*. Cambridge Univ. Press.

Aitkin, M., & Longford, N. (1986). Statistical modelling in school effectiveness studies. *Journal of the Royal Statistical Society, 149*, 1–43.

Alfaro, L., & Chen, M. X. (2010). *Surviving the global financial crisis: Foreign direct investment and establishment performance*. Harvard Business School BGIE Unit Working Paper No. 10.

Alvarez, R., & Görg, H. (2007). *Multinationals as stabilizers?: Economic crisis and plant employment growth*. University of Nottingham, Research Working Paper No.15.

Bevan, A. A., & Estrin, S. (2004). The determinants of foreign direct investment into European transition economies. *Journal of Comparative Economics, 32*, 775–787.

Cantwell, J., Dunning, J., & Lundan, M. S. (2010). An evolutionary approach to understanding international business activity: The co-evolution of MNEs and the institutional environment. *Journal of International Business Studies, 41*, 567–586.

Chao, M. C. H., & Kumar, V. (2006). The impact of institutional distance on the international diversity-performance relationship. *Journal of World Business, 45*(1), 93–103.

Child, J., & Markuczy, L. (1993). Host-country managerial behaviour and learning in Chinese and Hungarian joint ventures. *Journal of Management Studies, 30*, 611–631.

Choi, J. J., Lee, M. L., & Shoham, A. (2016). The effects of institutional distance on FDI inflow: General environmental institutions (GEI) versus minority investor protection institutions (MIP). *International Business Review, 25*, 114–123.

Chung, C. C., & Beamish, P. W. (2005). The impact of institutional reforms on characteristics and survival of foreign subsidiaries in emerging economies. *Journal of Management Studies, 42*(1), 35–62.

Congressional Research Service. (2020). *U.S.-EU trade and investment ties: Magnitude and scope*. Congressional Research Service. Retrieved from http://www.oig.hhs.gov/oei/reports/oei-05-05-00240.pdf

Courvisanos, J. (2009). Political aspects of innovation. *Research Policy, 38*(7), 1117–1124.

Delios, A., & Beamish, P. W. (1999). Ownership strategy of Japanese firms: Transactional, institutional, and experience influences. *Strategic Management Journal, 20*, 915–932.

Dorneana, A., Işan, V., & Oanea, D.-C. (2012). The impact of the recent global crisis on foreign direct investment. Evidence from Central and Eastern European countries. *Emerging Markets Queries in Finance and Business, 3*, 1012–1017.

Dunning, J. H. (1980). Towards an eclectic theory of international production: Some empirical tests. *Journal of International Business Studies, 11*(1), 9–31.

Dunning, J. H. (1988). *Explaining international production*. Unwin Hyman.

Dunning, J. H. (1993). *Multinational enterprises and the global economy*. Addison Wesley.

Dunning, J. H. (2000). The eclectic paradigm as an envelope for economic and business theories of MNE activity. *International Business Review, 9*, 163–190.

Dunning, J. H., & Fortanier, F. (2007). Multinational enterprises and the new development paradigm: Consequences for host country development. *Multinational Business Review, 15*(1), 25–46.

Dunning, J. H., & Lundan, S. M. (2008). Institutions and the OLI paradigm of the multinational enterprise. *Asia Pacific Management, 25*(4), 573–593.

European Economy Series. (2014). *Market reforms at work in Italy, Spain, Portugal and Greece*. European Commission Directorate-General for Economic and Financial Affairs, Brussels, European Economy Series. http://www.oig.hhs.gov/oei/reports/oei-05-05-00242.pdf

Ferrera, M. (1996). The "Southern Model" of welfare in social Europe. *Journal of European Social Policy, 6*(1), 7–37.

Filippetti, A., & Archibugi, D. (2011). Innovation in times of crisis: National systems of innovation, structure, and demand. *Research Policy, 40*(2), 179–192.

Gaur, A. S., Delios, A., & Singh, K. (2007). Institutional environments, staffing strategies, and subsidiary performance. *Journal of Management, 33*, 611–636.

Ghemawat, P. (2001). Distance still matters: The hard reality of global expansion. *Harvard Business Review, 9*, 137–147.

Håkanson, L., & Ambos, B. (2010). The antecedents of psychic distance. *Journal of International Management, 16*(3), 195–210.

Henisz, W. J., & Delios, A. (2004). *Following the herd and sleeping with the enemy: Strategies for managing political uncertainty*. University of Pennsylvania, Working Paper Series of the Wharton School.

Hotho, J. H., & Pedersen, T. (2012). Beyond the "rules of the game": Three institutional approaches and how they matter for international business. In G. Wood & M. Demirbag (Eds.), *Handbook of institutional approaches to international business* (pp. 236–273). Edward Elgar.

Johnston, A., & Regan, A. (2014). Introduction: Is the European Union capable of integrating diverse models of capitalism? *New Political Economy, 23*(2), 145–159.

Kogut, B., & Singh, H. (1988). The effect of national culture on the choice of entry mode. *Journal of International Business Studies, 19*(3), 411–432.

Konzelmann, S., & Fovargue-Davie, M. (2012). Anglo-Saxon capitalism in crisis? Models of liberal capitalism and the preconditions for financial stability. In G. Wood & M. Demirbag (Eds.), *Handbook of institutional approaches to international business* (pp. 236–273). Edward Elgar.

Kostova, T., Beugelsdijk, S., Scott, W. R., Kunst, V. E., Chua, C. H., & Essen, M. (2019). The construct of institutional distance through the lens of different institutional perspectives: Review, analysis, and recommendations. *International Business Studies, 51*, 467–497.

Lee, Y., Hemmert, M., & Kim, J. (2014). What drives the international ownership strategies of Chinese firms? The role of distance and home-country institutional factors in outward acquisitions. *Asian Business & Management, 13*(3), 197–225.

McGuiness, M., & Demirbag, M. (2012). The multinational enterprise, institutions and corruption. In G. Wood & M. Demirbag (Eds.), *Handbook of institutional approaches to international business* (pp. 236–273). Edward Elgar.

Mody, A. (1999). *Industrial policy after the East Asian crisis: From outward orientation to new internal capabilities?* Policy Research Working Paper Series of the World Bank, Washington, DC: The World Bank No. 2112.

Newman, K. L. (2000). Organisational transformation during institutional upheaval. *Academy of Management Review, 25*, 602–619.

Nugent, N. (2010). *The government and politics of the European Union* (7th ed.). Palgrave Macmillan.

Peng, M. (2003). Institutional transitions and strategic choices. *Academy of Management Review, 28*, 275–296.

Persson, T., & Tabellini, G. (2003). *The economic effects of constitutions*. The MIT Press.

Phillips, N., Tracey, P., & Karra, N. (2009). Rethinking institutional distance: Strengthening the tie between new institutional theory and international management. *Strategic Organisation, 7*(3), 339–348.

Poulsen, L. N. S., & Hufbauer, G. C. (2011). *Foreign direct investment in times of crisis*. Peterson Institute for International Economics Working Paper No. 11-3.

Powell, W. (1991). Expanding the scope of institutional analysis. In W. Powell & P. DiMaggio (Eds.), *The new institutionalism in organisational analysis*. University of Chicago Press.

Rhodes, R. A. W. (1996). The governance: Governing without government. *Political Studies, 3*, 652–667.

Scott, W. R. (1995). *Institutions and organisations*. Sage.

Tong, H., & Wei, S.-J. (2009). The composition matters: Capital inflows and liquidity crunch during a global economic crisis. *The Review of Financial Studies, 24*(6), 2023–2052.

Tsang, E. W. K., & Yip, P. S. L. (2007). Economic distance and survival of foreign direct investments. *Academy of Management Journal, 50*(5), 1156–1168.

Ucal, M., Özcan, K. M., Bilgin, M., & Mungo, J. (2010). Relationship between financial crisis and foreign direct investment in developing countries using semiparametric regression approach. *Journal of Business Economics and Management, 11*(1), 20–33.

United Nations Conference on Trade and Development. (2017). WID country profile: Belgium, world investment report 2017. *UNCTAD World Trade Organisation, 2017*.

Villaverde, J., & Maza, A. (2015). The determinants of inward foreign direct investment: Evidence from the European regions. *International Business Review, 24*(2), 209–224.

Wan, W. P., & Hoskisson, R. (2003). Home country environments, corporate diversification strategies, and firm performance. *Academy of Management Journal, 46*, 27–45.

Williams, C., & Martinez, C. A. (2012). Government effectiveness, the global financial crisis, and multinational enterprise internationalization. *Journal of International Marketing, 20*(3), 65–78.

Wooldridge, J. M. (2015). *Introductory econometrics: A modern approach*. South-Western, Cengage Learning.

World Bank. (2020). World Bank Group – International development, poverty, & sustainability. [Online]. Retrieved November 19, 2020, from http://www.worldbank.org

Wright, M., Filatotchev, I., Hoskisson, R. E., & Peng, M. W. (2005). Guest editor's introduction: Strategy research in emerging economies: Challenging the conventional wisdom. *Journal of Management Studies, 42*(1), 1–33.

Xu, D., & Shenkar, O. (2002). Institutional distance and the multinational enterprise. *Academy of Management Review, 27*(4), 608–618.

3

Litigation Risk, Audit Fees and the Financial Crisis Impact: Empirical Evidence from the UK

Panagiotis E. Dimitropoulos

3.1 Introduction

The worldwide recession in 2008, referred as the Great Financial Crisis (GFC), started with the bankruptcy of Lehman Brothers in September 2008 and then resulted in a great disaster on various industries around the world, including the auditing market. World's economic condition declined greatly and the financial market became illiquid (Xu et al., 2013). At the height of GFC, the UK government was concerned with the fact that their citizens were almost unable to withdraw money from British banks at that time and in order to survive from this crisis, the UK authority had injected more than £375 million to bail out banks through quantitative easing programs and borrowing expansion and £500 billion

P. E. Dimitropoulos (✉)
Department of Sport Organization and Management, University of Peloponnese, Sparta, Greece
e-mail: dimitrop@uop.gr

D. Vrontis et al. (eds.), *Business Under Crisis Volume I*, Palgrave Studies in Cross-disciplinary Business Research, In Association with EuroMed Academy of Business, https://doi.org/10.1007/978-3-030-76567-5_3

to support financial enterprises. Also the government implemented a number of high-profile institutional reforms and fiscal rules to end this long-term stagnation in the economy (Mabbett & Hodson, 2009; NIESR, 2009).

This crisis influenced not only the British financing industries but also numerous supporting regimes such as British regulatory agencies and auditing practices (Sikka, 2015). A great number of inquiries were sparked into the role of auditors and their work efficiency. More and more attention has been put on the unsatisfied capabilities of auditors and on the need to reform the audit quality control regulation (Alderman & Jollineau, 2020; Chy et al., 2020; Humphrey et al., 2009; Sikka, 2009). Auditors are seriously accused of delivering "dodgy auditing" to take advantage of this catastrophe to demand more liability concession and increase their profits thereby (Sikka, 2008, 2009). Different parties, such as the government, regulators and shareholders, heavily criticized the high level of auditing fees charged on the auditee clients during GFC.

However, the current evidence on the impact of GFC on auditing pricing is mixed in the countries of Sweden, China, Australia and America (Alexeyeva & Svanström, 2015; Ettredge et al., 2014; Kang et al., 2019; Xu et al., 2013; Zhang & Huang, 2013) and there is little evidence found on GFC impact on non-auditing service (NAS) pricing in the literature. In addition, the relatively high level of litigation risks on auditors under such incredibly unstable environment and how auditors would adjust their fees to deal with their future exposed liability during GFC is still unknown. It is often expected that auditors would be more professionally skeptical and make more audit effort to deal with more audit risks and litigation risks. And the audit and non-audit fees are expected to be large enough to cover the "after the fact" litigation costs and reputation losses (Mautz & Sharaf, 1961; Simunic, 1980; Simunic & Stein, 1996). Therefore, this study is motivated to identify this gap in the literature. In this study, the UK's auditing market was selected as the primary target because London is at the top of Global Financial Centers' ranking and one of the first market that the GFC struck, since it has a longstanding connection and integration with the New York Stock Exchange (French et al., 2009; Sikka, 2015).

This study contributes to the existing literature from three aspects. Firstly, due to the limited study on the joint effect on both auditing and non-audit fees during the GFC, this chapter adds to the existing literature by using firm-year observations spanning the period of pre-GFC (2006–2007), GFC (2008–2009) and post-GFC (2010–2011) so as to examine the fee structure of auditing services firms. Meanwhile, analyzing auditing and non-auditing fees is important to understand the pricing policies of accounting firms and understand how auditors decide their charges based on the specific conditions of their clients and markets. Secondly, the existing literature on the effect of the GFC on audit pricing is contradictory. The results from the less influenced countries such as Sweden and China are different from studies within the USA, which was the center of that crisis. This study chooses UK auditing market in which there is no prohibition on most non-audit services during the recession, and therefore, the level of pricing is largely determined by the client-specific needs. Thirdly, the fee level is often determined by the auditors who would take their litigation risks into consideration, and GFC is such a suitable setting in which auditors are exposed to an extremely high level of litigation liability. This study would provide evidence of how the disclosed auditing and non-auditing fees would shift in the response to the increased litigation and audit risk induced by the financial crisis.

The remainder of the chapter is organized as follows. The study's background and literature review would be described in Sect. 3.2. Thereafter, Sect. 3.3 presents the methodology adopted in this study and results would then be presented in Sect. 3.4. Finally, Sect. 3.5 would conclude the chapter with a discussion of the main findings, along with the implications, limitations and potential avenues for future research.

3.2 Literature Review and Hypothesis Development

Simunic (1980) has firstly proposed a framework for audit fee model in which audit fees must equal the auditors' expected costs. In the framework of Simunic (1980), the quality and quantity of resources invested by auditors to conduct their work should be considered, because there is a positive relationship between audit effort and audit fees. When determining their services charges, the auditors have to exercise their professional judgment to assess the likelihood of their responsibility to bear future losses and how much they need to invest to gain a marginal profit (Pratt & Stice, 1994). Therefore, the litigation risk factor is important when deciding their fees because the return from the engagements relies on the fees paid by clients, which need to be large enough to cover the possible litigation and reputation losses (Simunic, 1980; Simunic & Stein, 1996).

For clients, auditing and non-audit service (NAS) fees are similar in the way that they have the quality of services which are difficult to verify when they negotiate the purchase decision with auditors (Dasgupta, 2000; Shapiro, 1983). NAS refers to services of tax advice, management consultancy and others. However, the characteristics of the two services are different as the auditing is mandatory especially for public companies, while the NASs are purchased if needed. In terms of the joint determination of the audit fees with total management advisory services or non-audit fees, many studies confirm there is a significant positive association (Bell et al., 2001; Davis et al., 1993; Ezzamel et al., 1996). Simunic (1984) suggested that the provision of audit and non-audit services would cause knowledge spill-overs so that cost savings could be achieved by way of a lower audit fee but it is the audit firms who would retain such cost-saving as part of their earnings. However, there is another opinion from Abdel-Khalik (1990) and Barkess and Simnett (1992) who suggest that there is no statistical relationship between audit fees and the provision of NAS.

As mentioned earlier, in the model of Simunic (1980), the cost of gathering audit evidence and forming an audit opinion is often broken down into two parts. This first is the resource cost component, which would increase with the level of auditor efforts. Another is the expected loss component as the product of the likelihood of litigation risks and the expected present value of the future loss. Auditors have to bear the litigation risks because financial statements can easily hide undetected material misstatements manipulated by financial managers. Litigation risk would occur when managers, shareholders and any other third parties try to recover their business losses from a material misstatement by ascribing them in the audited financial statement and making auditors responsible for such business losses. This "after the fact" litigation costs may make the realized return unprofitable both for the specific engagement and even over the whole portfolio of clients, resulting in the bankruptcy of auditing firms due to high reputation costs. Therefore, when auditors decide their charges, they normally take into consideration the clients specific nature of audit costs and the expected liability loss components (Simunic & Stein, 1996). During GFC, many businesses have collapsed after receiving the unqualified audit reports. Stakeholders started having doubts on whether auditors are worthwhile to trust or not. Along with the demise of the Enron scandal, the issue of "auditors" became prevalent again (Humphrey et al., 2009; Sikka, 2009).

Xu et al. (2013) found that the increased client business risk in Australia led to higher auditing pricing and procedures during the period of 2008 to 2009. And auditors have responded to be more conservative reporting to protect themselves from higher risk exposure during GFC. Higher auditing fees were also found in China and Sweden (Alexeyeva & Svanström, 2015; Zhang & Huang, 2013). Alexeyeva and Svanström (2015) also found a change in the audit fee model by comparing the period from pre-GFC to post-GFC; however, they do not identify any more audit efforts in Sweden. Nevertheless, these countries are less impacted by this crisis, as French et al. (2009) discovered that GFC is a very geographic crisis, in which the UK and the USA are the global financial centers, which are hit more hardly, and the evidence from the USA by Krishnan and Zhang (2014) point to the opposite direction. In their research, they revealed that financial companies exert fee pressures on auditors with curtailing audit quality and effort. Additionally, Ettredge et al. (2014) suggested that in 2008, almost half of clients exerted fee pressures; however, their study selected publicly listed companies without specifying the countries of the samples, and such mixture may distort the results as GFC has a particular geographic effect.

Simunic and Stein (1996) figure out that the audit fee is the reflection of litigation risk. Seetharaman et al. (2002) have identified a higher audit fee for their UK auditee companies that are listed on the US markets in which a stricter liability regime is exposed. During the GFC, the number of dissatisfaction from financial statement users has increased significantly and thus auditors bear more litigation risk. Courts might change their attitude toward auditors' negligence due to all sues filed from financial statement users and the public (Seetharaman et al., 2002). Therefore, the first hypothesis in this study is formed as follows:

H1 *Audit fee increases from the pre-GFC period to GFC and post-GFC period to offset higher litigation risks.* At the same time, Srinidhi and Gul (2007) argued that non-audit fees dropped from 2000 to 2001 during the USA economic downturns, since clients restrict their expenses when surviving from GFC and the consultancy service was not the prioritized choice. While the existing literature provides little evidence regarding how non-audit fees change during GFC, Alexeyeva and Svanström (2015) identify that there is a decrease in the level of non-audit fees due to the financial constraints. However, their samples are only drawn from small and midcap listed companies in the Swedish economy, which faced a relatively small impact by the crisis. Meanwhile, the companies selected are quite small in size, which renders the generalizability of the results. This limited evidence shows that when companies face a drop in their risk management quality along with a shortage of capital, they may have no choice but to decrease their cash outflows by refraining their consultancy services (Aldamen et al., 2012). However, there is another opinion that when there is a change in economic conditions such as a financial crisis, companies are forced to restructure their operation, which hence needs more consultancy services from professional bodies (Firth, 2002). Therefore, the second research hypothesis is formed as follows:

H2 *Non-audit fees decrease from the pre-GFC period to GFC and post-GFC period.*

3.3 Data Selection and Research Design

In order to examine the aforementioned hypotheses, a quantitative analysis approach (empirical analysis) is chosen. The sample in this study consists of companies listed on the London Stock Exchange (LSE). A total number of 148 firms are analyzed with the exclusion of the financial institutions and banks for which have different asset structure and accounting treatments relative to other sectors. Companies are obliged to develop their individual financial statements following the International Financial Reporting Standards (IFRS). In order to capture the impact on economic fluctuations on auditing and NAS pricing model and to ensure the uniformity and comparability of statistics, the sample is restricted to companies having the same fiscal accounting year end (December 31). Observations with incomplete financial data on asset value and non-audit fees are omitted. As a result of these pre-conditions, the final sample incudes 93 companies that were chosen for analysis. The GFC period (2008–2009) would be evaluated by comparing the results with pre-GFC (2006–2007) and post-GFC (2010–2011) periods. Therefore, a total of 558 firm-year observations for the entire period would be identified. Financial data are collected from the annual reports and DataStream database.

In this study, the total fees charged by the auditing firms are analyzed from auditing and non-auditing fees categories. The aforementioned hypotheses will be tested by the following cross-sectional audit fee and non-audit service fee linear regression models. The models are set up based on the fee model of Leventis and Dimitropoulos (2010) and Alexeyeva and Svanström (2015) as follows:

$$\begin{aligned}\mathrm{LNAF}_{it} &= a_0 + a_1\mathrm{GFC}_{it} + a_2\mathrm{POSTGFC}_{it} + a_3\mathrm{LNTA}_{it} \\ &+ a_4\mathrm{INVREC}_{it} + a_5\mathrm{CUR}_{it} + a_6\mathrm{QUICK}_{it} + \\ &a_7\mathrm{ROA}_{it} + a_8\mathrm{ROE}_{it} + a_9\mathrm{LEV}_{it} + a_{10}\mathrm{LOSS}_{it} \\ &+ a_{11}\mathrm{BIG4}_{it} + a_{12}\mathrm{ALTMAN}_{it} + e_{it}\end{aligned} \tag{3.1}$$

$$\begin{aligned}LN\mathrm{NAF}_{it} &= a_0 + a_1\mathrm{GFC}_{it} + a_2\mathrm{POSTGFC}_{it} + a_3\mathrm{LNTA}_{it} \\ &+ a_4\mathrm{INVREC}_{it} + a_5\mathrm{CUR}_{it} + \\ &a_6\mathrm{QUICK}_{it} + a_7\mathrm{ROA}_{it} + a_8\mathrm{ROE}_{it} + a_9\mathrm{LEV}_{it} \\ &+ a_{10}\mathrm{LOSS}_{it} + a_{11}\mathrm{BIG4}_{it} + a_{12}\mathrm{ALTMAN}_{it} + e_{it}\end{aligned} \tag{3.2}$$

where

LNAF: Natural logarithm of audit service fees.

LNNAF: Natural logarithm of non-audit service fees.

GFC: Dummy variable that is coded 1 if the fiscal year is for 2008–2009 and 0 otherwise.

POSTGFC: Dummy variable that is coded 1 if the fiscal year is for 2010–2011 and 0 otherwise.

LNTA: Natural logarithm of auditee's total assets.

INVREC: The ratio of inventory plus accounts receivable to total assets.

CUR: The ratio of the current asset to current liabilities.

QUICK: The ratio of current asset minus inventory, divided by current liabilities.

DA: The ratio of net debt to total assets.

ROA: Return on assets, calculated as operating income divided by total assets.

ROE: Return on equity, calculated as net income divided by average shareholders' equity.

LEV: The ratio of debt to capital.

LOSS: Dummy variable that is coded 1 if the net profit is negative in the previous year, and 0 otherwise.

ALTMAN: The ratio of Altman z-score capturing bankruptcy risk.

BIG4: Dummy variable that is coded 1 if the audit firm is PwC, E&Y, KPMG or Deloitte and 0 otherwise.

The constant term α has been referred in the two linear regression models to demonstrate the fixed cost of having an audit engagement and to capture specification errors as a result of the functional form of the models. Meanwhile, the stochastic disturbance e would function as the comprehensive effect of all variables that are deduced from the models but could also impact on audit and non-auditing service fees. ε is seen to be independent and distributed with the same variance (Leventis & Dimitropoulos, 2010). In the UK, companies are required to disclose auditor fees in their financial reports. Chan et al. (1993) point out that such disclosure may just be an estimate for the current year because there would be some adjustment for any over or under-estimate for the previous year. Therefore, in this study, the natural logarithm of audit (LNAF) and non-audit (LNNAF) fee are used as the dependent variables. In order to mitigate such inaccuracies, the cross-sectional data pooled over a two-year period would be analyzed from pre-GFC (2006–2007), GFC

(2008–2009) and post-GFC (2010–2011) periods. In these two regression models, GFC and POSTGFC would be evaluated as the independent variables to indicate litigation risks as a result of the recession.

To control cross-sectional differences in different financial conditions and overcome the problem caused by the likely high correlation between absolute levels of profits and company size, the leverage and profitability are taken into consideration. Simunic (1980) suggest that leverage could also be a measurement of clients risks, which potentially makes auditors exposed to losses. The most popular proxies for leverage has been the net debt to the total asset (DA) and equity-debt ratio (LEV) and the sign is expected to be positive as companies' higher debt exposure exposes auditors to higher risks. Excessive leverage has the potential to increase liquidity risk and jeopardize their survival (Sikka, 2009). The profitability of clients is analyzed as the reduced profitability of companies enhances risks exposure for auditors, so higher audit fees are expected. Therefore, the profitability is a great measurement of litigation risk because it would reflect the extent to auditor's exposure to future losses under the circumstance that clients are not financially visible (Hay et al., 2006; Simunic, 1980). Therefore, the presence of previous year loss (LOSS) is also considered because the threshold of moving from profit to loss could signal auditors need to conduct a more intensive and costly auditing work, therefore a positive relationship is expected with fees charged (Firth, 1997; Zaman et al., 2011).

The ROA variable is calculated as profits before taxes divided by total assets and the return on shareholders' equity (ROE) are expected to have a negative relationship with the fees (Chan et al., 1993; Seetharaman et al., 2002). Besides, Altman z-score is used to predict the possibility of bankruptcy (ALTMAN) at the end of the fiscal year (Altman, 1968). Referring to the other control variables, the most dominant factor is the auditee size, which is expected to have a positive impact on fees (Chan et al., 1993; Ferguson et al., 2003; Pereira et al., 2020; Simunic, 1980). Total assets in the balance sheets typically measure the size of companies, so the natural logarithm of total assets (LNTA) is used in this study. Additional controls are the combination of inventory plus receivables divided by total assets (INVREC) and the ratio of the current asset to current liability (CUR) and quick ratio (QUICK) following Dengleri et al. (2019). Apart from the auditee factor, the auditor's attribute is also important in determining the fees of auditing firms. Francis and Stokes (1986) found that Big 4 audit firms charge more fees than non-Big 4. Also, Roussy and Mayer (2018) state that Big 4 firms are often experts within specific industries who could handle complex auditee situations compared to the non-Big 4 firms. Therefore, such superior quality would normally charge more fees to their clients. Moreover, Big 4 auditors would ask more fees for their greater audit effort costs than non-Big 4 ones (Choi et al., 2008). Therefore, in order to control auditor characteristics, the dummy variable BIG4 is used in this test and a positive coefficient is expected.

3.4 Empirical Results

Table 3.1 reports the descriptive statistics of the dependent and independent variables used in the regression covering the whole period of investigation with the means, the median, and the standard deviation. This table includes 93 UK listed companies with three investigated periods: the pre-GFC (2006–2007), GFC (2008–2009), post-GFC (2010–2011) period and the whole sample period (2006–2011). In terms of dependent

Table 3.1 Descriptive statistics of sample variables

	PRE-GFC (2006–2007)			GFC (2008–2009)		
	Mean	Median	Std. Dev.	Mean	Median	Std. Dev.
AF(£)	3,676,627.15	800,000.00	16,648,958.31	3,140,685.63	1,155,078.50	6,501,154.78
NAF(£)	2,861,165.00	800,000.00	8,966,046.86	2,677,747.24	805,000.00	9,375,652.42
LNAF	13.49	13.59	2.47	13.73	13.99	2.00
LNNAF	13.09	13.59	2.86	13.28	13.60	2.36
LNTA	14.48	14.25	1.73	14.79	14.68	1.67
INVREC	0.26	0.23	0.20	0.53	0.24	1.52
CUR	1.47	1.25	1.42	1.40	1.23	1.50
QUICK	1.03	0.83	1.20	0.95	0.77	1.06
DA	0.21	0.19	0.16	0.19	0.19	0.22
ROE	33.52	24.65	75.33	19.19	14.17	62.33
ROA	12.30	10.08	10.56	6.57	5.64	11.99
LEV	34.14	33.37	23.23	38.66	36.71	25.64
ALTMAN	0.63	0.31	0.90	0.86	0.74	0.93
BIG4	0.06	0.00	0.24	0.20	0.00	0.40
LOSS	0.99	1.00	0.10	0.99	1.00	0.10

variables, it shows the mean of total AF has decreased from pre-GFC to GFC by 15 percent, but then increased slightly by 6 percent in the post-GFC period. This result indicates that clients have exerted fee pressure on their auditors so as to survive during GFC. Meanwhile, NAF has the same decreasing trend by 6 percent from pre-GFC to GFC period, but it then goes down sharply by 42 percent for more than 1.1 million pounds from GFC to post-GFC period. All averages of NAF for the investigated period is lower than AF, while the gap is largest for over 1,577,660 pounds during the GFC period, compared to 815,462 and 462,938 pounds in pre-GFC and GFC periods, respectively.

Turning to the control variables, it can be seen that the mean of the logarithm of the total assets (LNTA) remains quite stable at around 14.7, along with the minimum and maximum at 9.9 and 19.7, respectively, for the investigated periods. The gap between the largest and the smallest firm is not quite large so it suggests that the observations chosen in the sample are comparable in size. The median of INVREC remains stable from 2006 to 2011 at the level of around 0.24, but the median was the largest at 0.53 during GFC with around 0.25 both during the pre-GFC and post-GFC periods. In terms of liquidity ratio, the median of current ratio (CUR) remains quite steady at the level of 1.4 while the maximum

POST-GFC (2010–2011)			FULL SAMPLE (2006–2011)		
Mean	Median	Std. Dev.	Mean	Median	Std. Dev.
3,155,278.89	1,200,000.00	5,447,700.71	3,324,197.23	1,024,500.00	10,771,310.83
1,577,617.97	582,500.00	3,407,383.09	2,372,176.74	725,402.78	7,750,756.51
13.99	14.00	1.71	13.74	13.86	2.09
12.65	13.27	3.34	13.00	13.50	2.89
14.88	14.73	1.68	14.72	14.53	1.70
0.53	0.24	1.52	0.44	0.24	1.25
1.40	1.23	1.50	1.42	1.24	1.47
0.97	0.80	0.92	0.99	0.80	1.06
0.19	0.19	0.22	0.20	0.19	0.20
19.19	14.17	62.33	23.97	17.02	67.16
6.57	5.64	11.99	8.48	7.19	11.83
38.66	36.71	25.64	37.16	35.74	24.91
0.86	0.74	0.93	0.79	0.65	0.93
0.20	0.00	0.40	0.16	0.00	0.36
0.99	1.00	0.10	0.99	1.00	0.10

has increased annually from 8.65 to 13.97. While the mean of the quick ratio (QUICK) decreases from 0.211 to 0.19 from pre-GFC to GFC period and remains stable during the post-GFC period, the mean of ROE for the entire period (2006–2011) is 23.97, and this figure decreased during the GFC and post-GFC period at 19.19. Similar to the trend of ROE, the median of ROE decreased from pre-GFC (12.3) to GFC (6.57), followed by a slight increase to 9.96 in the post-GFC period.

It is interesting to find that the minimum of DA is 0.45 in the GFC and post-GFC period. DA is the ratio of net debt divided by the total asset. In addition, the mean of DA keeps quite stable at the level of around 0.2. The variable LEV does not fluctuate too much in these six years, and it has its largest figure at 38.66 during GFC. The mean and median of Altman Z-score (ALTMAN) are all below 1.8 during the investigated period, showing that most companies are heading for bankruptcy from pre-GFC to GFC and post-GFC periods. However, the level of average Z-score is increasing gradually from 0.6 to 0.86. The dummy variable LOSS indicates that during the periods of pre-GFC and post-GFC, the mean of LOSS is 0 while during GFC is 0.989, indicating companies have already received the indicator of going concern before the crisis. Finally, Table 3.1 also shows that almost all companies have been audited by Big 4 accounting firms.

The Pearson correlation coefficients of the sample variables are presented in Table 3.2, and since all correlations are lower than 0.8, multicollinearity is not a serious problem (Alin, 2010). We can see GFC do not have a significant association with LNAF and LNNAF, while POSTGFC has a significant relationship with LNAF. Both LNTA and LEV have a strong positive relationship with the LNAF and LNNAF. ROA and LOSS are the two factors that are most influenced by GFC and POSTGFC simultaneously. In terms of dependent variables, LNAF and LNNAF are positively and significantly correlated to LNTA, LEV and ALTMAN. At the same time, LNAF has a significant negative association with INVREC and CUR. On the other hand, ROA have a strong relationship with LNNAF while BIG 4 is positive. The correlations among the rest of the control variables are economically meaningful and with expected signs.

Tables 3.3 and 3.4 illustrate the results of the audit and non-auditing fee regression models as presented in equations (3.1) and (3.2) to test the

Table 3.2 Pearson correlation coefficients of sample variables

Variables	1	2	3	4	5	6	7	8	9	10	11	12	13	14	15
1. GFC	1														
2. POSTGFC	**-0.50**	1													
3. LNAF	-0.00	**0.08**	1												
4. LNNAF	0.05	-0.08	**0.53**	1											
5. LNTA	0.03	0.07	**0.52**	**0.41**	1										
6. INVREC	0.05	0.05	**-0.08**	-0.07	**-0.19**	1									
7. CUR	0.01	0.01	**0.16**	-0.05	**-0.28**	-0.01	1								
8. QUICK	-0.02	0.01	-0.05	-0.06	**-0.29**	-0.00	**0.67**	1							
9. DA	-0.02	-0.02	0.04	0.02	**0.09**	-0.02	**-0.18**	**0.16**	1						
10. ROE	-0.05	-0.05	0.00	0.01	**-0.09**	0.00	-0.02	0.02	0.05	1					
11. ROA	**-0.11**	**-0.11**	-0.04	**-0.09**	**-0.32**	**0.22**	**0.22**	**0.34**	**-0.10**	**0.39**	1				
12. LEV	0.04	0.04	**0.13**	**0.13**	**0.18**	0.06	**0.31**	**-0.27**	**0.45**	**0.12**	**-0.10**	1			
13. ALTMAN	0.06	0.05	**-0.09**	**-0.11**	**-0.31**	**0.15**	**0.56**	**0.42**	**-0.23**	**0.09**	**0.52**	**-0.34**	1		
14. LOSS	**0.09**	**0.09**	-0.06	-0.05	0.07	-0.06	-0.06	**-0.16**	**0.17**	**-0.20**	**-0.47**	**0.16**	**-0.28**	1	
15. BIG4	0.00	0.00	0.03	0.00	**0.14**	-0.02	**0.14**	**-0.20**	**0.08**	-0.00	**-0.13**	**0.15**	**0.16**	0.04	1

Note: Correlation coefficients in bold indicate statistical significance at the 5 percent significance level at least (two-tailed test)

Table 3.3 Regression results of the audit fee model (1)

Variables	Exp. sign	Coeff.	t-Test	p-Value	VIF
(Constant)		0.039	3.665	0.000[b]	
GFC	+	0.029	0.642	0.521	1.601
POSTGFC	+	0.069	1.537	0.125	1.607
LNTA	+	0.550	13.813	0.000[b]	1.251
INVREC	-	-0.022	-0.568	0.570	1.140
CUR	-	-0.130	-2.457	0.014[a]	2.202
QUICK	+	0.141	2.912	0.004[b]	1.853
DA	+	0.005	0.116	0.908	1.296
ROE	-	-0.003	-0.081	0.936	1.256
ROA	-	0.070	1.290	0.198	2.355
LEV	+	0.063	1.444	0.149	1.514
BKRP	+	0.057	1.049	0.295	2.358
LOSS	+	-0.064	-1.516	0.130	1.384
BIG4	+	-0.026	-0.718	0.473	1.067
No. of obs			558		
Adjusted R^2			0.295		
F-value			18.860[b]		
F-sig			0.000		

Note: Dependent variable: LNAF
[a]Indicates significance at the 0.05 level (2-tailed)
[b]Indicates significance at the 0.01 level (2-tailed)

Table 3.4 Regression results of the non-audit fee model (2)

Variables	Exp. sign	Coeff.	t-Test	p-Value	VIF
(Constant)		0.031	2.169	0.031[b]	
GFC	-	-0.023	-0.485	0.628	1.601
POSTGFC	-	-0.125	-2.566	0.011[b]	1.608
LNTA	+	0.435	10.164	0.000[c]	1.253
INVREC	-	0.014	0.337	0.736	1.141
CUR	-	0.068	1.189	0.235	2.206
QUICK	+	0.037	0.718	0.473	1.855
DA	+	-0.039	-0.888	0.375	1.298
ROE	-	0.031	0.716	0.474	1.257
ROA	-	-0.056	-0.948	0.343	2.357
LEV	+	0.116	2.459	0.014[b]	1.512
BKRP	+	0.004	0.065	0.949	2.358
LOSS	+	-0.088	-1.951	0.052[a]	1.383
BIG4	+	-0.061	-1.546	0.123	1.067
No. of obs			558		
Adjusted R^2			0.204		
F-value			10.692		
F-sig			0.000		

Note: Dependent variable: LNNAF
[a]Indicates significance at the 0.10 level (2-tailed)
[b]Indicates significance at the 0.05 level
[c]Indicates significance at the 0.01 level (2-tailed)

hypothesis 1 and 2. The tables include the estimation of the model covering the entire period (2006–2011) by including GFC and POSTGFC as independent variables. In addition, the variance inflation factors (VIF) is helpful in determining the existence of multicollinearity in the results. The largest VIF in both tables is 2.358, which is far lower than 10, indicating the multicollinearity would not be a major impediment in the interpretation of the results and thus standard interpretations of the regression coefficients could be made (Alin, 2010; Firth, 1997).

In the audit fee model, we can see that the independent variables GFC and POSTGFC do not show a significant coefficient with LNAF. This finding is different from many studies indicating that GFC has a significant impact on the audit fees, in a positive or negative way (Alexeyeva & Svanström, 2015; Krishnan & Zhang, 2014; Zhang & Huang, 2013). Consequently, the first hypothesis that audit fees would increase from pre-GFC to GFC and post-GFC period should be rejected.

Moving on to the control variables, we can see that some results are consistent to most of the previous literature, while others are not. We found that client size is one of the most significant explanatory variables in determining audit fees. It appears that the size of the auditee client is an important factor on explanation of the level of audit fees, which is consistent with previous studies (Chan et al., 1993; Ferguson et al., 2003; Leventis & Dimitropoulos, 2010; Simunic, 1980). The results also provide evidence that the current ratio (CUR) is negatively associated with LNAF with coefficient equals to -0.13, corroborating findings of Gul (1999) and Ghosh and Pawlewicz (2009). The variable QUICK is positive and significant as expected, which is consistent with previous studies (Seetharaman et al., 2002). The coefficients of DA and LEV do not show a significant association with LNAF, which is in contrast with the prior literature, which indicates that the higher leverage level could result in higher litigation risks on auditors and, in turn, to higher audit fees (Hay et al., 2006; Sikka, 2009; Simunic, 1980).

Table 3.4 reports the results from the non-audit fee model, showing that the explanatory power of the non-audit fee model is nearly up to 20 percent. Similar to the result of the audit fee model, the independent variable GFC does not have a significant association with LNNAF, while POSTGFC has also a particularly strong negative coefficient in the non-audit fee model. This result confirms the part of the second hypothesis that non-audit fees decrease from GFC (2008–2009) to post-GFC (2010–2011) period, but rejects the other part of decreasing from pre-GFC (2006–2007) to GFC (2008–2009) period. The highly significant negative coefficient of POSTGFC shows that clients restricted their expenses for surviving from GFC and the consultancy service is not the prioritized choice, which is similar to previous studies (Srinidhi & Gul, 2007; Alexeyeva & Svanström, 2015). The fee pressure from clients does not allow auditors to charge more fees to compensate for the higher litigation risks during the post-GFC period. Similar to the result of audit fee model, auditors are also not prepared to charge more on their clients without realizing the increased litigation risks exposed on them in the future during the GFC period.

The variable LNTA is also an important positive driver for the non-audit fee model, suggesting that non-audit service fees are higher for larger clients. Meanwhile, the level of leverage (LEV) seems to be an important driver for the non-audit service fee. This confirms that companies who borrow more would be exposed to higher audit risk and litigation risk, and this result is consistent with other studies (Seetharaman et al., 2002). We can also see that LOSS is a significant factor determining non-audit fees as well. It could be easily explained that the higher the likelihood of companies going bankrupt, the higher the possibility of audit firms who provide management advisory services to bear higher responsibility from shareholders, and so the fee pressure on those auditors would be greater.

3.5 Conclusion

The current research aims to explore how auditors' response to the changing macroeconomic conditions, especially during the global financial crisis, and the increased litigation risks that this crisis created, by adjusting their audit fees and non-audit fees from the year 2006 to 2011 in the UK. The GFC period which begins at the year of 2008 influenced not only the British financing industries but also numerous supporting regimes such as regulatory agencies and auditing practices (Sikka, 2015).

The role of auditors and their work efficiency have been questioned seriously from different parties around the world. The large amount of the unqualified opinions given by auditors during GFC does not satisfy the society due to the large losses that came without any notice from the auditors. The increased litigation risks exposed on auditors have become higher than ever.

In this study, we considered how the audit and non-audit service pricing are decided by taking the litigation risk factor into consideration, as highlighted in the literature review part. The regression results of this study do not find that auditors have changed their audit fees and non-audit fees in response to their higher exposed legal liability during the GFC period (2008–2009) or post-GFC (2009–2011) periods. Therefore, the increased litigation risk during GFC do not make auditors require more fees from their clients who are also struggling to survive from this crisis. On the other hand in terms of non-audit fees, auditors indicated a rather small change on the fees charged on the clients for management advisory services after the GFC period.

The findings of this study could be proved useful for the shareholders and other stakeholders of companies, as well as the regulators because they could help them to understand how the impact of macroeconomic fluctuations would shape the judgments of auditors by analyzing the cost structure of their audit and non-audit fees. It could enhance decisions of the related regulators in the UK when they judge the performance of the auditors, so as to improve the existing auditing standards, especially during turbulent periods such as the GFC. The study is also important to the accounting literature as it firstly considers how the litigation risks during GFC impacts the level of both audit and non-audit fees in the UK.

Nevertheless, there are some limitations in the study, which can impact the conclusions and generalizability of the obtained results. First, the sample is restricted within public companies, which survived successfully from GFC. There are numerous small- and medium-sized companies, which went through a hardship because of this crisis among the six-year period from 2006 to 2011. The attitudes of auditors toward these companies could be considered in more detail as these companies could pose a higher litigation risk compared to their larger counterparts. Finally, the reaction toward the litigation risk during GFC may differentiate within different countries; thus further studies could investigate the determinants of audit and non-audit fees in other developing countries along with various political, cultural and economic factors.

References

Abdel-Khalik, A. R. (1990). The jointness of audit fees and demand for MAS: A self-selection analysis. *Contemporary Accounting Research, 6*(2), 295–322.

Aldamen, H., Duncan, K., Kelly, S., McNamara, R., & Nagel, S. (2012). Audit committee characteristics and firm performance during the global financial crisis. *Accounting & Finance, 52*(4), 971–1000.

Alderman, J., & Jollineau, S. J. (2020). Can audit committee expertise increase external auditors' litigation risk? The moderating effect of audit committee independence. *Contemporary Accounting Research, 37*(2), 717–740.

Alexeyeva, I., & Svanström, T. (2015). The impact of the global financial crisis on audit and non-audit fees, evidence from Sweden. *Managerial Auditing Journal, 30*(4/5), 302–323.

Alin, A. (2010). Multicollinearity. *Computational Statistics, 2*(3), 370–374.

Altman, E. I. (1968). Financial ratios, discriminant analysis and the prediction of corporate bankruptcy. *The Journal of Finance, 23*(4), 589–609.

Barkess, L., & Simnett, R. (1992). *An empirical investigation of the relationship between audit fees and the provision of other services by the incumbent auditor – Australian evidence.* Working Paper University of New South Wales.

Bell, T. B., Landsman, W. R., & Shackelford, D. A. (2001). Auditors' perceived business risk and audit fees: Analysis and evidence. *Journal of Accounting Research, 39*(1), 35–43.

Chan, P., Ezzamel, M., & Gwilliam, D. (1993). Determinants of audit fees for quoted UK companies. *Journal of Business Finance & Accounting, 20*(6), 765–786.

Choi, J., Kim, J., Liu, X., & Simunic, D. A. (2008). Audit pricing, legal liability regimes, and Big 4 premiums: Theory and cross-country evidence. *Contemporary Accounting Research, 25*(1), 55–99.

Chy, M., De Franco, G., & Su, B. (2020). The effect of auditor litigation risk on clients' access to bank debt: Evidence from a quasi-experiment. *Journal of Accounting and Economics, 101354*. https://doi.org/10.1016/j.jacceco.2020.101354

Dasgupta, P. (2000). Trust as a commodity. In D. Gambetta (Ed.), *Trust: Making and breaking cooperative relations* (pp. 49–72). Electronic edition. Department of Sociology, University of Oxford, Chapter 4, www.sociology.ox.ac.uk/papers/dasgupta

Davis, L. R., Ricchiute, D. N., & Trompeter, G. (1993). Audit effort, audit fees, and the provision of non-audit services to audit clients. *The Accounting Review, 68*(1), 135–150.

Dengleri, K., Lois, P., Thrassou, A., & Repousis, S. (2019). Industry application of assessment and forecasting theories through comparative financial analysis: The case of Greek pharmaceutical industries under crisis conditions. In A. Thrassou et al. (Eds.), *The synergy of business theory and practice, Palgrave studies in cross-disciplinary business research* (pp. 175–198). In Association with EuroMed Academy of Business.

Ettredge, M., Fuerherm, E. E., & Li, C. (2014). Fee pressure and audit quality. *Accounting, Organizations and Society, 39*(4), 247–263.

Ezzamel, M., Gwilliam, D. R., & Holland, K. M. (1996). Some empirical evidence from publicly quoted UK companies on the relationship between the pricing of audit and non-audit services. *Accounting and Business Research, 27*(1), 3–16.

Ferguson, A., Francis, J. R., & Stokes, D. J. (2003). The effects of firm-wide and office-level industry expertise on audit pricing. *The Accounting Review, 78*(2), 429–448.

Firth, M. (1997). The provision of non-audit services and the pricing of audit fees. *Journal of Business Finance & Accounting, 24*(3), 511–525.

Firth, M. (2002). Auditor – Provided consultancy services and their associations with audit fees and audit opinions. *Journal of Business Finance & Accounting, 29*(5-6), 661–693.

Francis, J. R., & Stokes, D. J. (1986). Audit prices, product differentiation, and scale economies: Further evidence from the Australian market. *Journal of Accounting Research, 24*(2), 383.

French, S., Leyshon, A., & Thrift, N. (2009). A very geographical crisis: The making and breaking of the 2007–2008 financial crisis. *Cambridge Journal of Regions, Economy and Society, 2*(2), 287–302.

Ghosh, A., & Pawlewicz, R. (2009). The impact of regulation on auditor fees: Evidence from the Sarbanes-Oxley Act. *Auditing: A Journal of Practice and Theory, 28*(2), 171–197.

Gul, F. (1999). Audit prices, product differentiation and economic equilibrium. *Auditing: A Journal of Practice and Theory, 18*(1), 90–100.

Hay, D. C., Knechel, W. R., & Wong, N. (2006). Audit fees: A meta-analysis of the effect of supply and demand attributes. *Contemporary Accounting Research, 23*(1), 141–191.

Humphrey, C., Loft, A., & Woods, M. (2009). The global audit profession and the international financial architecture: Understanding regulatory relationships at a time of financial crisis. *Accounting, Organizations and Society, 34*(6), 810–825.

Kang, M., Lee, H.-Y., Mande, V., & Woo, Y.-S. (2019). Audit firm attributes and auditor litigation risk. *Abacus, 55*(4), 639–675.

Krishnan, G. V., & Zhang, Y. (2014). Is there a relation between audit fee cuts during the global financial crisis and banks' financial reporting quality? *Journal of Accounting and Public Policy, 33*(3), 279–300.

Leventis, S., & Dimitropoulos, P. E. (2010). Audit pricing, quality of earnings and board independence: The case of the Athens stock exchange. *Advances in Accounting, 26*(2), 325–332.

Mabbett, D., & Hodson, D. (2009). UK economic policy and the global financial crisis: Paradigm lost? *Journal of Common Market Studies, 47*(5), 1041–1061.

Mautz, R. K., & Sharaf, H. A. (1961). *The philosophy of auditing*. American Accounting Association.

National Institute of Economic and Social Research. (2009). *National institute economic review*. NIESR.

Pereira, J. M., Ribeiro, H., Silva, A., & Alves, S. R. (2020). To fail or not to fail: An algorithm for SME survival prediction using accounting data. In A. Thrassou et al. (Eds.), *The changing role of SMEs in global business* (pp. 83–108). Palgrave Studies in Cross-disciplinary Business Research, In Association with EuroMed Academy of Business.

Pratt, J., & Stice, J. D. (1994). The effects of client characteristics on auditor litigation risk judgments, required audit evidence, and recommended audit fees. *The Accounting Review, 69*(4), 639–656.

Roussy, M., & Mayer, M. (2018). Conventions of audit quality: The perspective of public and private company audit partners. *Auditing: A Journal of Practice & Theory, 37*(2), 51–71.

Seetharaman, A., Gul, F. A., & Lynn, S. G. (2002). Litigation risk and audit fees: Evidence from UK firms cross-listed on US markets. *Journal of Accounting and Economics, 33*(1), 91–115.

Shapiro, C. (1983). Premiums for high quality products as returns to reputations. *The Quarterly Journal of Economics, 98*(4), 659–680.

Sikka, P. (2008). Watching the detectives. *The Guardian*. http://www.guardian.co.uk/commentisfree/2008/mar/14/watchingthedetectives

Sikka, P. (2009). Financial crisis and the silence of the auditors. *Accounting, Organizations and Society, 34*(6), 868–873.

Sikka, P. (2015). The corrosive effects of neoliberalism on the UK financial crises and auditing practices: A dead-end for reforms. *Accounting Forum, 39*(1), 1–18.

Simunic, D. A. (1980). The pricing of audit services: Theory and evidence. *Journal of Accounting Research, 18*(1), 161–190.

Simunic, D. A. (1984). Auditing, consulting, and auditor independence. *Journal of Accounting Research, 22*(2), 679–702.

Simunic, D. A., & Stein, M. T. (1996). Impact of litigation risk on audit pricing: A review of the economics and the evidence. *Auditing, 15*, 119.

Srinidhi, B. N., & Gul, F. A. (2007). The differential effects of auditors' non-audit and audit fees on accrual quality. *Contemporary Accounting Research, 24*(2), 595–629.

Xu, Y., Carson, E., Fargher, N., & Jiang, L. (2013). Responses by Australian auditors to the global financial crisis. *Accounting & Finance, 53*(1), 301–338.

Zaman, M., Hudaib, M., & Haniffa, R. (2011). Corporate governance quality, audit fees and non-audit services fees. *Journal of Business Finance & Accounting, 38*(1-2), 165–197.

Zhang, T., & Huang, J. (2013). The risk premium of audit fee: Evidence from the 2008 financial crisis. *China Journal of Accounting Studies, 1*(1), 47–61.

4

SMEs Facing Crisis: Ideal Response or Equifinal Reactions?

Diego Campagnolo, Martina Gianecchini, Paolo Gubitta, Simona Leonelli, and Alessandra Tognazzo

4.1 Introduction

Small and medium enterprises (SMEs) constitute the backbone of the European economy since they provide a large source of jobs and economic growth. According to the European Commission (2019), SMEs account for 99% of all enterprises, generate 67% of European employment, and produce 55% of the entire GDP.

D. Campagnolo (✉)
Department of Economics and Management "M. Fanno", University of Padova, Padua, Italy

ICRIOS Bocconi University, Milan, Italy
e-mail: diego.campagnolo@unipd.it

M. Gianecchini • P. Gubitta • S. Leonelli • A. Tognazzo
Department of Economics and Management "M. Fanno", University of Padova, Padua, Italy
e-mail: martina.gianecchini@unipd.it; paolo.gubitta@unipd.it; simona.leonelli@unipd.it

D. Vrontis et al. (eds.), *Business Under Crisis Volume I*, Palgrave Studies in Cross-disciplinary Business Research, In Association with EuroMed Academy of Business, https://doi.org/10.1007/978-3-030-76567-5_4

According to part of the literature, SMEs generally face a liability of smallness and a liability of newness because they have more difficulties in obtaining resources compared to larger firms (Freeman et al., 1983). SMEs are more vulnerable than larger companies because of a lack of planning; relative shortcomings in terms of technological, managerial, and human capabilities; lower diversification opportunities; and a strong dependence on a few customers and suppliers (Branicki et al., 2018; Chowdhury, 2011). Moreover, they are more susceptible to competition than large companies, which generally benefit from economic conditions associated with economies of scale, barriers to entry, and stronger financial positions (Gunasekaran et al., 2011).

Despite these liabilities, SMEs also show some features that could help in times of crisis (Eggers, 2020). They can be more flexible than large firms when opportunities or threats arise because they are less affected by inertia, rigidity, and sunk costs (Tan & See, 2004). Also, thanks to their limited size, decision-makers are closer to the ground and may quickly adapt to constantly changing customers' and other stakeholders' needs (Eggers et al., 2012). Furthermore, it is easier for them to exploit market niches than larger firms (e.g., Hodorogel, 2009). Finally, SMEs typically rely on informal credit and are often more flexible with respect to the management of their financial position (e.g., Ter Wengel & Rodriguez, 2006).

In periods of prolonged economic crisis, SMEs' weaknesses may be exacerbated. They are generally the first to feel the effects of the crisis and those which undergo the most critical consequences (Branicki et al., 2018; Chowdhury, 2011; Juergensen et al., 2020). Because of their lower level of formalisation and the absence of crisis management planning, SMEs are more exposed to the risk of failure than larger companies (Herbane, 2013; Marshall et al., 2015; Smith & Fischbacher, 2009). For instance, the coronavirus pandemic period affected both the supply and demand side of several supply chains. SMEs, more than other firms, have suffered from supply chain interruptions, leading to shortages of goods, and from staff reduction because workers were ill, in quarantine, or needed to look after children. Again, SMEs have experienced a dramatic reduction of revenues on the demand side due to consumers' income losses (Etemad, 2020; Juergensen et al., 2020).

From the extant literature, it is unclear what the most relevant causes of adversity for SMEs are or how they react to such events. In this chapter, we try to explore how SMEs respond to different sources of potential crises. Unlike large firms, which through prevention activities can anticipate future threats and reduce their vulnerability (Sullivan-Taylor & Branicki, 2011; Weick & Sutcliffe, 2015), SMEs could have more difficulties in coping with such adversities. Indeed, they might experience further challenges in anticipating and planning for a crisis because of the resource scarcity and the informal administrative systems which typically sustain their strategies (Iborra et al., 2019; Sullivan-Taylor & Branicki, 2011). In order to explore this issue and to answer the call of Etemad (2020) for further studies on how SMEs manage uncertainties, in this chapter we investigate the types of causes which undermine SMEs' survival and the kinds of actions SMEs undertake to counter the effects of crises and thrive. We use a descriptive approach, focusing on a sample of Italian SMEs that have successfully gone through a crisis that threatened their survival in the period 2014–2018. Our findings advance the current understanding of the types of adversities that SMEs face and how they face such adversities. The chapter contributes to the resilience and crisis management literature on SMEs, advancing current understanding of the relationship between sources of threats and response actions.

The chapter begins with a review of the literature on the external and internal environmental factors that may impact on SMEs' vulnerability; it then continues with an explanation of the different actions SMEs can adopt as a response to a crisis. Then, the methods and the analyses of the empirical research are presented. Finally, we end the chapter with a discussion of the results, managerial implications, and conclusions.

4.2 Environmental Factors Impacting on Firms' Vulnerability

The environment embraces the totality of the factors which affect and influence firms' strategic choices, performance, and survival (Boyd et al., 1993). Interpreting and understanding environmental uncertainties is vital for firms (Miller, 1992; Thompson, 2003).

Seminal studies on organisations' environments conceptualised the environment as a single entity, focusing only on firms' external environments (Dill, 1958; Lawrence & Lorsch, 1967). Subsequent studies started to consider the environment to include all the physical and social factors that should be considered by firms' decision-makers (Duncan, 1972). Duncan (1972) underlined the importance of firms' internal and external environments as collections of factors that impact on a firm's performance and survival. A study by Miller (1992) developed a conceptual framework for classifying environmental uncertainty according to the environment from which uncertainty arises. In this vein, Miller distinguished the macro-, micro-, and internal environment.

The macro-environment includes political, economic, socio-cultural, technological, legal, and environmental forces that are outside a firm's boundaries. These forces have an indirect influence on each firm; that is, they affect the trends surrounding a firm's specific environment (e.g., the industry it is in). Again, firms take the macro-environment for granted and cannot affect it. Uncertainties in the macro-environment are generated from changes at the legislative or economic level that are hardly predictable but that can severely impact on a firm's strategy (Miller, 1992). Losing sight of the above forces, or even underestimating their effects, threatens the survival of a firm in the medium and long run. Recent research on SMEs suggests that crises emerging from changes in the macro-environment can impact several interconnected levels of a firm's network of relationships, including those with employees, with other firms in the supply chain, and with the local community in which a firm is embedded (Marshall & Schrank, 2014). Local communities are represented either by a geographically bounded area (which includes essential services such as infrastructure and utilities, government services, and housing) or by the social capital (which includes the network of relationships) among community members. For example, the Small Business Disaster Recovery Framework developed by Schrank et al. (2013) considers that in a disaster due to the macro-environment, firms face family as well as business and community challenges. This suggests that when a crisis comes from outside the boundaries of the organisation, it can severely impact on SMEs' viability because of the overlap between the firm and the family that often characterises SMEs.

The micro-environment is the nearby environment of the industry in which a firm operates, and it encloses all forces at the client, supplier, and competitor levels. Hence, micro-environmental uncertainties could derive, among others, from changes in clients' demands, suppliers' policies, or increasing competition (Miller, 1992). Differently from the macro-environment, forces at the micro-environment level directly affect a firm's strategy and operations. Moreover, the opposite is also true: a firm's individual choices can impact on the forces surrounding its micro-environment through product, process, or business model innovations or through vertical and horizontal integration strategies. Moreover, compared to changes at the macro-environment level, changes at the micro-environment level are easier to detect and more predictable since firms constantly interact with their customers and suppliers. SMEs can identify potential threats arising from the micro-environment even without formal processes of regular monitoring, thus increasing the possibility of taking preventive action and adjusting accordingly.

Finally, the internal environment is composed of elements within the organisation, including organisational structure, employees' competences and motivation, management practices, and corporate culture. The internal environment is "under the control" of the top management team or the business leader of a firm, whose choices and behaviours, as a consequence, directly influence such an environment. This makes the internal environment substantially different from the external environments, which cannot (the macro-environment) or can only partially (the micro-environment) be affected by the firm. Uncertainties from the internal environment are associated with the leader's situation or with the relationships with employees (Miller, 1992). Some studies support the argument that the viability of SMEs depends specifically on factors related to the internal environment. Although the internal environment is supposed to be directly impacted by the owner or the top management team, SMEs rely greatly on the resources and social capital of their owners and managers. This makes SMEs more vulnerable to crises associated with the owners' competences and professional and personal life cycle (Danes et al., 2009; Stafford et al., 1999). For instance, Winter et al. (2004) showed that SMEs' failure is often related to non-business situations that impact the owner, such as divorce and other life events (Arrondo-García et al., 2016; Di Zhang & Bruning, 2011; Marshall & Schrank, 2014).

4.3 How Firms Respond to a Crisis: Proactive and Concurrent Actions

Bundy et al. (2017) synthesised the literature on firms' crisis management around three primary stages: pre-crisis prevention, crisis management, and post-crisis outcomes.

The pre-crisis prevention stage includes the preparation and implementation of planned organisational solutions to reduce the impact of a potential crisis. In particular, organisations can adopt scenario planning practices to promote a continual analysis of the external environment and can adjust their organisational structure by creating planning units to prevent system breakdowns and the associated crises. Such changes are aimed at improving, among other things, communication systems and governance structures, which, in turn, enhances an organisation's anticipation culture and capabilities. In fact, cognitive and behavioural processes of collective managerial "mindfulness" are essential traits of "high-reliability organizations" (i.e., of those organisations that are exceptionally consistent in accomplishing goals and avoiding unexpected events whose consequences are potentially catastrophic even if of limited scope (Weick & Sutcliffe, 2001)). Again, by maintaining positive relationships with the overall network of their stakeholders, organisations develop anticipation capabilities, which according to Duchek (2020) are essential components of organisational resilience. Specifically, anticipation capabilities include "the ability to observe internal and external developments, the ability to identify critical developments and potential threats, and—as far as possible—to prepare for unexpected events" (p. 225).

The second stage—crisis management—includes the resources and capabilities that firms utilise in the short term aimed at containing the consequences of adverse events; these resources include financial resources, processes, and job redesign. In other words, crisis management requires coping capabilities, which are abilities to effectively handle unforeseen adversities to resist destruction. Coping capabilities involve two steps: first, accepting that a problem exists and second, developing and implementing solutions to face it, which can entail new investments (Duchek, 2020). The effectiveness of coping capabilities largely depends on leaders' crisis perceptions (e.g., the way leaders frame a crisis as an opportunity rather than a threat), leaders' traits and team composition (e.g., leaders who are more or less charismatic, flexible and open-minded), and crisis features (e.g., origin and size).

Finally, the post-crisis stage requires adaptation capabilities that are able to adapt to critical situations and to leverage organisational change to foster future success (Limnios et al., 2014). A crisis impacts on several organisational dimensions, such as outcomes (e.g., turnover and financial performance), processes (e.g., creativity and innovation), and intangible resources (e.g., reputation, legitimacy, and trust). Each of the previous dimensions is expected to enhance a firm's ability to successfully prevent or cope with adverse events. Firms develop adaptation capabilities by reflecting on crisis situations and incorporating the associated insights into their existing knowledge base through processes of accumulation and articulation (Zollo & Winter, 2002). The final objective is to increase organisational change capabilities by incorporating adaptability into the values of the organisational culture (Duchek, 2020).

In line with the above discussion, in this chapter we study the types of crises SMEs face, the actions they implement to face such adversities, and the perceived effectiveness of those actions. As we discussed earlier, such actions can be adopted before a crisis emerges (i.e., proactive actions) or during a crisis (i.e., concurrent actions). Proactive actions enable an organisation to control and act before the crisis happens rather than adjusting when a crisis manifests. Problem prevention and strategic scanning are examples of practices through which firms manifest proactive actions (Parker & Collins, 2010). Firms prevent problems by adopting scenario planning methodologies and developing corresponding contingency plans or by subscribing to insurance policies. Proactively examining the (external) environment is a first step to understanding its changes and to maintaining a dynamic fit between organisation and environment. Firms can identify the main forces that are likely to threaten their survival in the short and medium term and can anticipate strategic and organisational trajectories along which the organisation should evolve.

In contrast, concurrent actions include those coping and reacting practices that firms adopt during a crisis. Coping refers to the ability to adjust to changes in order to moderate potential damages (Coleman & Adim, 2019). Coping actions are short-term strategies and include, for example, the use of financial resources which act as an effective bridge to overcome times of turbulence when a crisis is temporary and does not entail a "structural break" with past trends (Rumelt, 2009). Reacting actions include new investments to get prepared to take advantage of the economic opportunities that adversities eventually create. These investments provide above-average results when the crisis marks a noticeable discontinuity with the past. Examples of reactive actions include new investments in tangible or intangible resources and capabilities.

Current empirical studies on resilience as a process are scarce and focus mostly on large firms (Annarelli & Nonino, 2016; Bhamra et al., 2011; Linnenluecke, 2017). In contrast to large firms, SMEs' limited resources and capabilities penalise their capability to prepare for adversity and to sustain periods of prolonged crisis, even if their informal decision-making processes might improve their reaction. Overall, the empirical evidence on the subject is limited, both on the sources of crises and on the actions SMEs adopt when confronting adverse events (Annarelli & Nonino, 2016; Battisti & Deakins, 2017; Conz et al., 2017). What are the main sources of crises that threaten SMEs' survival? Again, even if both proactive and concurrent actions are essential to achieving a high level of resilience, SMEs can hardly dedicate resources to all stages. Do SMEs adopt proactive or concurrent actions? Are SMEs better off adopting single actions or combining different types of actions? These are the questions we try to answer in the remaining part of the chapter.

In this chapter, we focus only on the pre-crisis prevention and crisis management phases identified by Duchek (2020) and Battisti and Deakins (2017)—thus on proactive, coping, and reactive actions. We decided not to focus on the post-crisis phase as it requires a longitudinal approach, studying if and how firms leverage their past experience to develop adaptive capabilities that affect their preventive and crisis management practices over time.

4.4 Method

Sample and Procedure

In this chapter, we use the data collected through the research project "Building Better Business Resilience", a two-year (2018–2019), five-country study into small business resilience funded by the JPMorgan Chase Foundation and carried out by the Enterprise Research Centre from the UK in collaboration with academic partners from France, Germany, Spain, and Italy (Wishart & Hopley, 2020). The authors of this chapter are the Italian group of researchers. Data were collected in five European cities: London, Frankfurt, Madrid, Milan, and Paris. The research project was aimed at studying the ways in which small and medium enterprises experience and respond to adversity. In this chapter, we use the data we collected in the Metropolitan City of Milan (Campagnolo et al., 2019) based on the following procedure.

First, we extracted all SMEs between 3 and 99 employees located in the metropolitan area of Milan from the AIDA database, which contains data on all limited liability Italian firms. The survey was administered between January 2019 and March 2019, using computer-assisted telephone interview (CATI) to collect 600 observations randomly extracted from the universe of 7319 firms. The final database contains 560 valid observations; the remaining 40 were excluded due to missing data. The respondents were all entrepreneurs or leaders of their businesses. We concentrated on them since they are the epicentre of their businesses, both in "business as usual" times and when navigating through adverse times. Entrepreneurs and top management leaders know exactly what they have done, why they have done (or not done) something and can better report what worked well and what did not. For these reasons, the use of secondary data cannot fully capture the nuances of SMEs' crises. The questionnaire consisted of two parts. The first part collected general information about the respondents (e.g., age, education, nationality, individual resilience) and the firm (e.g., industry, economic and financial data, organisational structure, firm's objectives). The second part focused on the firm's behaviour in situations that endangered their regular activity or their survival (e.g., past sources of crises, actual responses and their effectiveness, and current sources of threats).

4.5 Results

Table 4.1 (Panel A) lists the main characteristics of SMEs and entrepreneurs. The SMEs in our sample belong to the service industry (54.11%), the manufacturing industry (35.71%), and the construction industry (10.18%). The 41.07% of the firms are older than 21 years, while 36.25% are younger than 10 years old. Small firms (less than 50 employees) account for the great majority of the sample (96.96%), while medium-sized firms represent the remaining 3.04%. Concerning the entrepreneur's characteristics, the sample is balanced on gender: 50.89% of entrepreneurs are males, while 49.11% of the entrepreneurs are females. A third (33.21%) of the interview respondents are between 46 and 55 years old, while 38.75% of them are younger than 45 years old and 28.04% are older than 55. Finally, most of the entrepreneurs hold a high school diploma (57.50%), while around a quarter (27.67%) hold a bachelor's degree or higher (master's or PhD).

In our sample, 127 SMEs (22.68%) report that they had experienced a crisis in the five years between 2014 and 2018 (Table 4.1: Panel B). We asked entrepreneurs what sources of crises threatened their firm survival from among sixteen causes. These 16 causes belong to three categories on the basis of the environment from which they originate: macro-environment, micro-environment, and internal environment (Miller, 1992). The macro-environment includes all events of economic and social nature, changes in regulations or legislation, natural disasters like extreme weather events or floods, and crimes such as theft and cyber-crime. The micro-environment includes threats that originate in the relationships with customers, suppliers, and competitors. Finally, the internal environment includes threats arising from firms' internal dynamics, such as loss of key staff members, recruiting issues, equipment problems, production or technical failures, and cash flow shortages. In our sample, the majority of SMEs (44.88%) identified the micro-environment as the primary source of crisis, followed by the macro-environment (37.01%), and

Table 4.1 Characteristics of the survey sample

Panel A					
SME characteristics	*N*	%	*Entrepreneur characteristics*	*N*	%
Industry			Gender		
Service	303	54.11	Male	285	50.89
Manufacturing	200	35.71	Female	275	49.11
Construction	57	10.18	Total	560	100.00
Total	560	100.00			
Age			Age		
≤ 3 years old	28	05.00	≤ 35 years old	68	12.14
4–5 years old	54	09.64	36–45 years old	149	26.61
6–10 years old	121	21.61	46–55 years old	186	33.21
11–20 years old	127	22.68	56–65 years old	113	20.18
>21 years old	230	41.07	>65 years old	44	07.86
Total	560	100.00	Total	560	100.00
Employees			Education		
3–4	126	22.50	None	11	1.69
5–9	176	31.43	Elementary or middle school	72	12.86
10–19	137	24.46	High school	322	57.50
20–49	104	18.57	Bachelor's degree	74	13.21
50–99	17	03.04	Master's degree or PhD	81	14.46
Total	560	100.00	Total	560	100.00
Panel B			*Panel C*		
Crisis information	*N*	%	*During the crisis*	*N*	%
Experienced a crisis			Cause of crisis		
Yes	127	22.68	Macro-environment	47	37.01
No	433	77.32	Micro-environment	57	44.88
Total	560	100.00	Internal environment	23	18.11
			Total	127	100.00
			Choices to face the crisis		
			Proactive action	13	7.65
			Concurrent actions of coping	92	54.12
			Concurrent actions of reacting	65	38.24
			Total	170	100.00

lastly 18.11% of respondents reported the internal environment as the major source of crisis (Table 4.1: Panel C).

We also collected information on how firms faced the crisis they experienced. Respondents could select multiple choices among a list of ten alternatives that can be divided into proactive actions, concurrent actions of coping, and concurrent actions of reacting (Duchek, 2020). Proactive actions include the implementation of contingency plans prepared ahead of a crisis and the claiming on insurance policies (that they took out ahead of an event to protect against a future crisis). The concurrent actions of coping consist of the use of financial resources; staff reduction; seeking advice from specialists, colleagues, or informal networks; and working hours reduction. Finally, the reactive actions include developing a crisis management plan, investing in new equipment and technical systems, and hiring additional staff. In our sample, the majority of SMEs implemented concurrent actions of coping (54.12%), followed by concurrent actions of reacting (38.24%), and by proactive actions (7.65%) (Table 4.1: Panel C).

Figure 4.1 shows the percentage of each choice that SMEs adopted to face a crisis, grouped into proactive actions, concurrent actions of coping, and concurrent actions of reacting, matched with the perceived effectiveness that each adopter reported.

As we argued earlier, very few SMEs adopted proactive actions, whose effectiveness is on average lower than that of other actions: 33.33% of the adopters of a plan prepared ahead of the crisis and 50% of those who claimed on an insurance policy they previously took out considered their actions to be effective. Among concurrent actions of coping, the use of financial resources is the most cited (45.67%) as well as the most effective (63.79%). Staff reduction, seeking advice from specialists, and working hours reduction have been adopted by 30.71%, 19.69%, and 14.71% of respondents, respectively. Working hours reduction and staff reduction

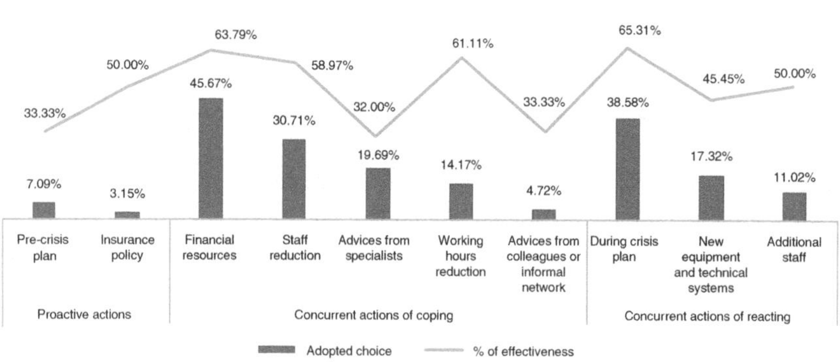

Fig. 4.1 Entrepreneurs' adopted choices to cope with the crisis and percentages of effectiveness

have also been effective for six out of ten adopters. Seeking advice from specialists, colleagues, or informal networks was reported as effective by only one-third of the adopters. Finally, among concurrent actions of reacting, only 38.58% of respondents developed a crisis management plan, which was effective for 65.31% of the adopters. This positions such a practice at the highest level of effectiveness among all actions in the study. About half of the adopters of the remaining concurrent actions of reacting (new equipment and additional staff) also considered them effective. These results confirm that SMEs are less likely to adopt proactive actions; instead they mainly adopt concurrent actions of coping or reacting (Iborra et al., 2019; Sullivan-Taylor & Branicki, 2011; Weick & Sutcliffe, 2015).

In Table 4.2 (Panel A), we combined the data on the sources of crises and the type of actions firms undertook to navigate adversities. Specifically, firms adopted proactive actions mainly to face crises whose principal cause arose from the macro-environment (53.85% of respondents), while only 23% of respondents that had taken targeted actions to anticipate and prevent the effects of crisis did that to face crises originating in the micro- or internal environments. Differently, firms used concurrent actions of coping mainly to counter the effects of crises arising from the micro-environment (46.74%). Similar actions have been used by 35.87% and 17.39% of the adopters to deal with macro- and internal environment crises, respectively. Finally, concurrent actions of reacting are uniformly used both with macro-environment (44.62%) and micro-environment (40%) causes of crises. Reacting actions are used by only 15.38% of adopters to counter the effect of a crisis in the internal environment.

In Panel B of Table 4.2, we explored the combinations of different actions (proactive, coping, and reacting). The majority of firms adopted only one type of action. Overall, 89 out of 127 (70.07%) firms whose survival has been threatened successfully addressed the crisis using only proactive, coping, or reacting actions. The most frequently cited are the coping actions that were used by 54 firms out of 127 (42.52%), followed by reacting actions reported by 33 out of 127 firms (25.98%). Interestingly, all firms that used only one type of action reported a high level of effectiveness that ranged from 83.33% to 100%. Only 33 firms out of 127

Table 4.2 Choices implemented to cope with the crisis compared to the crisis' cause

		Cause of crisis			
		Macro-environment	Micro-environment	Internal environment	Total
Panel A: Choices to face the crisis					
Proactive action		53.84%	23.08%	23.07%	100%
Concurrent actions of coping		35.87%	46.74%	17.39%	100%
Concurrent actions of reacting		44.62%	40.00%	15.38%	100%
Panel B: Combination of choices to face the crisis					
Only Proactive actions	Adopters	–	1	1	2
	Effectiveness	–	100%	100%	
Only Coping actions	Adopters	15	29	10	54
	Effectiveness	100%	100%	90%	
Only Reacting actions	Adopters	14	13	6	33
	Effectiveness	100%	100%	83.33%	
Proactive & Coping actions	Adopters	3	1	2	6
	Effectiveness	33.33%	0%	0%	
Proactive & Reacting actions	Adopters	–	–	–	–
	Effectiveness	–	–	–	
Coping & Reacting actions	Adopters	11	12	4	27
	Effectiveness	9.09%	8.33%	0%	
All three actions	Adopters	4	1	–	5
	Effectiveness	0%	0%	–	
Total		47	57	23	127

(25.98%) indicated that they used a combination of two types of actions. In detail, 27 firms combined concurrent actions of coping and concurrent actions of reacting to counter the effects of the crisis and bounce forward compared to the situation pre-crisis. Only six firms reported a combination of proactive and coping actions. No firm reported a combination of proactive and reacting actions. Differently from the data on the effectiveness of sole actions, firms that utilised a combination of two types of actions reported on average a very low degree of effectiveness, which ranged from 0% to 33.33%. This might suggest that firms did not correctly detect the source of the crisis and that they used combinations of actions as a sort of trial-and-error approach to deal with it. Further evidence in favour of this interpretation comes from the five firms (3.94%) that adopted all three types of actions as they reported no effectiveness.

Overall, the results in Table 4.2 provide some evidence that SMEs in our sample have adopted diverse types of actions to cope with similar types of crises (i.e., crises that originated in the same environments). This advances the hypothesis that equifinal instead of ideal responses might be possible.

4.6 Discussion and Managerial Implications

This chapter investigates the types of causes that undermine SMEs' survival and the actions they take to counter the effects of a crisis. In doing so, we used a descriptive approach analysing the data of 560 Italian SMEs. The main results of our study are illustrated in Fig. 4.2, which summarises the adoption and the efficacy of the three categories of actions adopted by SMEs in order to prevent and react to crises (i.e., proactive actions, concurrent actions of coping, concurrent actions of reacting), highlighting (see the grey colour) in response to which source of crisis (i.e., macro-environment, micro-environment, internal environment) they have been implemented.

Our research indicates that the primary cause of the crisis that has undermined firm survival derives from the micro-environment. Even if the result is somewhat surprising, since the micro-environment is partially under the control of the firm, this result is in line with the study of Arasti et al. (2014), who showed that changes in buying patterns, decreases in the purchasing power of customers, shortage of raw materials, customer strikes, low price competitors, and product and technology substitution commonly impact on SMEs' survival. Furthermore, very few studies have focused on these sources of crises compared to those which analysed the role of the macro-environment (e.g., numerous studies have investigated the impact of natural disasters and conflicts in a

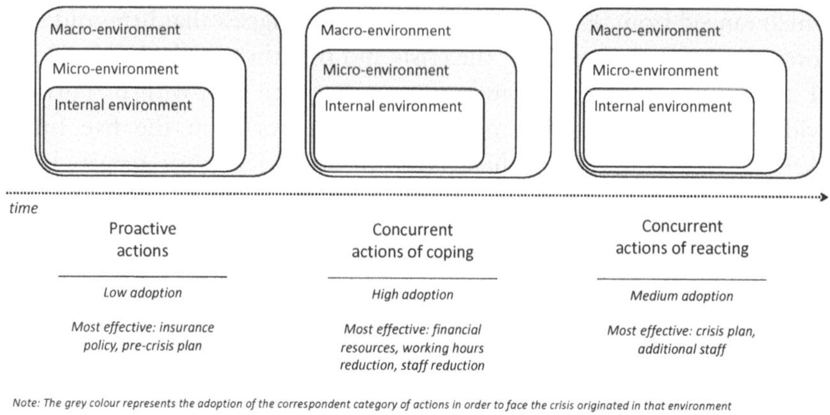

Fig. 4.2 Actions adopted and their effectiveness by crisis sources

variety of countries). Therefore, our results call for further studies on how SMEs face crises associated with the micro-environment.

The second result of our study underlines that SMEs implemented mainly concurrent actions of coping and of reacting instead of proactive ones to deal with adversities. This result is in line with previous studies demonstrating that, generally, SMEs cope or react when a crisis emerges due to their liability of smallness that constrains the adoption of preventive processes, such as planning for adversities (Branicki et al., 2018; Chowdhury, 2011).

The third outcome of our study reveals that firms' actions are associated with the environment from which the crisis arises. Our results show that if the crisis is determined by macro-environmental causes, SMEs mainly adopt proactive and reacting actions. Conversely, if the crisis is determined by micro-environmental sources, SMEs' main responses hinge on concurrent actions of coping. This might be associated with the fact that macro-environmental crises are more likely to be path-breaking of previous trends than changes at the micro-environmental level. Therefore, while anticipation and new investments are essential to bounce forward from the former sources of crises, actions aimed at resisting destruction are sufficient to navigate through the (temporary) adversities originating from the micro-environment.

Facing the consequences of a crisis might also entail balancing the benefits and costs of short-term versus long-term reactions (Rhodes & Stelter, 2009). According to Asel et al. (2011), implementing short-term actions such as massive cost-cutting and tight budget control could be necessary in the short term to cope with a sudden decline in revenues, but those actions could come at the expense of long-term growth as key stakeholder relationships might be compromised. In our study, short-term reactions can be concurrent actions of coping. We suggest that adopting solely coping actions might be an effective response to a crisis only if the crisis is limited in time and if it leaves unchanged the key success factors of the industry. For these reasons, proactive actions aimed at anticipating potential threats as well as a thorough understanding of the features of a crisis (e.g., root causes and expected duration) are crucial factors for identifying adequate responses and the ability to thrive in the long run.

Finally, implementing single types of actions rather than a mix of types can affect the effectiveness of the overall response to a crisis. Our results showed that those SMEs that implemented only one type of action (either proactive, coping, or reacting actions) reported a higher level of effectiveness than those firms that combined different responses. This result might suggest that those that adopted one action better understood the real sources of a crisis and further points out the importance of correctly detecting such determinants to implement an effective response strategy.

Furthermore, our findings advance the hypothesis that overcoming crises does not require the identification of an ideal response but that equifinal actions might be possible.

4.7 Conclusion

Our study deepens the current understanding of the sources of potential threats for SMEs and of how they face such adversities. We contribute to the resilience literature and the crisis management literature, underlining the importance for SMEs of analysing the sources of a crisis to implement the right choice to cope with it (Williams et al., 2017). Specifically, due to their limited resources, SMEs can hardly increase their resilience in advance leveraging on proactive actions for anticipating and preparing for a crisis. Therefore, knowing the main sources of adversities and the corresponding most effective choices of dealing with enhances the empirical knowledge on how SMEs strengthen their resilience during the management of a crisis. Moreover, improving the understanding of the link between sources of and responses to a crisis facilitates both learning processes within firms and imitation processes across firms. Moreover, such knowledge can be even more useful to cope with unexpected shocks, such as that due to the coronavirus pandemic that affects both the internal and external environments.

Our study suffers from a number of limitations that can represent avenues for future research. First, our sample is limited to data collected in the metropolitan area of Milan in Italy. To improve the generalisability of the results, future studies might compare data from different countries. Second, our analysis is only descriptive. Future studies could test the relationships among the variables. Third, our analysis, albeit adopting a process perspective, does not consider the post-crisis phase of adaptation through reflection and learning. Future studies might collect longitudinal data to investigate whether, and under what circumstances, SMEs activate processes of learning that enhance firms' capabilities of anticipation and crisis management. Fourth, our sample uses observations of firms that successfully went through a crisis that threatened their survival. Future studies might compare the actions adopted by firms that survived and those of firms that did not.

References

Annarelli, A., & Nonino, F. (2016). Strategic and operational management of organizational resilience: Current state of research and future directions. *Omega, 62*, 1–18.

Arasti, Z., Zandi, F., & Bahmani, N. (2014). Business failure factors in Iranian SMEs: Do successful and unsuccessful entrepreneurs have different viewpoints? *Journal of Global Entrepreneurship Research, 4*(1), 10–24.

Arrondo-García, R., Fernández-Méndez, C., & Menéndez-Requejo, S. (2016). The growth and performance of family businesses during the global financial crisis: The role of the generation in control. *Journal of Family Business Strategy, 7*(4), 227–237.

Asel, J. A., Posch, A., & Speckbacher, G. (2011). Squeezing or cuddling? The impact of economic crises on management control and stakeholder management. *Review of Managerial Science, 5*(2–3), 213–231.

Battisti, M., & Deakins, D. (2017). The relationship between dynamic capabilities, the firm's resource base and performance in a post-disaster environment. *International Small Business Journal, 35*(1), 78–98.

Bhamra, R., Dani, S., & Burnard, K. (2011). Resilience: The concept, a literature review and future directions. *International Journal of Production Research, 49*(18), 5375–5393.

Boyd, B. K., Dess, G. G., & Rasheed, A. M. (1993). Divergence between archival and perceptual measures of the environment: Causes and consequences. *Academy of Management Review, 18*(2), 204–226.

Branicki, L. J., Sullivan-Taylor, B., & Livschitz, S. R. (2018). How entrepreneurial resilience generates resilient SMEs. *International Journal of Entrepreneurial Behavior & Research, 24*(7), 1244–1263.

Bundy, J., Pfarrer, M. D., Short, C. E., & Coombs, W. T. (2017). Crises and crisis management: Integration, interpretation, and research development. *Journal of Management, 43*(6), 1661–1692.

Campagnolo, D., Gianecchini, M., Gubitta, P., Leonelli, S., & Tognazzo, A. (2019). *Building better business resilience. Report Italiano.* University of Padova.

Chowdhury, S. R. (2011). Impact of global crisis on small and medium enterprises. *Global Business Review, 12*(3), 377–399.

Coleman, R., & Adim, C. (2019). Entrepreneurial proactiveness and organizational resilience in mobile telecommunication firms in Rivers State, Nigeria. *The Strategic Journal of Business & Change Management, 6*(3), 454–465.

Conz, E., Denicolai, S., & Zucchella, A. (2017). The resilience strategies of SMEs in mature clusters. *Journal of Enterprising Communities: People and Places in the Global Economy, 11*(1), 186–210.

Danes, S. M., Lee, J., Amarapurkar, S., Stafford, K., Haynes, G., & Brewton, K. E. (2009). Determinants of family business resilience after a natural disaster by gender of business owner. *Journal of Developmental Entrepreneurship, 14*(04), 333–354.

Di Zhang, D., & Bruning, E. (2011). Personal characteristics and strategic orientation: entrepreneurs in Canadian manufacturing companies. *International Journal of Entrepreneurial Behavior & Research, 17*(1), 82–103.

Dill, W. R. (1958). Environment as an influence on managerial autonomy. *Administrative Science Quarterly, 2*(4), 409–443.
Duchek, S. (2020). Organizational resilience: A capability-based conceptualization. *Business Research, 13*, 215–246.
Duncan, R. B. (1972). Characteristics of organizational environments and perceived environmental uncertainty. *Administrative Science Quarterly, 17*(3), 313–327.
Eggers, F. (2020). Masters of disasters? Challenges and opportunities for SMEs in times of crisis. *Journal of Business Research, 116*, 199–208.
Eggers, F., Hansen, D. J., & Davis, A. E. (2012). Examining the relationship between customer and entrepreneurial orientation on nascent firms' marketing strategy. *International Entrepreneurship and Management Journal, 8*(2), 203–222.
Etemad, H. (2020). Managing uncertain consequences of a global crisis: SMEs encountering adversities, losses, and new opportunities. *Journal of International Entrepreneurship, 18*(2), 125–144.
European Commission. (2019). *Annual report on European SMEs 2018/2019: Research & development and innovation by SMEs*. https://ec.europa.eu/docsroom/documents/38366/attachments/2/translations/
Freeman, J., Carroll, G. R., & Hannan, M. T. (1983). The liability of newness: Age dependence in organizational death rates. *American Sociological Review*, 692–710.
Gunasekaran, A., Rai, B. K., & Griffin, M. (2011). Resilience and competitiveness of small and medium size enterprises: An empirical research. *International Journal of Production Research, 49*(18), 5489–5509.
Herbane, B. (2013). Exploring crisis management in UK small-and medium-sized enterprises. *Journal of Contingencies & Crisis Management, 21*(2), 82–95.
Hodorogel, R. G. (2009). The economic crisis and its effects on SMEs. *Theoretical & Applied Economics, 16*(5), 79–88.
Iborra, M., Safón, V., & Dolz, C. (2019). What explains resilience of SMEs? Ambidexterity capability and strategic consistency. *Long Range Planning, 101947*.
Juergensen, J., Guimón, J., & Narula, R. (2020). European SMEs amidst the COVID-19 crisis: Assessing impact and policy responses. *Journal of Industrial and Business Economics, 47*(3), 499–510. https://doi.org/10.1007/s40812-020-00169-4
Lawrence, P. R., & Lorsch, J. W. (1967). *Organization and environment*. Harvard Business School Press.

Limnios, E. A. M., Mazzarol, T., Ghadouani, A., & Schilizzi, S. G. (2014). The resilience architecture framework: Four organizational archetypes. *European Management Journal, 32*(1), 104–116.

Linnenluecke, M. K. (2017). Resilience in business and management research: A review of influential publications and a research agenda. *International Journal of Management Reviews, 19*(1), 4–30.

Marshall, M. I., Niehm, L. S., Sydnor, S. B., & Schrank, H. L. (2015). Predicting small business demise after a natural disaster: An analysis of pre-existing conditions. *Natural Hazards, 79*(1), 331–354.

Marshall, M. I., & Schrank, H. L. (2014). Small business disaster recovery: A research framework. *Natural Hazards, 72*(2), 597–616.

Miller, K. D. (1992). A framework for integrated risk management in international business. *Journal of International Business Studies, 23*(2), 311–331.

Parker, S. K., & Collins, C. G. (2010). Taking stock: Integrating and differentiating multiple proactive behaviors. *Journal of Management, 36*(3), 633–662.

Rhodes, D., & Stelter, D. (2009). Seize advantage in a downturn. *Harvard Business Review, 87*(2), 50–58.

Rumelt, R. P. (2009). Strategy in a "structural break". *The McKinsey Quarterly, 1*, 35–42.

Schrank, H. L., Marshall, M. I., Hall-Phillips, A., Wiatt, R. F., & Jones, N. E. (2013). Small-business demise and recovery after Katrina: Rate of survival and demise. *Natural Hazards, 65*(3), 2353–2374.

Smith, D., & Fischbacher, M. (2009). The changing nature of risk and risk management: The challenge of borders, uncertainty and resilience. *Risk Management, 11*(1), 1–12.

Stafford, K., Duncan, K. A., Dane, S., & Winter, M. (1999). A research model of sustainable family businesses. *Family Business Review, 12*(3), 197–208.

Sullivan-Taylor, B., & Branicki, L. (2011). Creating resilient SMEs: Why one size might not fit all. *International Journal of Production Research, 49*(18), 5565–5579.

Tan, H. H., & See, H. H. (2004). Strategic reorientation and responses to the Asian financial crisis: The case of the manufacturing industry in Singapore. *Asia Pacific Journal of Management, 21*(1–2), 189–211.

Ter Wengel, J., & Rodriguez, E. (2006). SME export performance in Indonesia after the crisis. *Small Business Economics, 26*(1), 25–37.

Thompson, J. D. (2003). *Organizations in action: Social science bases of administrative theory*. Transaction publishers.

Weick, K. E., & Sutcliffe, K. M. (2001). *Managing the unexpected: Assuring high performance in an age of complexity*. Jossey Bass Publishers.
Weick, K. E., & Sutcliffe, K. M. (2015). *Managing the unexpected: Sustained performance in a complex world*. John Wiley & Sons.
Williams, T. A., Gruber, D. A., Sutcliffe, K. M., Shepherd, D. A., & Zhao, E. Y. (2017). Organizational response to adversity: Fusing crisis management and resilience research streams. *Academy of Management Annals, 11*(2), 733–769.
Winter, M., Danes, S. M., Koh, S.-K., Fredericks, K., & Paul, J. J. (2004). Tracking family businesses and their owners over time: Panel attrition, manager departure and business demise. *Journal of Business Venturing, 19*(4), 535–559.
Wishart, M., & Hopley, L. (2020). *Building resilience in under-represented entrepreneurs: A European comparative study. A European comparative study*. https://www.enterpriseresearch.ac.uk/publications/building-resilience-in-under-represented-entrepreneurs-a-european-comparative-study-summary-report/
Zollo, M., & Winter, S. G. (2002). Deliberate learning and the evolution of dynamic capabilities. *Organization Science, 13*(3), 339–351.

5

Changes in Consumption Patterns of Tourists After the COVID-19 Pandemic

Mara Franco

5.1 Introduction

In December 2019, the world met a reported novel case of coronavirus pneumonia (COVID-19) in Wuhan, China, which rapidly became a public health problem all over the world. On March 11, 2020, the World Health Organization (WHO) classified COVID-19 as a pandemic (WHO, 2020). On January 5, 2021, the WHO issued a status report indicating that COVID-19 had a cumulative number of 83 million reported cases and over 1.8 million deaths since the beginning of the pandemic. New variants of the virus, such as the United Kingdom and South Africa variants, were also detected in other countries and regions of the world, as being more contagious and fast spreading (WHO, 2021b). The COVID-19 vaccination campaigns continue worldwide, and despite

---

M. Franco (✉)
University of Madeira & Centre for Tourism Research, Development and Innovation, Funchal, Portugal
e-mail: mara.franco@staff.uma.pt

D. Vrontis et al. (eds.), *Business Under Crisis Volume I*, Palgrave Studies in Cross-disciplinary Business Research, In Association with EuroMed Academy of Business, https://doi.org/10.1007/978-3-030-76567-5_5

being an important tool that can help to slow down this virus spread, its production and subsequent application in people is still a slow process.

The tourism sector is highly vulnerable to events and crises, as it is greatly influenced by external factors, such as political instability, economic conditions, environmental events and social impacts (Gudurav, 2014). Historically, terrorist attacks, pandemic and epidemic events and global financial crises affect consumer behaviour, bringing about changes in their consumption patterns (Reeves et al., 2020). Due to COVID-19 transmissibility through human-to-human contact, many countries have imposed travel restrictions, as international tourism has suffered considerable losses. In 2020, international tourist arrivals declined 74% due to the pandemic crisis, leading to an estimated loss of USD 1.3 trillion in international travel revenues and putting between 100 and 120 million direct tourism jobs at risk (UNTWO, 2021). Hotels, restaurants, travel agencies, tour operators, airlines, cruise ship companies and tourist entertainment companies have seen their activity suspended or massively reduced, raising unemployment rates across the globe.

The impact on the tourism industry is colossal worldwide; however, on the demand side, some changes are taking place in consumer behaviour, entailing changes in the consumption patterns in the years to come, and will shape a new consumer, even after the COVID-19 pandemic disappears. New words and habits have become part of everyone's life, as the social and physical distancing, mask-wearing and hand sanitising have given rise to new rules that are now part of people's routine (WHO, 2021a). From this, consumers have made some adaptations to their consumption, adopting a territorial and ethnocentric behaviour (Kirk & Rifkin, 2020) and, with the advances in technology and supply chains, e-commerce has become widely accepted by the consumer (Sheth, 2020).

To understand these consumption changes, it is vital to understand consumer behaviour changes in past crises, specifically in the tourism sector. Then, some COVID-19 changes in individuals' behaviour and impacts on the tourism industry are examined. Lastly, insights about the new tourists are provided, specifically changes in their consumption patterns that will last even after COVID-19 is declared to be over.

5.2 Impacts of Outbreaks on Tourist Behaviour

Throughout history, pandemics, from the Black Death in the Middle Ages to the Spanish Flu in the early twentieth century, have resulted in a massive change in the social behaviours of consumers (Reeves et al., 2020), and the COVID-19 pandemic will do likewise. Several crisis events have affected consumer behaviour, such as terrorist attacks (September 11 attacks in 2001), epidemics and pandemics (Spanish Flu, Hong-Kong Flu, SARS, H1N1, H5N1) and financial crises (global economic crisis of 2008–2014). All these major crisis events have long-lasting effects and shape consumer behaviour.

The 9/11 terrorist attacks in 2001 were felt worldwide due to its new dimension, mode and magnitude. Immediately, consumption behaviours became more compulsive and materialistic (Choi et al., 2007). While terrorism has the ability to shift consumer behaviour in the short term, it does not change consumer plans for the long term (Baumert et al., 2020). Having said that, consumers that were physically close to terror attacks experience high degrees of panic, anxiety, catastrophe and a sense of being lost, where they take self-protective measures, as consumers return to a daily routine over time. However, terror attacks also have impacts on customers that are physically distant from the event and also undergo changes, as they become more vigilant, but quickly return to the daily routine (Seger Guttmann et al., 2021).

Regarding pandemics and disease outbreaks that became widespread due to human-to-human infection, they had major negative impacts on health, the economy, politics, society and the security of global communities. The most lethal pandemic was the Spanish Flu in 1918–1919 (caused by the influenza virus), causing up to 100 million deaths worldwide. Still, this pandemic also had impacts on individuals' social trust, which is a vital emotional response for long-term economic development (Aassve et al., 2021). For example, the H1N1 influenza in 2009 has threatened health-care systems, animal health, education, transport and tourism sectors. Likewise, the SARS epidemic in 2003 has caused quite a bit of damage in Asian economies and society, resulting in illness and death. Although the economic impacts of a pandemic are significant, the social impacts can be more severe and long-lasting, as individual mobility can be conditioned with travel restrictions, schools, markets and sporting venues closing (Qiu et al., 2017). In terms of psychological factors affecting consumer behaviour, media coverage of these disease outbreaks creates unnecessary fear and an exaggeration of the perceived risk of a country or region (Rittichainuwat & Chakraborty, 2009). So, consumer behaviour also undergoes changes after these pandemic events, most of them being careful to prevent an infection. For instance, during the SARS outbreak, online shopping demand grew, thus empowering consumers, providing an alternate and safe channel to shop (Forster & Tang, 2005). So, the internet and the spread of the ecommerce infrastructure can play a major role, reducing the social and economic impact of crises.

Likewise, the global economic crisis that began in 2008 and lasted until 2014 had major economic and social impacts on consumers, contributing to shaping a new consumer behaviour. Essentially, consumers have lost confidence and become more economical, responsible and demanding. These new consumers question themselves what they are buying and, more importantly, why they are buying, being more involved and vigilant in all the buying processes, from design of products to their social and economic impacts. These new consumers are now aware that their consumption choices have impacts on the world, being more responsible in their consumption (Filip & Voinea, 2011). Mansoor and Akram (2011) state that the main changes in consumer behaviour as a result of the economic recession include the following:

- The need for simplicity: due to limited offers during the recession, consumers simplify their demands, so, after the crisis, consumers keep looking for simple offers, but with greater utility.
- Temperance: consumers show dissatisfaction with overconsumption, so they begin to recycle and to reuse.
- Smart consumption: consumers act more quickly, have the ability to change brands and look for the lowest price while sacrificing quality and brand loyalty.

- Green consumerism: this trend gets slowed down during the recession, because these products are more expensive. However, these products recover after the recession.
- Ethical consumerism: consumers are more worried about the welfare of their families and less willing to participate in charity initiatives.

The mindset of consumers after the international economic crisis was moulded in order to search for the most competitive offer, where online tools had a major role, from websites with consumer reviews, group-buying promotions to price comparison sites. These new consumers now need more reasons to justify the purchase, regarding aspects of quality, comfort, brand and price segment (Egol et al., 2010).

Tourism is a phenomenon that has economic, environmental, social and cultural impacts on places and people. External factors such as those of a political, social, technological, economic, natural and human events-related nature, with the interaction of international forces and trends, can lead to changes in tourist behaviour (Gudurav, 2014). The decision-making process of a tourist regarding a destination choice is influenced by external factors, where the awareness of terrorism can be included and plays a serious constraint on tourist behaviour. This awareness is built up by media coverage, travel advisories and social interaction sources, and the tourist determines the level of perceived risks. Then, potential tourists match their needs to the least perceived risk destinations (Sönmez & Graefe, 1998). The unprecedented 9/11 terrorist attack has caused major shock waves in several economic sectors, especially in the travel and tourism sector. By using commercial jetliners as weapons, terrorists made people wary of travelling by airplane, causing a huge impact on tourism and airline industry around the world (Garg, 2013). The vast majority of travellers are concerned about their safety, avoiding places that recently suffered terrorist attacks, as the perceived risk is higher. In the long term, the perceived risk decreases and terrorism does not impact travellers' choices as much (Rittichainuwat & Chakraborty, 2009).

Asian countries had a massive tourism impact due to the SARS epidemic in 2003 and the H1N1 influenza pandemic in 2009. Because of the fast spread of infections, tourists reflect on the decision of the specific time of travelling and the destination choice (Garg, 2013). When the

SARS epidemic was over, the tourism sector quickly recovered, due to accurate information delivered to potential visitors about safety and to change travel motivation based on natural landscape attributes (B. Zeng et al., 2005). However, even throughout a global pandemic, the intention of travelling is resilient, because potential international tourists easily perceive non-pharmaceutical interventions that can be taken during a trip, such as hand-washing, mask-wearing and information-gathering (Lee et al., 2012), with safety and security being the leading conditions determining destination choice.

This travel resilience also was shown during the global economic crisis, where tourists affected by the crisis did not quit travelling, as they adjusted their choices to closer or cheaper destinations, and, when choosing a traditional destination, they reduce the length of stay (Campos-Soria et al., 2015; Gudurav, 2014; Sedmark & Planinc, 2011; Smeral, 2010). Tourists gain awareness when searching for the most competitive offer and also have the tools that aid in that online search. However, only a global public health crisis, such as the COVID-19 pandemic, has had an impact on the international tourist network.

5.3 COVID-19 Changes in Individuals' Behaviour and Impacts on the Tourism Industry

Understanding consumers' consumption patterns is crucial to the success of any business organisation of any industry. Consumer behaviour has been attracting academics over the years, as it is highly influenced by economic and social external aspects. So, during and after an event, such as a crisis, consumer behaviour changes, giving rise to a new consumer. COVID-19 turned out to be not only a global health crisis but also a political, social and economic crisis, where the new consumer behaviour has undergone a series of changes. Before looking at the changes that COVID-19 has made to consumption behaviour, it is important to primarily understand the changes that people have undergone in their daily lives and routines. Table 5.1 shows the harsh proactive measures taken to

Table 5.1 Proactive measures to contain COVID-19 and changes in individuals' behaviour

Author	Proactive measures to contain COVID-19	Changes in individual's behaviour
Li et al. (2020)	Spatial distance	Individuals are more sensitive regarding the spatial or physical distance with others.
	Temporal distance	Individuals pay close attention to pandemic-related context and details.
	Social distance	Even in closer groups, such as family and friends, people have begun to take protective measures to keep themselves as well as their loved ones safe.
	Quarantine measures imposed by governments	People were forced to stay at home, reducing social contacts.
Kirk and Rifkin (2020)	Multi-functional homes	People work, exercise, learn, meditate and buy from home using technology equipment.
Sigala (2020)	Mask-wearing	People have to wear masks before going shopping, boarding mass transit or for just being on the street.
	Screening	Such as taking an individual's temperature when boarding a flight or testing for the presence of the virus before boarding.
Gössling et al. (2021)	Closed international borders (air, land and sea)	Travel restrictions and borders closed to movement of non-citizens and non-residents.
WHO (2021a)	Sanitary precautions	Frequently washing hands with alcohol-based sanitisers or soap, keeping a distance of 1 metre or more from others, wearing a mask, not going to crowded places and adhering to respiratory hygiene.

contain the COVID-19 global outbreak and the subsequent changes in individuals' behaviour.

Since the beginning of the COVID-19 pandemic, in a matter of weeks, the nature and the level of human interaction has been highly modified around the world. As the psychological distance (including spatial, temporal and social distances) imposed by the COVID-19 entered people's daily lives (Li et al., 2020), overnight, people started to turn their homes into workplaces, classrooms, gyms, meditation sites or places of worship, doctor's offices and shops, all of that using their own technological equipment. Such equipment is now the doorway for human interaction and socialisation, on top of the family that live in the same space (Kirk & Rifkin, 2020). Everything became virtual: entertainment, parties, events, festivals, dining and even visiting destinations and attractions (Sigala, 2020). Psychologically, individuals report effects of post-traumatic stress symptoms, confusion and anger, as a result of the quarantine and psychological distance measures (Brooks et al., 2020).

Although the proactive measures taken by health authorities and governments became essential for containing the quick spread of COVID-19, it has a negative impact on several industries around the world, particularly tourism (Crossley, 2020). The WHO has warned nations worldwide to restrict individuals' movements, to close tourist attractions, to suspend public events and business activities (Ioannides & Gyimothy, 2020). So, government authorities quickly started to implement health-related measures to isolate travellers arriving from the most affected countries, to suspend visas, to request medical certificates, to test for the presence of COVID-19 in travellers upon arrival, to call for travel bans from selected countries and to demand self-isolation or quarantine (Gössling et al., 2021). As a result, the tourism and hospitality industries were forced to suspend operations and to lay off their workforces (Wen et al., 2020).

During the pandemic, travellers have experienced traumatic tourism experiences, with trip cancellations, loss of money from paid trips, trip disruptions, loss of frequent-flyer benefits and imposed quarantines and isolation periods. Even if some travellers did not experience any of these events, they also went through these experiences through media channels and social networks (Sigala, 2020). Tourists have viewed their activity (travelling) as a perceived risk. The health risk can be a travel inhibitor. However, the psychological risk that travellers suffer is higher during the COVID-19 and can reflect anxiety or mental discomfort, which can lead to affective reactions of worry and regret after purchasing a tourism product (Li et al., 2020). Given this perceived risk, business meetings went from face-to-face to online conference calls, restricting business travel (He & Harris, 2020). However, the travel intention is greater than the travel anxiety (Wachyuni & Kusumaningrum, 2020). Recent reports state that tourists are ready to travel, especially engaging in activities linked to camping, recreational vehicles, walking and cycling (De Vos, 2020), related to nature-based activities forced by social distancing and perceived as safer. Hence, according to Wachyuni and Kusumaningrum (2020) most potential travellers want to travel again, and more than half will do it right after the end of the pandemic (0 to 6 months). Tourists will prefer natural attractions and will travel for a shorter period of time (1 to 4 days), choosing destinations based on cleanliness and safety factors.

5.4 Changes in Consumption Patterns of Tourists After the COVID-19 Pandemic

In this pandemic period, it is important to highlight the main changes that are occurring in the consumption patterns of tourists and to portray the new tourist behaviour after the COVID-19 pandemic. Overall, consumers had to adapt to the new market rules and circumstances. Recent studies have stated that consumers tend to exaggerate when buying essential products, adopting a territorial behaviour (Kirk & Rifkin, 2020) and tend to buy local, raising an ethnocentric consumption movement. So, the consumer decision-making during crises can be irrational due to a high level of uncertainty regarding the near future, driven by self-interest and emotions, such as fear, anger and anxiety (He & Harris, 2020), leading to changes in consumption. This disruption of consumer purchasing habits will lead to learning and improvising in new habits due to technological advances, social changes and mostly due to a global pandemic, such as COVID-19, as consumers do not go to the store, but the store comes to their home (Sheth, 2020).

Sheth (2020) summarised eight immediate effects of the COVID-19 pandemic on consumption and consumption behaviour. The first one was hoarding, as consumers started to stockpile essential products for daily consumption (toilet paper, water, meat and disinfecting products) as a reaction to future uncertainty of product supply. This was a panic-buying answer to individuals' perception of the threat of a health crisis and scarcity of products, fear of the unknown and uncertainty, anxiety that lead to coping behaviour, and influence from individuals' social network (Yuen et al., 2020). Then consumers started to improvise when facing constraints (improvisation effect) and new habits were invented, such as Zoom weddings or funeral services (Sheth, 2020). The third effect was the pent-up demand, as consumers postponed purchases of discretionary products, such as automobiles, homes and appliances (Sheth, 2020). The fourth was the embracing of digital technology, duc to the need to keep up with family, friends, work and school. Besides these virtual meetings, the internet helped to spread the electronic word of mouth, recommendations and information sharing, with social media as the main tool. Also, robotics, artificial intelligence and human-robot interactions utilisation increased in hospitals, at airports, in transportation systems, recreation areas, hotels, restaurants and communities in general, to manage the spread of COVID-19 (Sheth, 2020; Z. Zeng et al., 2020). This led to two other effects: the store coming home (due to lockdowns, consumers were unable to go grocery shopping) and gatherings with family and friends. Another effect is the blurring of work-life boundaries, as consumers are "prisoners" at home engaging in several activities (working, learning, shopping and socialising). And, lastly, the discovery of talent, because consumers have experimented with new recipes, new ways to share learning, spreading them online through videos on YouTube (Sheth, 2020).

Specifically regarding travel behaviour, Miao et al. (2021) also stated eight travel behaviours: the abstinence behaviour (postponing or cancelling travel plans), the disruptive travel behaviour (violating every precautionary measure when travelling), the rational travel behaviour (adopting every precautionary measure when travelling), the compensative travel behaviour (making up for lost time and deprivation of travel), the bounded travel behaviour (travelling locally and domestically), the voluntary de-crowding behaviour (reducing over-tourism), mindful tourism behaviour (sustainable tourism experiences) and travel as a quest for meaning (looking for a genuine experience in tourism).

Regarding the past crises, the changes that the COVID-19 pandemic has brought about in individuals' behaviour and routines, the impacts on the tourism sector and general consumer behaviour changes, the following main changes in consumption patterns of tourists after the COVID-19 pandemic are put forth:

- **Greater responsibility:** tourists will shift to a more responsible and prosocial consumption, reflecting on their choices and their impacts on themselves, on society and on the environment. This will reflect a more responsible and sustainable tourism and travel consumption.
- **Greater emotion:** tourists will pursue a pleasant experience to satisfy emotional needs that arise during the pandemic.
- **Greater ethnocentricity:** during and even shortly after the end of the pandemic, tourists can show preference for domestic destinations, as they can consider them safer and the right choice, manifesting a sentiment of nationalism.
- **Greater anxiety:** the tourist can demonstrate mental discomfort and pressure to make the right destination choice.
- **Greater thrill:** when safety issues are surmounted by tourists and when they consider it safe to travel, there will be a surge in the travel market. A sense of urgency to get out of the house and visit places, people and to dine out.
- **Less business travel:** the effectiveness of meetings and conferences online turned out to be a pleasant experience that can be extended to a non-pandemic situation.
- **Greater openness to technology:** the tourist will not think twice and will choose to buy online book visits online, purchase tickets through QR codes and compare prices online.
- **Greater respect:** it will be easy to respect new measures in destinations, accommodations and transports (e.g., marks with distance on the floor or testing rules for COVID-19).
- **More nature based:** the tourist can prefer wide-open and natural settings or destinations that are less populated, as well as tourism activities that take place outdoors.
- **Greater ethics:** the tourist becomes more aware of ethical and safety issues regarding unethical and excessive food consumption, towards a sustainable development of destinations and worrying about the welfare of their own families.
- **New mindset:** the tourist can embrace a new mindset focusing on health and wellbeing, searching for a genuine experience when travelling and engaging in a quest for their own meaning.

- **Less is more:** tourists will pursue simple offers that prevent overcrowding and avoid over-tourism destinations, using navigation technology to automatically re-route tourists.
- **More high-tech and high-touch:** a human-centred, highly personalised, but touch-free experience maintaining social distancing and reducing anxiety regarding contagion through human interaction.
- **Greater caution:** tourists will be more mindful about spending their money, paying careful attention to companies' social responsibility strategies and actions, and also taking economic instability and uncertainty into account.
- **Smarter:** tourists will be quicker in their reactions regarding brand utility and quality; if the brand does not fulfil this new tourist mindset, another brand will easily be preferred, as they also become less loyal to brands.
- **Less travel time:** the duration of trips is expected to be shortened or divided into several small trips.
- **Greater individualism:** individuals will avoid travelling in groups or purchasing tour packages, due to the fear and anxiety of being in a space with unfamiliar people.
- **Greater health awareness:** tourists will be concerned with cleanliness, access conditions and quality of care offered by the destination.
- **Lower income:** with the economic crisis, tourists will reduce travel expenses.
- **More information needs:** tourists will need to learn more about the destination before making a decision.
- **Greater vigilance:** as in previous crises events, due to feelings of anxiety and panic, tourists will take self-protective measures when travelling, such as social distancing, mask-wearing and health precautions.

5.5 Conclusion

The COVID-19 pandemic outbreak that emerged in December 2019 in China quickly affected the whole world (WHO, 2020). Several crises have happened in the past, and all of them had direct and indirect impacts on the tourism sector, but in the long term tourists always returned to their travel plans. The difference is that tourists had experienced new events that shaped old habits, presenting themselves as new consumers (Campos-Soria et al., 2015; Gudurav, 2014; Sedmark & Planinc, 2011; Smeral, 2010). During the COVID-19 disease outbreak, several measures were taken by health authorities and governments to slow down the quick spread of COVID-19 among humans, such as lockdowns and closure of international and national borders. Due to those restrictions, individuals were forced to reinvent themselves and to modify and learn new habits, such as working from home, learning from home and shopping from home (Sheth, 2020; Z. Zeng et al., 2020). These behaviours were regarded as alternatives at the beginning of the COVID-19 pandemic; however, they have become core habits. Henceforth, tourist consumption patterns will also change, as tourists are resilient and will adapt their behaviour to travel safely. It is important for destinations to rethink and redesign travel journeys and experiences in light of the proposed changes in tourist behaviour. Accurate information should be provided to potential visitors regarding safety, to offer natural-based activities, to focus on genuine experiences, avoiding overcrowded activities and, most importantly, focusing, more than ever, on sustainability issues.

References

Aassve, A., Alfani, G., Gandolfi, F., & Le Moglie, M. (2021). Epidemics and trust: The case of the Spanish Flu. *Health Economics, n/a*(n/a). https://doi.org/10.1002/hec.4218

Baumert, T., de Obesso, M. M., & Valbuena, E. (2020). How does the terrorist experience alter consumer behaviour? An analysis of the Spanish case. *Journal of Business Research, 115*, 357–364. https://doi.org/10.1016/j.jbusres.2019.11.085

Brooks, S. K., Webster, R. K., Smith, L. E., Woodland, L., Wessely, S., Greenberg, N., & Rubin, G. J. (2020). The psychological impact of quarantine and how to reduce it: Rapid review of the evidence. *The Lancet, 395*(10227), 912–920.

Campos-Soria, J. A., Inchausti-Sintes, F., & Eugenio-Martin, J. L. (2015). Understanding tourists' economizing strategies during the global economic crisis. *Tourism Management, 48*, 164–173. https://doi.org/10.1016/j.tourman.2014.10.019

Choi, J., Kwon, K.-N., & Lee, M. (2007). Understanding materialistic consumption: A terror management perspective. *Journal of Research for Consumers, 13*.

Crossley, É. (2020). Ecological grief generates desire for environmental healing in tourism after COVID-19. *Tourism Geographies, 22*(3), 536–546. https://doi.org/10.1080/14616688.2020.1759133

De Vos, J. (2020). The effect of COVID-19 and subsequent social distancing on travel behavior. *Transportation Research Interdisciplinary Perspectives, 5*, 100121. https://doi.org/10.1016/j.trip.2020.100121

Egol, M., Clyde, A., Rangan, K., & Sanderson, R. (2010). The new consumer frugality: Adapting to the enduring shift in US consumer spending and behavior. *Booz & Company, 24*.

Filip, A., & Voinea, L. (2011). Analyzing the main changes in new consumer buying behavior during economic crisis. *International Journal of Economic Practices and Theories, 1*, 14–19.

Forster, P. W., & Tang, Y. (2005). The role of online shopping and fulfillment in the Hong Kong SARS crisis. *Proceedings of the 38th Annual Hawaii International Conference on System Sciences*, 271a-271a.

Garg, A. (2013). A study of tourist perception towards travel risk factors in tourist decision making. *Asian Journal of Tourism and Hospitality Research, 7*, 47–57.

Gössling, S., Scott, D., & Hall, C. M. (2021). Pandemics, tourism and global change: A rapid assessment of COVID-19. *Journal of Sustainable Tourism, 29*(1), 1–20. https://doi.org/10.1080/09669582.2020.1758708

Gudurav, D. (2014). Economic crisis and tourism: Case of the Greek tourism sector. *Ekonomska Misao i Praksa, 23*, 613–632.

He, H., & Harris, L. (2020). The impact of Covid-19 pandemic on corporate social responsibility and marketing philosophy. *Journal of Business Research, 116*, 176–182. https://doi.org/10.1016/j.jbusres.2020.05.030

Ioannides, D., & Gyimothy, S. (2020). The COVID-19 crisis as an opportunity for escaping the unsustainable global tourism path. *Tourism Geographies, 22*(3), 624–632.

Kirk, C. P., & Rifkin, L. S. (2020). I'll trade you diamonds for toilet paper: Consumer reacting, coping and adapting behaviors in the COVID-19 pandemic. *Journal of Business Research, 117*, 124–131. https://doi.org/10.1016/j.jbusres.2020.05.028

Lee, C.-K., Song, H.-J., Bendle, L. J., Kim, M.-J., & Han, H. (2012). The impact of non-pharmaceutical interventions for 2009 H1N1 influenza on travel intentions: A model of goal-directed behavior. *Tourism Management, 33*(1), 89–99. https://doi.org/10.1016/j.tourman.2011.02.006

Li, Z., Zhang, S., Liu, X., Kozak, M., & Wen, J. (2020). Seeing the invisible hand: Underlying effects of COVID-19 on tourists' behavioral patterns. *Journal of Destination Marketing & Management, 18*, 100502. https://doi.org/10.1016/j.jdmm.2020.100502

Mansoor, D., & Akram, J. (2011). The global business crisis and consumer behavior: Kingdom of Bahrain as a case study. *International Journal of Business and Management, 6*(1). https://doi.org/10.5539/ijbm.v6n1p104

Miao, L., Im, J., Fu, X., Kim, H., & Zhang, Y. E. (2021). Proximal and distal post-COVID travel behavior. *Annals of Tourism Research, 88*, 103159. https://doi.org/10.1016/j.annals.2021.103159

Qiu, W., Rutherford, S., Mao, A., & Chu, C. (2017). *The Pandemic and its Impacts, 2017*, 11. https://doi.org/10.5195/hcs.2017.221

Reeves, M., Carlsson-Szlezak, P., Whitaker, K., & Abraham, M. (2020). Sensing and shaping the post-COVID era. *The BCG Henderson Institute.*

Rittichainuwat, B. N., & Chakraborty, G. (2009). Perceived travel risks regarding terrorism and disease: The case of Thailand. *Tourism Management, 30*(3), 410–418. https://doi.org/10.1016/j.tourman.2008.08.001

Sedmark, G., & Planinc, T. (2011). The effect of economic crisis on tourist behavior. *Academica Turistica, 4*, 35–42.

Seger Guttmann, T., Gilboa, S., & Partouche-Sebban, J. (2021). "I live with terror inside me": Exploring customers' instinctive reactions to terror. *International Journal of Hospitality Management, 92*, 102734. https://doi.org/10.1016/j.ijhm.2020.102734

Sheth, J. (2020). Impact of Covid-19 on consumer behavior: Will the old habits return or die? *Journal of Business Research, 117*, 280–283. https://doi.org/10.1016/j.jbusres.2020.05.059

Sigala, M. (2020). Tourism and COVID-19: Impacts and implications for advancing and resetting industry and research. *Journal of Business Research, 117*, 312–321. https://doi.org/10.1016/j.jbusres.2020.06.015

Smeral, E. (2010). Impacts of the world recession and economic crisis on tourism: Forecasts and potential risks. *Journal of Travel Research, 49*(1), 31–38. https://doi.org/10.1177/0047287509353192

Sönmez, S. F., & Graefe, A. R. (1998). Influence of terrorism risk on foreign tourism decisions. *Annals of Tourism Research, 25*(1), 112–144. https://doi.org/10.1016/S0160-7383(97)00072-8

UNTWO. (2021). All regions barometer. Retrieved January 30, 2021, from https://www.unwto.org/news/2020-worst-year-in-tourism-history-with-1-billion-fewer-international-arrivals

Wachyuni, S. S., & Kusumaningrum, D. A. (2020). The effect of COVID-19 pandemic: How are the future tourist behavior? *Journal of Education, Society and Behavioural Science*, 67–76.

Wen, J., Wang, W., Kozak, M., Liu, X., & Hou, H. (2020). Many brains are better than one: The importance of interdisciplinary studies on COVID-19 in and beyond tourism. *Tourism Recreation Research, 46*, 1–4.

WHO. (2020). Director-General's opening remarks at the media briefing on COVID-19 – 11 March 2020. Retrieved January 4, 2021, from https://www.who.int/director-general/speeches/detail/who-director-general-s-opening-remarks-at-the-media-briefing-on-covid-19%2D%2D-11-march-2020

WHO. (2021a). Coronavirus disease (COVID-19) advice for the public. Retrieved February 15, 2021, from https://www.who.int/emergencies/diseases/novel-coronavirus-2019/advice-for-public

WHO. (2021b). *Weekly epidemiological update – 5 January 2021*. https://www.who.int/publications/m/item/weekly-epidemiological-update%2D%2D-5-january-2021

Yuen, K. F., Wang, X., Ma, F., & Li, K. X. (2020). The psychological causes of panic buying following a health crisis. *International Journal of Environmental Research and Public Health, 17*(10), 3513.

Zeng, B., Carter, R. W., & De Lacy, T. (2005). Short-term perturbations and tourism effects: The case of SARS in China. *Current Issues in Tourism, 8*(4), 306–322. https://doi.org/10.1080/13683500508668220

Zeng, Z., Chen, P.-J., & Lew, A. A. (2020). From high-touch to high-tech: COVID-19 drives robotics adoption. *Tourism Geographies, 22*(3), 724–734. https://doi.org/10.1080/14616688.2020.1762118

6

e-mobility in the Age of COVID-19

Alessandro Augurio, Clelia Mazzoni, Laura Castaldi, and Teresa Cerchiello

6.1 Introduction

The pressing need to reduce greenhouse gas (GHG) emissions has been shifting the transport sector towards e-mobility (Mazzoni et al., 2020), which means adopting electrically powered technologies for the propulsion of vehicles (Gartner, n.d.). Electric vehicle (EV) sales have been increasing for years, and in 2019, 2.9 million EVs were sold worldwide. China is the biggest market, followed by the United States. In Europe sales increased by 50% in 2019 (IEA, 2020).

The COVID-19 outbreak in 2020 had strongly affected the automotive industry through value chain disruption and a fall in demand. The

A. Augurio (✉) • C. Mazzoni • L. Castaldi • T. Cerchiello
Department of Economics, University of Campania "Luigi Vanvitelli", Capua, Italy
e-mail: alessandro.augurio@unicampania.it; clelia.mazzoni@unicampania.it; laura.castaldi@unicampania.it; teresa.cerchiello@unicampania.it

D. Vrontis et al. (eds.), *Business Under Crisis Volume I*, Palgrave Studies in Cross-disciplinary Business Research, In Association with EuroMed Academy of Business, https://doi.org/10.1007/978-3-030-76567-5_6

health crisis has pushed consumers to opt for safer individual mobility forms (PWC, 2020a; Bert et al., 2020).

This work discusses the future of e-mobility, investigating whether the pandemic, with all its consequences, could hinder the diffusion of EVs. We use a literature review approach. We also undertake, on the one hand, an analysis of the latest industry reports for supply and demand data and trends, and on the other hand, a study of the European Union's (EU) and its member states' directives, laws, and other documentation for public policy determinants.

The work is structured as follows. Section 1 consists of an introduction to the issue of e-mobility based on a literature review of the main works about the environmental impact of EVs and the new business models that were born with the advent of e-mobility. Sections 2 and 3 discuss the main effects of COVID-19 on mobility and the automotive industry. Section 4 contains an analysis of the European policy to sustain e-mobility during the pandemic, with examples of incentives and bonuses from national governments. The analysis suggests that e-mobility remains at the centre of governments' agenda, despite the crisis. This section is followed by concluding remarks to the effect that the combination of policy from governments, new mobility patterns, and the introduction of new EV models by car manufacturers has enabled e-mobility to tackle the consequences of the pandemic.

6.2 e-mobility: A New Pattern for Transportation

E-mobility is raising governments' interest, as it represents a chance to reduce greenhouse gas (GHG) emissions. EVs consist of different types of vehicles that are fully or partially powered by electricity:

- Battery electric vehicles (BEVs), which are completely electric, where the motor exploits the energy stored in batteries.

- Plug-in hybrid electric vehicles (PHEVs), which have both an electric motor and an internal combustion engine, where the former is charged by an external source of energy.
- Hybrid electric vehicles (HEVs), which have an electric motor that supports the conventional engine and is charged by regenerative breaking.

In contrast, internal combustion engine vehicles (ICEVs) consist of traditional cars that are powered only by an internal combustion engine.

EVs are deemed by the European Commission (EC) as a pivotal instrument to decarbonise transport emissions by 2050 and to reduce the Union's dependence on oil and carbon in accordance with the European Strategy "Transport 2050" objectives (European Commission, 2011, 2018a). In particular, road transport, which accounts for a significant part of European GHG emissions (EEA, 2020), is subject to strict regulations that consist of banning conventionally fuelled vehicles in cities by 2050 and converting freight transport to zero-emission by 2030 (European Commission, 2011).

Fully electric vehicles such as BEVs produce no emissions from the tailpipe, so they reduce air pollution in the urban context (Biresselioglu et al., 2018; Hawkins et al., 2013). Moreover, electric powertrains are more efficient, and thus EVs require less maintenance.

However, EVs have a non-negligible environmental impact, raising two main issues when taking into consideration all the stages of the life cycle of these vehicles (Mazzoni et al., 2020). The life cycle of EVs consists of the manufacture of their components and their assembly, the production of the electricity and the combination of the energy mix that fuels them, the usage of vehicles by drivers, and their maintenance and disposal (Danielis, 2015).

The first issue is about the electricity mix, which consists of the combination of fuels used to generate the electricity. It is estimated that BEVs fuelled by an electricity mix with a higher share of renewable sources can reduce the GHG emissions by 10–24% compared to gasoline and diesel vehicles (Hawkins et al., 2013). On the contrary, when the electricity mix depends more on fossil fuels such as oil, lignite, and coal, BEVs do not reduce global GHG emissions. In this case, the only result of EVs is to shift pollution from the urban context to the places where the electricity is produced (Hawkins et al., 2013; Holland et al., 2015). In China, EVs produce even more GHG emissions than internal combustion engine vehicles (ICEVs) in Germany, the United States, and Japan due to the different energy mix (Asaithambi et al., 2017).

The second issue is about the manufacture of batteries, which has a strong environmental impact. Their production accounts for a significant amount of GHG emissions (Nealer & Hendrickson, 2015), and the mining and disposal activities produce very toxic chemicals (Abdul-Manan, 2015; Messagie, 2017). Thus, EVs increase the risks of toxicity for human beings, freshwater eco-toxicity, water eutrophication processes, and pollution from disposal of metals (Hawkins et al., 2013). The production of the batteries entails another problem, as the mining of cobalt, which is the main component of lithium batteries, has often taken place in Congo by exploiting people, including children, without respecting human rights, as denounced by an investigation by Amnesty International and AfreWatch in 2016. This denunciation has forced the Chinese company that owns those mining firms and the government of Congo to pledge to respect the international standard of human rights and ban child labour in future (Amnesty USA, 2017; Mazzoni et al., 2020).

The empirical studies about the benefits of EVs are characterised by different results due to the variety of the basic assumptions, namely the electricity source, the efficiency of the EVs and ICEVs used in the studies, and the drive cycles—which consist of all the testing conditions related to the vehicles' use, such as the engine speed, the ambient temperatures, the driving patterns, and many others (Abdul-Manan, 2015; Messagie, 2017). Nevertheless, these studies provide important guidance. The effective reduction of GHG emissions by EVs requires significant efforts by governments to increase the renewable share of the electricity mix and to promote further research, with the creation of public–private partnerships, to reduce the environmental impact of batteries. Research should identify second-life applications for batteries, such as their reuse as energy storage, in order to extend their lifetime and to improve their recycling and disposal. The successful contribution of EVs to reducing GHG emissions calls for measures that take into account and intervene in the environmental impact produced by the implementation of all the phases of the vehicle lifecycle (Danielis, 2015; Messagie, 2017).

Beyond the potential GHG emission reduction, e-mobility is also seen as an opportunity for the European car manufacturers to renew their technologies and to improve their competitiveness (Biresselioglu et al., 2018), as China does by supporting Chinese manufacturers' electrification of vehicles in order to undermine the role of the foreign car manufacturers in the country (Meissner, 2014).

Electrification has been affecting not only cars and public and freight transportation but also micro-mobility, which is based on small and light devices. The technological development of more efficient electric motors and batteries has allowed the development of several electric personal mobility devices (ePMDs), such as e-scooters, skate scooters, e-bikes, Segways, hoverboards, monowheels, and motor quadricycles, which are attracting the interest of an increasing number of people worldwide who seek alternative transportation modes to avoid traffic and to enter the low-emission zones in congested cities. EPMDs are deemed to reduce GHG emissions, as they require less energy than cars and public transportation, as well as to solve traffic and parking issues in great cities where they are as popular as traditional bicycles (Heineke et al., 2019; Zagorskas & Burinskienė, 2019). However, ePMDs are not completely safe for users yet, as their use is accompanied by the risk of severe injuries and hospitalisation for adopters (Heineke et al., 2019; Tan et al., 2019).

E-mobility is not only contributing to changes in mobility from a technology perspective. In fact, new business models are emerging to make EVs more attractive and affordable to consumers who need more services to support the charging, navigation, and parking of vehicles. E-mobility business models, which are characterised by a strong service orientation, make the usage of EVs easier (Laurischkat et al., 2016). For example, e-car sharing is considered a valid option for the diffusion of BEVs because it allows consumers to overcome barriers such as high costs, battery life limitations, and non-optimal charging infrastructures (Brendel et al., 2018). EPMDs are also provided by sharing, which is turning mobility, traditionally based on the purchase of vehicles, into the provision of a service, where consumers are especially interested in the provision of the transportation service rather than the purchase and ownership of vehicles (MSCI, 2020). Other business models are described in the literature. Consumers can purchase a vehicle together with a bundle of services, such as electricity services, parking services, discounted car rentals, and access to e-roaming providers that permits them to charge at every charging station. Charging stations can provide energy provision contracts by which consumers can charge their cars by paying a fixed amount per month. Companies that set out to electrify their fleets can be assisted by fleet electrifiers, which provide consulting services to manage the substitution of ICEVs with EVs. These vehicles can be also made available to the firms' employees for private use after work (Laurischkat et al., 2016).

Electric vehicles and sharing represent the future of mobility, which intersects with two other phenomena: vehicle connectivity and autonomous driving. Vehicles are becoming more connected and autonomous thanks to technologies that guarantee onboard entertainment, data sharing, and remote control (PWC, 2020a). Furthermore, the advancement of autonomous vehicle technologies will allow for reduction of transportation costs, increased safety, and making mobility more accessible to disabled and non-ambulatory people (Bagloee et al., 2016).

6.3 Mobility Change on Demand Side Post-COVID-19

The health crisis caused by COVID-19 caused a stop in everyday life, with an interruption of the movements (for work, study, pleasure, etc.) of millions of people around the world. With the lockdown, the use of almost all modes of public and private transport collapsed. Public transportation was guaranteed to provide low-cost transport for essential workers, with frequent disinfection of subways, trains, stations, rail cars, and buses, and contactless payments were established to avoid the exchange of currency, which can be a vector of contagion. Many e-scooter and car-sharing services have been temporarily suspended, while other operators have maintained them, taking care to carry out sanitisations and adapting services to new hygiene measures. Other players in the sector have reduced their rental fleets to reduce costs due to the decrease in the number of users, as people turned towards the use of private vehicles (cars, bikes, scooters, etc.), also stimulated by the existence of different bonuses supporting their purchase.

During the lockdown and in the post-lockdown period, lifestyles, consumption, and travel practices have changed, and there is a greater propensity to save due to the period's economic uncertainty. A study conducted by Bert et al. (2020) in Europe, the United States, and China shows that in the period of the freeze, people have preferred the use of bikes and private scooters, with an increase of bike-sharing, especially in the United States and China, thanks to the continuous disinfection and price reductions. Besides, bike use has been facilitated in some cities by closing roads to motorised vehicles and creating pop-up bike paths. This is because bicycles, in addition to providing a way to avoid contact with others, offer a healthy and above all convenient alternative to mobility and the possibility of being outdoors, where the risk of infection is minimal. The analysis by Bert et al. (2020) also shows that, on the whole, customers prefer individual mobility to relying on public transport. About 60% of respondents in all three regions said they would use public transport less or much less frequently, preferring to walk, ride a bicycle, or drive their own car. On the other hand, other modes of shared mobility, such as ride-hailing and car-sharing, will be used less, but will not suffer such steep declines as public transport. However, the health crisis has led to a change in the population's consumption and, after the lockdown, their willingness to buy (thanks also to state incentives) low-emission cars, including electric ones, as they represent a safer form of mobility.

Regarding the corporate market, in the first half of 2020, there was a decline in corporate sales at the European level. Companies stopped modernising their fleets of cars due to the lockdown. Companies are TCO (total cost of ownership) oriented, and before making any investment, they analyse the total cost of ownership, including operating costs, repairs, taxes, maintenance, depreciation, and resale values. EVs are associated to four categories of costs (or revenues) that may occur along the different stages of the life cycle, that is costs associated with shipping, charging infrastructure, taxation, and externalities (e.g., emissions).

Considering that the TCO of electric cars is much lower than that of ICE cars, electric cars could be preferred, not least because most European countries offer generous tax regimes for companies that buy electric vehicles.

6.4 The Consequences of the Pandemic on the Automotive Industry: e-mobility Outlook

Before analysing the outlook of e-mobility, a focus on the general impact of the pandemic on the automotive industry is provided.

The COVID-19 outbreak has hit the automotive industry hard worldwide, disrupting the global value chains and decreasing demand. Governments' containment measures, such as curfews and closing factories, to fight back the outbreak have caused car manufacturers to stop most of their plants and to reduce their production in the short-term (Accenture, 2020; PWC, 2020a).

Car sales are expected to decrease by 25% in Europe, from 12.8 million units in 2019 to 9.6 million in 2020 (ACEA, 2020). As a consequence, the top-20 original equipment manufacturers (OEMs) will face a reduction of their profits of up to $100 billion in 2020 (Hofstatter et al., 2020).

The supply shortage has added to those restrictions. The pandemic has demonstrated the fragility of the global automotive value chains, which are based on the just-in-time philosophy and are strictly dependent on Chinese suppliers (Accenture, 2020; Hofstatter et al., 2020). The flight cancellations and the Chinese government's quarantine measures prevented suppliers, including those with consistent stock, from delivering materials and components to their customers (Patò & Herczeg, 2020).

The economic crisis resulting from the pandemic has led to a decrease in sales, also due to reduced possibilities for consumers to borrow capital, decreasing their purchasing power. Moreover, the turbulent economic situation has negatively impacted the confidence of individuals, who—as a consequence—are postponing their intended purchases (ITF, 2020;

PWC, 2020a). The pandemic is also changing consumers' behaviour and purchasing process. Consumers are less available to acquire information and purchase cars by visiting dealers; thus, car manufacturers and car dealers have to use more digital channels to guarantee contactless customer engagement and online sales (Gartner, 2020). Digital technologies can be an important tool for firms giving them new opportunities to enhance their competitiveness (Thrassou et al., 2020).

The same solutions are required in aftermarket sales, where a not insignificant share of consumers are postponing maintenance and repair activities to avoid any contacts (Furcher et al., 2020).

The outbreaks of COVID-19 have created a potentially difficult scenario for e-mobility as well. Consumers' loss of confidence and reduced purchase power will negatively affect their decision to buy e-cars, which are still more expensive than ICEVs. Furthermore, the drop in oil prices will reduce the total cost of ownership of conventional vehicles, making EVs less attractive. Finally, OEMs could postpone or reduce investment in e-mobility considering the drop in sales and the shortage of liquidity (ITF, 2020).

However, e-mobility is expected to continue its development in the long term. Indeed, the pandemic has also provided some favourable conditions to e-mobility. The reduction of pollution during the lockdown period has emphasised people's awareness of environmental issues (Desomer & Walker, 2020). Many governments are providing incentives and policies for e-mobility to stimulate the economic recovery (Gersdorf et al., 2020). The positive long-term outlook is enhanced by other considerations. Car manufacturers had already made huge investments in e-mobility, and they are constrained for the future. Finally, the oil price is supposed to rise in the long term (ITF, 2020).

Months after the declaration of the pandemic by the World Health Organization (WHO), the e-mobility market has shown the ability to tackle the automotive crisis. Comparing the first nine months of 2020 with those of 2019, EV sales recorded an increase of 19% in the major markets (China, the United States, and the top-ten European ones, which are Germany, France, the United Kingdom, Spain, Italy, Norway, the Netherlands, Austria, Sweden, and Switzerland). From January to September 2020, EV sales were 2,770,500, almost half a million more than in the same period of the last year, when 2,331,600 electrified vehicles were sold. In particular, PHEV sales increased by 45%, from 342,000 to 495,800. In contrast, the growth of BEVs was a more moderate 7%. The largest increase is given by the top-ten European markets, where EV sales grew by 128% compared to the same period of 2019, with an increase of all the types of EVs, in particular of PHEVs, whose sales grew by 316% (PWC, 2020b). Similarly, there is a negative trend for the registration of petrol and diesel cars in Europe compared to the first half of 2019, confirming the orientation of consumers towards the "cleanest" vehicles. The confirmation of all the objectives in term of CO_2 emissions by the European leaders and the introduction of several electric models by European OEMs has allowed this growth (Gersdorf et al., 2020). The same effect occurred in Italy, where the share of registered EVs has grown by more than 2% compared to the same period in 2019 (Chiaroni et al., 2020).

In China, the growth of EV sales was 49%, mostly consisting of BEVs (PWC, 2020b). The Chinese e-mobility market can benefit from the efficacy of the country's containment measures, which are allowing a quick return to normal, and of the previous policies adopted to develop the e-mobility market and facilitate the birth of several EV startups before the outbreak (Gersdorf et al., 2020).

The US e-mobility market growth has been slower. In the first nine months of 2020, EV sales increased by only 8%. The market has been pushed by HEVs, as PHEV sales dropped, while those of BEVs were the same as in the last year. This slowdown is due to the postponing of new EV models by car manufactures (PWC, 2020b).

Although the health crisis due to COVID-19 has had a very negative impact on worldwide car registrations, electric vehicles have suffered less than the automotive sector as a whole. The long-term outlooks are also very positive for e-mobility in China and Europe, where the market share of EV sales will be respectively between 35% and 50% and between 35% and 45% by 2030. These markets will benefit from several more stable forms of incentives. European EV sales should rise also in 2021 and 2022, when they will reach between 2 million and 2.9 million vehicles. The European market share of EVs is expected to rise to 15%. The short-term outlook of the Chinese market is also positive because the number of EVs sold may reach between 2.4 and 3.5 million in 2022. The market share of EVs could reach between 11% and 14% (Gersdorf et al., 2020).

In the United States, the scenario is more complicated because recent policies towards emissions are less harsh, and taxes on gasoline are lower than in most other countries. Moreover, the falling oil price could make ICEVs cheaper than EVs (Gersdorf et al., 2020).

6.5 European Public Policy to Sustain e-mobility Pre- and Post-COVID-19

The changes in the transport industry in recent years have been very rapid, as there has been an increasing focus of international policy on environmental issues, which has pushed more and more towards sustainable, eco-friendly, and therefore electric mobility. Switching to electric mobility can help achieve environmental sustainability goals, such as reducing greenhouse gas emissions and oil dependence. In this direction, the European Union has worked and is working with legal, economic, and strategic measures to encourage the development and adoption of electric mobility.

Transport policy is a shared competence between the European Union (EU) and the Member States. EU lays down the common guidelines on the issue, the so-called European directives, and it is the duty, or rather the obligation, of Member States to intervene at the local level, implementing the same by identifying economic incentives and/or taxes for their citizens. Directive 2014/94/EU encourages public and private investments in vehicle technologies, fuels, and the construction of infrastructure aimed at promoting the circulation of cars powered by alternative energy sources. It represents a common framework of measures for the establishment of an infrastructure for alternative fuels in the Union to minimise oil dependence and environmental impact in the transport sector. The EU supports research and innovation in alternative fuel vehicles (e-mobility, LPG, hydrogen) and related infrastructure, in particular through the Horizon 2020 programme for smart, eco-sustainable, and integrated transport. In particular, with this directive, the EU called on member states to ensure that by 31 December 2020, an adequate number of publicly accessible charging points were set up to allow the movement of electric vehicles. The European Commission established the technical characteristics of national charging stations to provide electricity compatible with all electric vehicles in circulation in the European Union (Directive 2019/944).

As urban mobility has an impact on both economic growth and the environment, the EU is investing significant resources to help cities improve mobility and make it more sustainable by developing strategies that can foster a transition to ever cleaner and more sustainable modes of transport. The promotion takes place not only through specific directives, as set out above, but also through the financing of urban mobility by means of two Structural and Investment European (SIE) funds: (1) the European Regional Development Fund (ERDF) and (2) the Cohesion Fund.

The ERDF aims to strengthen economic and social cohesion in the European Union by correcting imbalances between its regions. The ERDF focuses its investments on several key priority areas:

- Innovation and research
- The digital agenda
- Support for small and medium-sized enterprises (SMEs)
- The low-carbon economy

The Cohesion Fund aims to reduce economic and social disparities and to promote sustainable development. For the 2014–2020 period, the Cohesion Fund focuses on Bulgaria, Croatia, Cyprus, the Czech Republic, Estonia, Greece, Hungary, Latvia, Lithuania, Malta, Poland, Portugal, Romania, Slovakia, and Slovenia. The Cohesion Fund allocates a total of €63.4 billion to activities under the following categories:

- Trans-European transport networks, notably priority projects of European interest as identified by the EU. The Cohesion Fund will support infrastructure projects under the Connecting Europe Facility, a funding programme that supports trans-European networks and infrastructures in the sectors of transport, telecommunications, and energy.

- Environment: Here, the Cohesion Fund can also support projects related to energy or transport, as long as they clearly benefit the environment in terms of energy efficiency, use of renewable energy, developing rail transport, supporting intermodality, strengthening public transport, and so on.

Other available financial resources come from the aforementioned Horizon 2020 programme, in the field of research and innovation, and from the Connecting Europe Facility (CEF), in the field of transport. The resources available for urban mobility, through all the SIE funds, amounted to €16.3 billion for the period 2014–2020 and included not only funding for clean urban transport (€12.8 billion for the period 2014–2020), but also for intelligent transport systems (ITS), bicycle lanes, and multimodal transport (European Court of Auditors, 2020). Of course, projects supported by the SIE funds are co-financed with resources allocated by national governments. The huge amount of funds that Europe disburses is directed in different directions, such as the green economy and the digital, that intersect with the theme of electric mobility because it is a central theme to achieve net zero CO_2 emissions by 2050, which will have strong overall benefits, altogether generating major health benefits for citizens and the European economy (European Commission, 2018b).

After the Directive 2014/94/EU, the EU—in the Directive 2019/944/EU—addressed the need to integrate electro-mobility with the electricity distribution network present in its territory to develop charging stations for electric vehicles in Europe in order to allow greater adoption of electric vehicles.

Between the end of 2019 and the first months of 2020, positive signs, albeit weak ones were highlighted for the e-mobility sector, which allowed it to withstand the "stress test" represented by the pandemic. Despite the general decline in the automotive sector, the growth of the electric car market in Europe can be attributed to the different policies that member states have put in place to encourage the purchase of eco-friendly vehicles. For example, in the Netherlands, there is a purchase tax with a fixed and a variable component. The variable component is based on g CO_2/km emissions and applies to all motor vehicles except pure electric cars (BEVs), while the fixed component from January 2020 is €366 for all motor vehicles except BEVs and PHEVs. Besides, to discourage the purchase of diesel cars (with emissions exceeding 59 g CO_2/km) from January 2020, a tax of more than €78 was introduced for each gram of CO_2 exceeding the limit. From March 2020, in the UK, the purchase incentive for cars with emissions of less than 50 g CO_2/km, with a range of at least 112 km and with a list price of less than £50,000, is equal to 35% of the list price, up to a maximum of £3000. In Sweden, since January 2020, the emission limit for accessing purchase incentives has been raised to 70 g CO_2/km (previously it was 60 g CO_2/km). The purchase incentive is almost €5600 for cars with zero emissions (BEV), and almost €935 for PHEV cars with emissions equal to 70 g CO_2/km.

Incentives for buying BEVs and PHEVs in Germany vary depending on the list price of the car. With a list price of less than €40,000, the incentive for a BEV is €9000, and for a PHEV is €6750; for cars with a list price between €40,000 and €65,000 and for used cars, the incentive for a BEV is €7500, and for a PHEV is €5625. In France, in January and May 2020, the amounts of incentives for the purchase of cars with emissions below 20 g CO_2/km were changed and parameterised by the list price of the car. Precisely, the incentive to purchase is €7000 for cars with a list price below €45,000, while if the list price is between €45,000 and €60,000, the incentive is €3000 (Chiaroni et al., 2020). In Italy as well, the growth in the number of users of electric vehicles has been driven by several factors, including the incentives for the purchase of such vehicles that are called Ecobonus (Ecobonus, 2020). Changes to the original "Ecobonus" were introduced, first foreseen by the budget law 2019 and subsequently modified by the Decree August 2020 of the Ministry of Economic Development, which again increased the funds available for 2020 by €50 million for the registration of eco-compatible vehicles between August and December 2020. The contribution provided by the Decree August 2020 varies according to the CO_2 emissions/km of the vehicle being registered. Besides, in Italy, with law no. 145/2018, a regulatory process aimed at promoting the spread of electric micro-mobility in Italian cities, road-testing of vehicles for personal mobility with predominantly electric propulsion (so-called electric scooters) was authorised, not subject to the Traffic Law. Subsequently, with law no. 160/2019, scooters were equated to bicycles and included in the Highway Code, and with law no. 8/2020 the circulation of electric scooters and last-mile vehicles was regulated allowing their use in the national territory, with the same rules as bicycles.

Finally, Decree of the Ministry no. 34/2020 has provided a fund to finance a bonus of €500 for those who buy bicycles, electric scooters, or other means of sustainable mobility. Among the measures included in this decree, there is a retroactive bonus for the purchase of classic bicycles with assisted pedalling, Segways, hoverboards, scooters, and electric monowheels, providing a discount of 60% on the final price of the vehicle, for a maximum refund of €500.

It should be noted that, in addition to the economic incentives for the adoption of electric cars by citizens, the local policies provide a series of indirect incentives, such as the possibility of free parking in paid parking zones, access to limited traffic areas with public funds for charging infrastructure, exemption from property tax and VAT (Germany, Austria, the Netherlands, and the United Kingdom), and reduction of the annual traffic tax (Spain) (Egnér & Trosvik, 2018; Mazzoni et al., 2020).

As can be seen from the aforementioned text, there exist several incentive policies at both the national and international levels, and they seem to work. Nonetheless, the recent COVID-19 health crisis and the consequent economic downturn have slowed the full adoption of e-mobility.

The EU's monetary and fiscal policy initiatives and measures to preserve the health of citizens and prevent the collapse of the economy are impressive and unprecedented. At the end of May, the Commission presented, at the request of the Heads of State or Government, a reform package combining the Multiannual Financial Framework (MFF) with the *NextGenerationEU* instrument to counter the effects of an economic crisis. To enable member states to recover from the crisis, Europe set up the Recovery Fund, or *NextGenerationEU*, on 21 July 2020, allocating €750 billion in addition to a targeted strengthening of the EU's long-term budget for the period 2021–2027. The goal is a greener, more digital and resilient Europe that can create jobs and repair the damage caused by the COVID-19 pandemic. The legal commitments of a programme integrated by *NextGenerationEU* must be entered into by 31 December 2023. The related payments will be made by 31 December 2026 (European Consilium, 2020a).

There are strong links in European policies between more sustainable urban mobility, economic growth, and environmental pollution reduction. In the *NextGenerationEU* tool, the environmental issue is present in the Device for Recovery and Resilience (€672.5 billion of loans and grants), REACT-EU (€47.5 billion), InvestEU (€5.6 billion), and Horizon Europe (€5 billion) (European Commission, 2020). The MFF for the period 2021–2027 is also structured into different headings and clusters, whose expenditure breakdown reflects the Union's political priorities for a greener and more resilient Europe. Under Headings (1) "Single Market, Innovation and Digital Agenda," (2) "Cohesion, Resilience and Values," and (3) "Natural Resources and Environment" (European Consilium, 2020a), actions aimed at achieving the objectives contained in the Paris Climate Agreement and the United Nations Sustainable Development Goals, with investments in clean energy and green transport, are included.

Given the importance of combating climate change, European programmes and instruments allocate at least 30% of the total budget expenditure of the Union and *NextGenerationEU* to support climate objectives. Therefore, all investments must comply with the EU's objective of climate neutrality by 2050 and contribute to the achievement of the Union's new climate targets for 2030. Hence, all EU expenditures should be consistent with the European Green Deal's objectives for the decarbonisation of Europe. The MFF as a whole contributes to the implementation of the Paris Agreement, and in order to address the social and economic consequences in terms of sustainability, competitiveness, and inclusive growth, a mechanism will be created for a transition right, which is included in the "Fund for the transition right." *NextGenerationEU* also allocates additional funding to other European programmes or funds such as Horizon 2020, InvestEU, the Rural Development Fund, and the Just Transition Fund to create a greener post-COVID-19 Europe. For the period 2021–2027, part of the InvestEU Fund (€2.8 billion) and the Connecting Europe Facility (€28.396 billion) are explicitly allocated to transport (€21.384 billion) and energy (€5.180 billion) (European Consilium,

2020b), stressing that the sustainable mobility systems cannot deviate from the protection of the environment and climate.

6.6 Conclusion

The pandemic has changed every citizen's way of life and the ways of working and moving. The travel restrictions imposed during the COVID-19 pandemic have had a significant impact on transport and mobility, leading to changes in consumer behaviour and attitudes and a reduction in disposable income that inevitably have substantial repercussions in the short, medium, and long term on the transport sector. The fear of contagion has prompted people to use more and more private cars, bikes, and scooters and opt for mobile sharing of bikes and scooters when managers guarantee continuous disinfection (Bert et al., 2020). Besides, the measures adopted by the governments of the different states, such as the increase in bonuses and incentives for the purchase of cars, bicycles, and Segways, have also contributed to changing the concept of mobility, moving more and more towards green mobility in the medium to long term. E-mobility is one of the great trends that are changing mobility, as it is more service oriented and less bound to the traditional transportation model based on the purchase of vehicles. The same introduction of EVs has stimulated new business models for the companies that work in the automotive industry.

The containment measures during the pandemic have significantly disrupted the automotive industry, which, during 2020, saw a general decrease in the number of car registrations. However, thanks to incentives, consumer sensitivity towards more sustainable forms of mobility, and introduction of new EV models in the European market by car manufacturers, it saw an increase in electric vehicle sales.

EVs were progressively established worldwide, and they were at the centre of worldwide governments' agenda to replace traditional vehicles. Their capability to reduce GHG emissions seems to require further actions by governments, such as the decarbonisation of the electricity mix and the identification of new ways to manufacture and dispose of batteries. Electric cars alone will not help reduce CO_2 emissions by 2050, as required by the EU and in line with the Paris Agreement targets, unless the way we produce the energy to build and power them is changed. The problems of battery production and disposal remain to this day. To significantly reduce greenhouse gas emissions from electric vehicles, the EU and its member states must adopt policies to increase the renewable share of the electricity mix and encourage research by creating public–private partnerships to reduce batteries' environmental impact. The effort to achieve the Paris Agreement's objectives must involve an integrated European policy, legislative and infrastructure reforms in the member states' territories, and precise management of the environmental budget for smart mobility.

In conclusion, the pandemic has demonstrated that economic development needs to go hand in hand with environmental sustainability due to the strong bond between the environment and the economy. This idea is supported by observed consumer behaviour, car manufacturers' choices, and governmental policies, which all together have allowed e-mobility to continue its positive trend despite the COVID-19 crisis (see Fig. 6.1). From the demand side, the environmental and health concerns seem to explain the consumer shift to e-mobility. From the supply side, car manufacturers have committed to electrifying their models by introducing

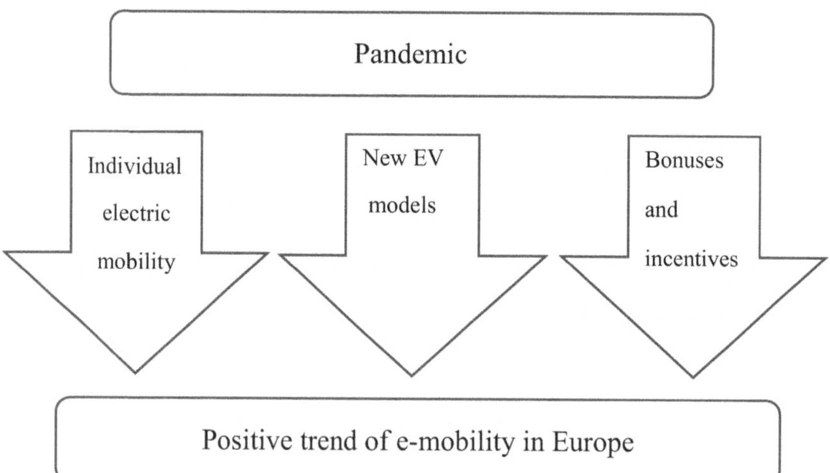

Fig. 6.1 The impact of COVID-19 on e-mobility

new models to the European market. Finally, the array of incentives and bonuses introduced in 2020 shows that Europe remains committed to the goal of reducing GHG emissions.

References

Abdul-Manan, A. F. N. (2015). Uncertainty and differences in GHG emissions between electric and conventional gasoline vehicles with implications for transport policy making. *Energy Policy, 87*, 1–7.

Accenture. (2020, May). *Impact on the automotive industry: Navigating the human and business impact of COVID-19.* https://www.accenture.com/_acnmedia/PDF-121/Accenture-COVID-19-Impact-Automotive-Industry.pdf

ACEA – European Automobile Manufacturers Association. (2020, June 23). *EU car sales forecast 2020: Record drop of 25% expected this year, says ACEA.* https://www.acea.be/press-releases/article/eu-car-sales-forecast-2020-record-drop-of-25-expected-this-year-says-acea

Amnesty International. (2017). *Time to recharge.* Amnesty USA. www.amnesty-usa.org/reports/time-to-recharge

Asaithambi, G., Treiber, M., & Kanagaraj, V. (2017). Life cycle assessment of conventional and electric vechicles. In M. Palocz-Andresen, D. Szalay, A. Gosztom, L. Sipos, & T. Taligas (Eds.), *International climate protection* (pp. 161–168). Springer International Publishing.

Bagloee, S. A., Tavana, M., & Asadi, M. (2016). Autonomous vehicles: Challenges, opportunities and future implications for transportation policies. *Journal of Modern Transportation, 24*, 284–303.

Bert, J., Schellong, D., Hagenmaier, M., Hornstein, D., Wegscheider, A. K., & Palme, T. (2020). *How COVID-19 will shape urban mobility.* Boston Consulting Group. https://www.bcg.com/it-it/featured-insights/coronavirus

Biresselioglu, M. E., Kaplan, M. D., & Yilmaz, B. K. (2018). Electric mobility in Europe: A comprehensive review of motivators and barriers in decision-making process. *Transportation Research Part A, 109*, 1–13.

Brendel, A. B., Lichtenberg, S., Brauer, B., Nastjuk, I., & Kolbe, L. M. (2018). Improving electric utilization in carsharing: A framework and simulation of an e-car sharing vehicle utilization management system. *Transportation Research Part D, 64*, 230–245.

Chiaroni, D., Frattini, F., Franzò, S., & Sgambaro, L. (2020, October). *Smart Mobility. La sostenibilità nei trasporti: opportunità e sfide per la filiera e gli end user*. Energy & Strategy Group – Politecnico di Milano.

Danielis, R. (2015). Inquinano maggiormente le auto elettriche o le auto convenzionali? Stime recenti, variabili determinanti e suggerimenti di politica dei trasporti. *Rivista di Economia e Politica dei Trasporti, 3*, 1.

Desomer, E., & Walker, A. (2020, May). *Future of mobility. COVID-19: Mobility in Belgium*. Deloitte Belgium. https://www2.deloitte.com/content/dam/Deloitte/be/Documents/strategy/Mobility_Covid%20report_2020.pdf

Directive 2014/94/EU of the European Parliament and of the Council of 22 October 2014 on the deployment of alternative fuels infrastructure. European Union Law. https://eur-lex.europa.eu/eli/dir/2014/94/oj

Directive (EU) 2019/944 of the European Parliament and of the Council of 5 June 2019 on common rules for the internal market for electricity and amending Directive 2012/27/EU. European Union Law. https://eur-lex.europa.eu/legal-content/EN/TXT/?uri=CELEX%3A32019L0944

Ecobonus. Le agevolazioni. (2020). *Le agevolazioni*. https://ecobonus.mise.gov.it/contributi/le-agevolazioni

Egnér, F., & Trosvik, L. (2018). Electric vehicle adoption in Sweden and the impact of local policy instruments. *Energy Policy, 121*, 584–596.

European Commission. (2011). *A growth package for integrated European infrastructure: Communication from the Commission to the European Parliament, the Council, the European Court of Justice, the Court of Auditors, the European Investment Bank, the European Economic and Social Committee to the Committee of the Regions, Bruselles*. https://ec.europa.eu/commission/presscorner/detail/en/IP_11_

European Commission. (2018a). *Communication from the Commission to the European Parliament, the European Council, the Council, the European Economic and Social Committee, The Committee of the Regions and the European Investment Bank. A clean planet for all: A European strategic long-term vision for a prosperous, modern, competitive and climate neutral economy*. https://ec.europa.eu/transparency/regdoc/rep/1/2018/EN/COM-2018-773-F1-EN-MAIN-PART-1.PDF

European Commission. (2018b). *In depth analysis in support of the Commission Communication COM*. https://ec.europa.eu/clima/sites/clima/files/docs/pages/com_2018_733_analysis_in_support_en_0.pdf

European Commission. (2020). *Recovery plan for Europe*. https://ec.europa.eu/info/strategy/recovery-plan-europe_en

European Consilium. (2020a). *Recovery and resilience facility: Council presidency and parliament reach provisional agreement.* https://www.consilium.europa.eu/it/press/press-releases/2020/12/18/recovery-and-resilience-facility-council-presidency-and-parliament-reach-provisional-agreement/

European Consilium. (2020b). *General Secretariat of the Council, Special meeting of the European Council (17, 18, 19, 20 and 21 July 2020) – Conclusions.* https://data.consilium.europa.eu/doc/document/ST-10-2020-INIT/en/pdf7

European Court of Auditors. (2020). *Sustainable Urban Mobility in the EU: No substantial improvement is possible without Member States' commitment, Special Report.* https://op.europa.eu/webpub/eca/special-reports/urban-mobility-6-2020/en/

European Environment Agency. (2020). *Greenhouse gas emissions from transport in Europe.* https://www.eea.europa.eu/data-and-maps/indicators/transport-emissions-of-greenhouse-gases/transport-emissions-of-greenhouse-gases-12

Furcher, T., Gruhn, B., Huber, I., & Tschiesner, A. (2020, September 22). *How consumers' behavior in car buying and mobility is changing amid COVID-19.* McKinsey & Company. https://www.mckinsey.com/business-functions/marketing-and-sales/our-insights/how-consumers-behavior-in-car-buying-and-mobility-changes-amid-covid-19

Gartner. (n.d.). *Electro-mobility (e-mobility).* https://www.gartner.com/en/information-technology/glossary/electro-mobility-e-mobility#:~:text=Electro%20mobility%20(or%20e%2DMobility,propulsion%20of%20vehicles%20and%20fleets

Gartner. (2020, March 30). *Gartner says automotive OEMs and car dealers must improve their online sales models to mitigate a Coronavirus related sales slump, Unprecedented situation also increases the need for contactless after-sales services.* https://www.gartner.com/en/newsroom/press-releases/2020-03-30-gartner-says-automotive-oems-and-car-dealers-must-imp

Gersdorf, T., Hensley, R., Hertzke, P., & Schaufuss, P. (2020, September). *Electric mobility after the crisis: Why an auto slowdown won't hurt EV demand.* McKinsey Center for Mobility. https://www.mckinsey.com/industries/automotive-and-assembly/our-insights/electric-mobility-after-the-crisis-why-an-auto-slowdown-wont-hurt-ev-demand

Hawkins, T. R., Singh, B., Majeau-Bettez, G., & Stromman, A. H. (2013). Comparative environmental life cycle assessment of conventional and electric vehicles. *Journal of Industrial Ecology, 17*(1), 53–64.

Heineke, K., Kloss, B., Scurtu, D., & Weig, F. (2019, January 29). *Micromobility's 15,000-mile checkup.* McKinsey & Company. https://

www.mckinsey.com/industries/automotive-and-assembly/our-insights/micromobilitys-15000-mile-checkup

Hofstatter, T., Krawina, M., Muhlreiter, B., Pohler, S., & Tschiesner, A. (2020, October 27). *Reimagining the auto industry's future: It's now or never*. McKinsey & Company. https://www.mckinsey.com/industries/automotive-and-assembly/our-insights/reimagining-the-auto-industrys-future-its-now-or-never

Holland, S. P., Mansur, E. T., Muller, N. Z., & Yates, A. J. (2015). Are there environmental benefits from driving electric vehicles? The importance of local factors. *American Economic Review, 106*(12), 3700–3729.

IEA. (2020). *Global EV outlook 2020*. https://www.iea.org/reports/global-ev-outlook-2020#the-global-electric-vehicle-fleet-expanded-significantly-over-the-last-decade-underpinned-by-supportive-policies-and-technology-advances

ITF. (2020). *COVID-19 Transport brief. Electric mobility: Taking the pulse in times of coronavirus*. International Transport Forum. https://www.itf-oecd.org/sites/default/files/electric-vehicles-covid-19.pdf

Laurischkat, K., Viertelhausen, A., & Jandt, D. (2016). Business models for electric mobility. *Procedia CIRP, 4*, 483–488.

Legge n. 145. 30 Dicembre, 2018. *Bilancio di previsione dello Stato per l'anno finanziario 2019 e bilancio pluriennale per il triennio 2019–2021*. Gazzetta Ufficiale. https://www.gazzettaufficiale.it/eli/gu/2018/12/31/302/so/62/sg/pdf

Legge n. 160. 27 Dicembre 2019. *Bilancio di previsione dello Stato per l'anno finanziario 2020 e bilancio pluriennale per il triennio 2020–2022*. Gazzetta Ufficiale. https://www.gazzettaufficiale.it/eli/id/2019/12/30/19G00165/sg

Legge n. 8. 28 Febbraio 2020. *Conversione in legge, con modificazioni, del decreto-legge 30 dicembre 2019, n. 162, recante disposizioni urgenti in materia di proroga di termini legislativi, di organizzazione delle pubbliche amministrazioni, nonché di innovazione tecnologica*. Gazzetta Ufficiale. https://www.gazzettaufficiale.it/eli/id/2020/02/29/20G00021/sg

Mazzoni, C., Cerchiello, T., & Castaldi, L. (2020). E-mobility e sostenibilità: Il mercato dell'auto elettrica. In *Contributi in onore di Gaetano Maria Golinelli* (pp. 1142–1166). Rogiosi Editore.

Meissner, M. (2014). *E-mobility: China planning fresh start for domestic automobile industry*. Mercator Institute for China Studies. https://merics.org/sites/default/files/2020-05/China_Monitor_17_E-Mobility_EN.pdf

Messagie, M. (2017). *Life cycle analysis of the climate impact of electric vehicles*. Transport and Environment White Paper. Vrije Universiteit Brussel. https://

www.transportenvironment.org/sites/te/files/publications/TE%20-%20draft%20report%20v04.pdf

MSCI. (2020). *Future mobility: Understanding a new transport system*. https://www.msci.com/documents/1296102/17292317/ThematicIndex-FutureMobility-cbr-en.pdf/38919606-41aa-cb2a-dd61-0a4c2972efb0?t=1582872708674

Nealer, R., & Hendrickson, T. P. (2015). Review of recent lifecycle assessments of energy and greenhouse gas emissions for electric vehicles. *Current Sustainable Energy Reports, 2*(3), 66–73.

Patò, B. S. G., & Herczeg, M. (2020). The effect of the COVID-19 on the automotive supply chains. *Studia Universitatis Babes-Bolyai Oeconomica, 65*(2), 1–11.

PWC. (2020a, May). *The impact of COVID-19 on the European automotive market. Learnings from past crises, future market outlook and recommended actions for OEMs*. Strategy &: Part of the PwC Network. https://www.strategyand.pwc.com/it/en/impact-of-covid-19-on-EU-automotive-market.html

PWC. (2020b, October). *E-mobility sales review Q4 2020*. Strategy &: Part of the PwC Network. https://www.strategyand.pwc.com/de/de/studien/2020/e-mobility-sales-review-q4/e-mobility-sales-review-q4.pdf

Tan, A. L., Chong, C. K., & Hassan, H. B. (2019). The price of personal mobility: Burden of injury and mortality from personal devices in Singapore. A nationwide cohort study. *BMC Public Health, 19*, 880.

Thrassou, A., Uzunboylu, N., Vrontis, D., & Christofi, M. (2020). Digitalization of SMSs: A review of opportunites and challenges. In A. Thrassou, D. Vrontis, Y. Weber, & S. M. R. Shams (Eds.), *The changing role of SMEs in global business. Volume II: Contextual evolution across markets, disciplines and sectors* (pp. 179–200). Palgrave Macmillan.

Zagorskas, J., & Burinskienė, M. (2019). Challenges caused by increased use of e-powered personal mobility vehicles in European cities. *Sustainability, 12*(1), 273.

7

Managing Climate Crisis in the Sport Sector: New Challenges and Opportunities for Sports Organisations

Rita Mura, Francesca Vicentini, and Giorgio Portaluri

7.1 Introduction

At the verge of 2020s, the global warming occurrence appears undoubted and as evident as ever: while the last four years (2015–2019) signed the highest ever world temperature records (UN, 2019), the average global temperature is now observed at 1°C higher with respect to the preindustrial era. As it is diffusely known, these issues provoke the occurrence of both gradual and radical dramatic environmental consequences of global, regional and local magnitudes. By looking at Italy, two Representative Concentration Pathways (RCP) scenarios reflecting hypothetical evolutions of greenhouse gas (GHG)

R. Mura (✉) • F. Vicentini • G. Portaluri
Department of Movement, Human and Health Sciences, University of Rome "Foro Italico", Rome, Italy
e-mail: rita.mura@uniroma4.it; francesca.vicentini@uniroma4.it; giorgio.portaluri@uniroma4.it

D. Vrontis et al. (eds.), *Business Under Crisis Volume I*, Palgrave Studies in Cross-disciplinary Business Research, In Association with EuroMed Academy of Business, https://doi.org/10.1007/978-3-030-76567-5_7

emissions, pollutants abuse and land use, namely RCP2.6 ("aggressive mitigation"—soft scenario) and RCP8.5 ("business as usual"—extreme scenario), show a general decrease in precipitation volumes in parallel with a general increase in precipitation intensity, particularly during summer and autumn (Spano et al., 2020). Both RCP-based projections forecast rise in hot days, heat waves, damages to critical coastal areas due to the sea-level rise as well as in average temperature (Spano et al., 2020). In consideration of such dramatic perspectives, the Italian National Strategy for Adaptation to Climate Changes has identified different critical areas, namely the Alpine and Apennine environments, the coastal regions and the Po Valley (MATTM, 2015). While world inhabitants are accustomed to generally referring to these alterations of the Earth System as climate changes, a conspicuous number of scientific voices keep warning that a proper "climate crisis has arrived and is accelerating faster than most scientists expected" (Ripple et al., 2019). This global climate emergency has serious potentialities to cause tremendous and widespread sanitary, social, political and economic side effects. Accordingly, some industries are labelled as climate dependent to highlight their anchor to some climate conditions such as stable temperatures or natural resources (like rainwater, solar light or snow)—more than others, thus being labelled climate dependent (Dingle & Mallen, 2020).

The sport sector is not free from environmental concerns, and sport organisations (in particular the National Sports Federations) are called to play an important role in using resources and adopting a sustainable approach for the environment. Given these assumptions, this research focuses on exploring the resources needed to develop a sustainable approach to address the challenges of the climate crisis. In particular, the main research questions are:

RQ1) How federations with climate-dependent facilities are able to include climate change in their strategic thinking?

RQ2) In which ways natural environment is affecting NSFs and how can they develop their (adaptive) capacity to accommodate changes in climate (and extend it to their sports organisations)?

In addressing these questions, we employ a semi-inductive approach (Trendafilova et al., 2013), using the Natural Resources Dependent Theory (NRDT) (Bergmann et al., 2016; Hillman et al., 2009). Existing theories tend to focus on how organisations can affect natural environment while NRDT focuses on the opposite direction: how the natural environment affects organisations is a new concept in management science (Bergmann et al., 2016). Climate change represents one of the most challenging risk of the natural environment (European Environment Agency, 2011) and is a strategically relevant issues to organisations (Whiteman et al., 2013).

This chapter is organised as follows. First it provides a brief overview of how climate crisis is affecting sports organisations in different ways. The second section discusses the methods used in the survey research. The next section presents key results and discussion, and the last one, a conclusion.

7.2 Literature Review

It has been argued that the general sport industry is a climate-dependent sector (Mallen & Dingle, 2017), and, consequently, sport's products, namely practice and events, and key assets are posed under increasing environmental risks. As a matter of fact, the sport industry is an interesting scenario to investigate how threats and affect all players placed in this industry, the world of sport has already started experiencing negative economic repercussions due to the global climate crisis; for example, to date sport organisations, communities and firms diffusely observe higher event cancellation or abandonment due to extreme weather, increased damages to playing surfaces and facilities, greater maintenance, water and energy expenditures (IOC, 2018). Since 1990s, through the lenses of CSR (Babiak & Trendafilova, 2011), sustainability theory (Mallen et al., 2010) and different streams of social theory (McCullough, 2013), sport management scholars have broadly been investigating how sport industries do leave environmental footprints—for example, sport events—induced greenhouse gas (GHG) emissions for fans' transportation, food procurement and energy consumption. More recently, the realisation of a bidirectional relationship between sport industry and the environment—sport is simultaneously causing and experiencing the climate crisis—has brought to development of a distinct climate on sport research field within sport management literature. Indeed, as it has become scientifically clear that the earth system keeps accelerating towards climatic alterations, a considerable number of sport management scholars have started questioning sport actors' and assets' vulnerability, adaptation and resilience to climate changes (Dingle & Mallen, 2020; Dingle & Stewart, 2018; Mallen & Dingle, 2017). Although this research stream remains rather unexplored, in the last 15 years climate-on-sport studies have been focusing on different topics: the latter encompass major and minor sport events' climate dependence (DeChano-Cook & Shelley, 2018; Scott et al., 2015), the climate vulnerabilities of specific sport disciplines (Scott & Jones, 2007), sub-sectors like ski tourism and outdoor sports (Brocherie et al., 2015; Scott & McBoyle, 2007) and facilities (Mallen & Dingle, 2017; McDonald et al., 2011). Despite the highly relevant granularity of sport-climate issues (global, industrial, organisational, individual), sport organisations appear to be the most investigated levels of analysis in the existing literature (Orr & Inoue, 2019). This is because organisations "have been described as central actors in the climate change adaptation process" (Dingle & Stewart, 2018). Several contributions have argued that this adaptation process is determined by sport organisations' adaptive capacity (Dingle & Mallen, 2020; Dingle & Stewart, 2018; Orr & Inoue, 2019). In the natural science and climate research, the latter term refers to "the ability of a system to adjust to climate change (including climate variability and extremes), to moderate potential damages, to take advantage of opportunities, or to cope with the consequences" (IPCC, 2001). Although "adaptive capacity" might appear a blurring term, it has been underlined that climate-proactive "awareness, skills, know-how and resourcefulness" (Orr & Inoue, 2019) within sport organisations might enable this latter's adaptation process. For what concerns sport organisations' awareness, skills and know-how on climate adaptation, crucial insights have been offered by Dingle and Stewart (2018) as well as Dingle and Mallen (2020). Both studies sought to explore the adaptative attitudes, awareness and responses of managers within different sport organisations and in different locations; while Dingle and Stewart (2018) investigated adaptive options and process of professional sport organisations managing Major Australian Sport Stadia (MASS), Dingle and Mallen (2020) focused on adaptive challenges and responses in community-level sport clubs. One more precise and comprehensive contribution has been recently provided by Orr and Inoue (2019) through the definition of the Climate Vulnerability of Sport Organisations (CVSO) framework. In the construction of the sole theoretical model pertaining to sport organisations' climate vulnerability, the authors translate adaptive capacity into organisational climate capacity (OCC) variable; in contrast to potential climate impacts on sport organisations (CIO), OCC is said here to consist in "a sport organisation's capacity to accommodate changes in climate with minimal disruptions or additional costs" (Orr & Inoue, 2019). As highlighted by Orr and Inoue (2019), adaptive capacity conceptualisation into climate—on—sport management research appears drawing from the existing literature concerning organisational capacity in nonprofit community sport organisations (Misener & Doherty, 2009), Olympic organisations (Robinson & Minikin, 2011) and National Sport Federations (NFSs).

For what concerns NSFs, different studies have used organisational capacity arguments and schemes to compare national federations' performances (Madella, 2002), and to investigate the elements conducive of change within federal organisational capacities—namely innovative leadership, knowledge and ability (Gobikas & Čingienė, 2019). To date, within sport management literature, there appears to exist no scientific attempt aimed at exploring NSFs' climate adaptive capacities, their peculiar characteristics and the responses to the environmental threats and opportunities witnessed by NSFs. Furthermore, a significant limitation in the climate-on-sport research stream appears to be the geographical concentration of investigated sport organisations; indeed, almost the totality of existing studies has explored sport organisations' adaptive capacity in North America, Europe and Australia. Despite the amount of scientific knowledge concerning the Italian peculiar and critical climatic scenario (Spano et al., 2020; ISPRA, 2015), no particular sport management academic attention has been posed on Italian sport organisations' and NFSs' sustainability strategies and adaptive capacities.

The National Sports Federations play a very important role within the Italian sport system. They enjoy technical, organisational and operational duties under the supervision of CONI (Italian National Olympic Committee) and they pursue their goals of organising and promoting their sports in accordance with national law and international sports regulations. In general, NSFs are designed in relation to their specific discipline, to organise, regulate, develop and promote their sports through regional sports clubs and associations. They are also responsible for organising their sports at an amateur and professional level where relevant.

7.3 Research Methods

Due to the heterogeneous frameworks of NSFs, our study divided the 44 Italian Sports Federations into three groups (large, medium, small). Clusters were set in relation to the size related to the number of individual members (using frequency distribution) that each federation counted (CONI, 2017). More specifically, the large-sized group concern federations (n = 5) that had a membership ranging from 288.015 to 419.413; the medium-sized group (n = 4) from 148.426 to 201.034 and the small-sized group (n = 34) from 3.999 to 135.561.

On the basis of the existing managerial literature on sport and environmental sustainability, purposive sampling was carried out. In the end the decision was taken to focus on the following federations: Italian Motorcycling Federation (IMF) and Italian Golf Federation (IGF). We chose these federations in relation to their high level of environmental impact (Dodson, 2005; Guo et al., 2007; Wheeler & Nauright, 2006). The Italian Motorcycling Federation (IMF) belongs to the medium-sized group (with 148.426 individual members) while the Italian Golf Federation is part of the small-sized group (with 94.642 individual members).

Data Collection

We used two primary approaches to data collection (semi-structured interviews and content analysis on official reports). The research primarily relied on a survey based on semi-structured interviews. The adoption of this type of method was deemed to be the most appropriate because it enabled the researchers to gather a large amount of information that could be used to provide a better understanding of the issues surrounding sustainability environment and organisational climate capacity (Yin, 2003). Qualitative methods address the "how" and "what" questions and are very good for "understanding the world from the perspective of those studied and for examining and articulating processes" (Pratt, 2009; Trendafilova et al., 2013). Asking questions based on "how" and "what" we found to be the best method of conducting interviews to acquire a qualitative understanding. Two semi-structured interviews were conducted with top-ranking officials within each federation.

The interviewees represented the most senior executives in their organisation responsible for creating and implementing their organisation's environmental efforts. They were intimately involved in their federations' environmental initiatives and were knowledgeable about the past and future plans for their environmental programmes. Due the involvement of a network of institutional relations that facilitated access to the NSFs, the interviews were preceded by informal web meeting with NSFs' managers and consultants in order to gather a higher level of information. Each interview ranged between 0.5 and 1 h and was conducted over cloud-based video meeting software (due to the outbreak of the COVID-19 pandemic).

The interview strategy applied by the researchers involved two areas of questioning. First, there were a number of key questions common to all federations. This was necessary to ensure a satisfactory degree of coherence within the interviews (Patton, 2002).

Interviewees answered questions relating to the reasoning behind their organisation's involvement in environmental initiatives. They were first asked to describe their operational roles and the tasks they were assigned in these roles as well as set out how long they have been working within the federation. This information was crucial because it allowed researchers to better understand the degree of knowledge relating to past environmental sustainability initiatives and strategies implemented by the federation. The second area of questioning focused on organisational changes in relation to the climate crisis (adaptive capacity). We asked in-depth questions not just about the sustainability awareness and the federation's commitment to the environment but also about the internal and external resources, external relationships, efforts to enhance sustainability policies, the federation's intentions to engage further in the future and what form this might take. We stimulated respondents to discuss the benefits, efforts and obstacles that they perceived regarding the implementation of their organisations' environmental strategy.

The data obtained from the interviews provided a unique and in-depth understanding of the awareness of the importance of sustainability for the federations' survival and the determination and resources needed to cope with climate crisis. The interviews were recorded and successively transcribed to aid analysis, and the transcription was sent out to respondents for approval.

Lastly, we analysed official documents related to the federations' environmental sustainability strategy. The contents of these documents provided additional explanation and support for the data and information gathered during the interviews.

Data Analysis

All official documents and interview transcripts were analysed using a manual coding method. An initial coding scheme was developed employing open coding where we identified and analysed consistent and recurring themes (and sub-themes) related to (1) sustainability approach (awareness) and (2) organisational climate capacity (infrastructures and venues, human, financial and other core resources, networks and external relationships). All issues regarding coding were discussed, debated and agreed upon by the authors. All codes, themes and sub-themes were then reviewed, confirmed and if necessary revised.

7.4 Results and Discussion

Result will be presented according to the following two themes and four sub-themes which emerged from our data analyses:

(1) The sustainability approach

(2) The organisational climate capacity: (a) infrastructure (status of facilities maintenance), (b) human resources (staff knowledge and education on environmental sustainability and climate crisis), (c) financial and other core resources (financial stability and governance), (d) networks and external relationship (interaction and collaboration between organisations)

The Sustainability Approach

Environmental sustainability is important because it supports valuable ecosystem services that are essential for the survival and healthy functioning of human society and its economic activities. Sport, through its global reach, can be an important catalyst for raising awareness about the need for the natural environment, and promoting and supporting efforts to enhance sustainability. There are a number of reasons underpinning the federations' decision to implement environmental strategies and policies in their programmes. The main reason is linked to the acknowledgement on the part of the management of the importance of developing sustainable programmes in order to increase the value of the environmental dimension of its action. The survival of NSFs depends on it.

Sports federations and organisations can negatively impact on environment through land use to build permanent (or temporary) sports venues and facilities, as well as through the pollution, noise, waste and resource demand resulting from the staging of sporting events attended by hundreds or thousands of spectators. Understanding and managing the potential negative impacts and opportunities for environment is vital for ensuring that sports venues and sporting events deliver successfully both from the financial and operational standpoint. Unmanaged environment sustainability impacts can lead to financial, operational and reputational risks. On the other hand, effective action to mitigate risks and enhance sustainability can help venues increase the long-term positive relationships with communities and stakeholders (e.g. media and sponsor).

In this regard interviews revealed that being sustainable for a federation has become *conditio sine qua non* for two fundamental reasons: the first derives from the reputation and corporate image (addressing the legitimate expectations of different stakeholders) and the second from an ethical perspective. The image of a federation also depends on what it can do to better manage its strategic resources.

In this vein, the passion for sport must be connected with sustainability by responding to the various external requests: alongside increasingly strict regulations, an increasing sensitivity to environmental issues has been developing rapidly in society in general and among the different stakeholders, who are less and less willing to accept forms of pollution (e.g. for the motorcycling federation, acoustic or atmospheric pollution or for the golf federation, the use of pesticides or the wastage of water). Addressing the stakeholders' needs means strengthening the federation's image and continuing to invest in good practices. This virtuous circle is triggered only if there is a push from within, by a management that has developed awareness and has clear objectives to be achieved in terms of sustainability. The following citation provides evidence of the federation awareness:

> The ethics issue of sporting discipline, certainly not secondary to the image, is based on the need to exercise legitimate passions (which can be defined as rights to sport practice), and to exercise them respecting the environment, thus also fulfilling duties. The balance between rights and duties is the key aspect of sustainability in motorcycling. (IMF, November 13, 2020)

The awareness and knowledge levels of NSFs help to determine the action they take, especially if they wish to move beyond compliance and into active prevention of environmental problems (Pfahl, 2010; Russo & Fouts, 1997; Shrivastava, 1995). Understanding awareness and knowledge levels allows for a more contextualised view of environmental initiatives (Barney, 1991; Judge & Douglas, 1998). The NSFs analysed in this research provide a good example of sustainable practices and strategies in the sport sector. For instance, the Italian Motorcycling Federation established the Environmental Regulation and Environmental Guidelines for sports clubs for the first time in 2019. Environmental Guidelines have been prepared with the aim of providing a guide document for all those working in the motorcycle sector, primarily motorcycle clubs, called upon to manage sporting events and adequately deal with all aspects organisational in environmental matters. Thus, Environmental Guidelines represent a document for a responsible conscious behaviour on roads and on competition circuits, providing useful tips to make motorcycling sport more environmentally sustainable. This highlights how the federation is strongly engaged in an education process addressed to develop a greater respect for the natural environment. This is important because alongside this new environmental regulation system a specific system of control has been developed (Gond et al., 2012; Simons, 1995), in order to reach the best sustainability performances in the whole country.

At the same time, the Italian Golf Federation has been active in different environment programmes at national and international levels. In accordance with the international programme GEO (Golf Environment Organization), the Italian Golf Federation signed—with five environmental associations—a memorandum of understanding on environment and biodiversity conservation, aimed at ensuring that the choice and construction of new golf facilities and the management of existing ones correspond to the strictest respect for environmental precautions:

> The federation, in addition to affirming and promoting these environmental values, intends to recognise and support the golf associations that most distinguish themselves in a virtuous path of environmental requalification or territorial recovery. (IGF, November 18, 2020)

In addition to this, the federation joined to the "Committed to green" project, promoted by the European Golf Federation and the Ecology Unit, with the contribution of the Commission of the European Community, in order to minimise the impact on the environment, from land use and resource consumption by a golf courses. The "Committed to green" project is an environmental certification programme which aims to provide environmental certification of environmental compatibility to all golf courses that adhere to the project criteria:

> The Committed to green project, which at European level involves all countries, is aimed at recognising the commitment by the clubs in implementing interventions on environmental sustainability and improving

their management performance through a responsible approach in the use of natural resources (saving water, abandoning waste products, energy, protecting the landscape and biodiversity). (IGF, November 18, 2020)

The Organisational Climate Capacity

The organisational climate capacity is defined as "the awareness, skill, know-how, and resourcefulness that allow organisations to adapt their operations to new threats and to proactively develop new capabilities to insulate the organisation from potential future threats" (Judge & Elenkov, 2005; Orr & Inoue, 2019). Following the aforementioned NRD theory, organisational behaviour is part of not only social system but also the natural environment (Tashman, 2011). In this vein, NRDT represent "a function of organisational ecosystem dependence, ecological impacts on organisations, and organisational impacts on ecosystems rather than organisational interdependence" (Tashman, 2011). Thus, climate change is both an intrinsic segment of the natural environment, as well a phenomenon that origins changes to the natural environment.

More specifically, due to climate crisis, sport federations and organisations are called upon to improve their sustainability strategy in order to cope with (1) damage to playing surfaces due to extreme temperatures, extended periods of drought, flooding and/or pest species extending their natural range; (2) damage to buildings and other infrastructure due to violent storms; (3) unseasonal rainfall forcing cancellation or abandonment of sport matches (IOC, 2018), just to name a few. These are real impacts that have happened and continue to happen across sports and throughout the world (IOC, 2018) affecting—in different ways—organisational changes in sports organisations.

Infrastructure

Due to climate crisis, adaption measures are being required in the design of new or refurbished sport venues and facilities.

NSFs offer a wide variety of specific disciplines and require different specific facilities with a substantial and variable environment impacts.

In terms of organisational climate capacity, both Italian Motorcycling Federation and Italian Golf Federation are considerate organisations with high level of climate-dependent facilities. The management of these outdoors sport facilities needs to anticipate a range of potential impacts arising from climate crisis. This means, for instance, that changes in rainfall patterns require modifications to drainage or irrigation system, and impacts from new pests and disease affecting turf grass.

The overall state of sport facilities in both federations is fragmented especially due to the size, the geographical area and so on. From interviews emerged a discrepancy between large facilities with a very effective sustainable management (e.g. Mugello circuit involved in the environmental sustainability programme of the Italian Grand Prix that engages teams, riders, spectators, enterprises, insiders, the community and nonprofit organisations), medium facilities with good attention to the sustainability, and smaller facilities managed locally (and at amateur level) where the difficulties in fulfilling the provisions increase, often due to lack of limited resources (human, infrastructural and financial).

> The size variable of the club is generally related to the availability of economic and financial resources, determining—above all to the detriment of the smallest—a strict priority of investments to be made over time. (IGF, November 18, 2020)

There are several climate actions that can be applied to the operational management of sport venues and their related facilities. These can vary significantly, and it is important to analyse relevant options in the planning process for new venues, or when reviewing the management and/or upgrading of existing facilities (IOC, 2018). Different strategic options can be considered for facilities in order to manage flood risk or drought and extreme heat. Even if the NSFs can't manage directly sports facilities, they can support in various ways their sports associations (motorcycle clubs or golf clubs).

For instance, due to the awareness and training activities carried out by the Italian Golf Federation in favour of its sport organisations (the affiliates), several interventions have been implemented in particular in relation to the maintenance of the turf which is the main object of the golf courses. The conversion of the turf from micro-therm (widespread in northern Europe and which requires continuous irrigation with a consequent increase in costs) to macro-therm (drought-tolerant turf cultivars) is a concrete action of facilities organizing change and adaptation to the climate crisis. Thanks to this strategy, the facilities can survive efficiently drought (due to the decrease in rainfall) and extreme heat (due to increase in temperature). The conversion into macro-therm therefore allows economic savings (with the recovery of the investment in the short term) and greater environmental sustainability.

Italian Federations have been actively supporting sports associations for several years, in order to contribute to a low carbon economy through the installation of on-site renewable energy (typically solar). For instance:

> In order to cope with climate crisis, the Italian Motorcycling Federation supports the use of energy from renewable sources and, in this vein, has promoted an awareness-raising campaign on the adoptions of solar energy systems (photovoltaic systems) for the facilities' needs. The initiative was possible also thanks to the partnership with leading companies in the energy sector. (IMF, November 13, 2020)

The latter point is very important because these installations require high capital investment, and through grants and subsidies is possible to promote uptake of renewable energy (the market for renewable energy has become much more competitive, capital costs have reduced and generation efficiency levels have improved). This would lead to less dependence on fossil energy sources that means substantial cost savings as well as important reductions in GHG emissions.

Results demonstrated the general great commitment of federations and the difficulties and challenges in developing a climate adaptation in their sports facilities. Basically, the Italian context is characterised by a great fragmentation of rules and regulations at national, regional and local level, sometimes different or in contrast with each other. This lack of homogeneity between the various national and local legislative and regulatory levels generates a series of difficulties at the operational level, because while informing and sensitising the sporting world on what should be done in compliance with national rules, federations often clash with local realities that require adaptation to their legislation.

Human Resources

The climate changes that have affected Italy in recent years have created a lot of damage in many contexts, with great inconvenience for fields completely flooded, others with trees razed to the ground, damages to stationary and mobile facilities. This required interventions to restore the prior conditions to the calamitous event that upset (e.g. the turf without which there would be no conditions for carrying out sporting activities) and to prevent future natural disasters. In this context human resources represent a strategic asset for federations. Both federations analysed in this study have created a specific team or internal unit, dedicated to environmental sustainability (Pfahl, 2010).

A "sustainability team" represents a primary driver for strategic changes to an organisation's environmental practices. The cross-functional sustainability team often comprises internal organisational members from across the organisation (Daily & Huang, 2001; Denison et al., 1996). They are charged with developing and conducting a variety of operational changes, organisational policies and daily/strategic practices. Their position allows them to act as the leaders of strategic environmental changes (Pfahl, 2010).

In this vein, the Italian Golf Federation has set up a scientific technical committee made up of professional experts belonging to internal and external resources (Italian universities) which support sports associations in their environmental activities. At the same time the Italian Motorcycling Federation established the "Environment Committee" in order to develop specific programmes and strategies on environmental sustainability in 2017. Its activity is aimed at increasing the environmental sustainability level in motorcycle sports associations during the races, regarding different areas: soil protection, chemical contaminations of soil, cleaning of motorcycling equipment, atmospheric emissions, energy consumption, the use of fuel and protection of natural habitats.

It was an important organisational change within the federation, testifying to a strong sensitivity of the management with respect to environmental sustainability issues as well as awareness that only with an ad hoc commission the environmental pressure of the motorcycling activity could have been better managed. Even if this specific sport is very impactful on the environment, the Italian Motorcycling Federation has only made great changes due to its foresight and vision in governance only in the last four years. The effective action of the measures issued by the Italian Motorcycling Federation "Environmental Regulations" is completed with the establishment of a specific figure aimed at supervising the sustainable compliance (Environment steward). This person has specific skills, training and experience as well as a propensity in the management of environmental issues.

In order to strengthen this strategic asset, the federations organise educational and training programmes addressed to internal (staff federation) and external resources (staff sports associations and others). In some cases, prevention natural disaster recovery programmes are planned. This is important demonstrating the proactive role of the federations towards the climate crisis.

In short, the mission of the sustainability teams is to develop environmental mission and vision statements, to develop an understanding of organisational practices as they relate to environmental issues and to act as a central repository and disseminator of information, practices and ideas (Kitazawa & Sarkis, 2000).

Financial Resources (Financial Stability)

Within the sporting system, NSFs enjoy technical, organisational and operational duties under the supervision of CONI. Sports associations can be affiliated to NSFs and in this way the NSFs can improve their financial revenues. For instance, the revenues of the membership fees for Italian Motorcycling Federation and Italian Golf Federation were, respectively, 55% and 32% of total incomes, in 2017. Basically, three critical objectives of the finances dimension emerged from interviews: (a) stable revenues, (b) stable expenses, (c) different sources of revenue. Analysing financial reports of NSFs in the past four years it emerged that the financial amount due to the Federations by CONI is based on a series of parameters that do not explicitly provide for funding measures for environmental sustainability actions. At the same time, the federations didn't provide directly financial support to associations in order to carry out environment sustainability investments. This is an important problem, because according to the interviews, impacts of climate change negatively affect organisational turnover and profits of sport associations in the short term, for instance, because of higher operation costs in facilities adaptation (e.g. adoption of new technologies and new soil treatments).

There is a common understanding that a higher level of resources in favour of the affiliates (sport organisations, golf clubs, motor clubs) that manage facilities would make it possible to carry out actions that very often remain partially fulfilled or incomplete due to lack of funds. This is even more significant given the role played by sports associations in Italy. Sports are typically started by participants themselves in response to an identified need in the community and they may be classified as grassroots membership associations, given their almost exclusive reliance on volunteers who tend to be drawn from the members, their local focus, their relatively informal structure, and their modest budgets, the largest proportion of which comes from membership fees (Doherty et al., 2014; Tschirhart, 2006).

However, a balance mechanism must be found so that investment in this sector is commensurate with something evident that gives feedback on the benefits obtained.

Networks and External Relationship

Federations adopt a multi-stakeholder approach to their partners and pursue sustainable and lasting growth while seeking to meet the expectations of all those interacting with the organisation, through ongoing dialogue and involvement. NSFs can be conceived as social system (Boulding, 1956), which exchange resources with their environment in order to achieve legitimacy. This is a prerequisite of the system within which they survive (Pfeffer & Salancik, 1978). To achieve their sustainable goals, federations have to respond to the institutional pressures by developing partnerships founded on shared principles and values. From the interviews emerged:

> The need that occurred was to involve external resources (institutional and private organisations, environmental experts) who could contribute to the development of the strategic path undertaken in terms of sustainability. (IMF, November 13, 2020)

Correspondingly, the Italian Golf Federation has been involving and engaging in numerous partnerships for several years with universities, environmental associations and environmental experts, in order to develop a positive dialogue for the whole sports system (Table 7.1).

7.5 Conclusion

The increased societal focus on issues of climate crisis and the drive by many organisations to implement environmental issues has stimulated scholars within the field of sport management to investigate the ways in which environmental sustainability can also further developed. However, there is less focus on the issues of environmental strategies in National Sports Federations to cope with climate change. This is an important managerial challenge. This study contributes to enhancing the understanding of the way in which the natural environment is affecting sports organisations, and it provides some good adaptation practices adopted by sports organisations with a high level of climate-dependent facilities, highlighting the importance to include climate change matter in their strategic thinking in order to survive.

This chapter has focused on the issues of awareness of sustainability in NSFs and their organisational climate capacity. More specifically, the study sought to analyse the dependence of the investigated federations on climate crisis in terms of (1) the status of facilities maintenance, (2) staff knowledge and education on environmental sustainability and climate crisis, (3) financial stability and (4) interaction and collaboration between organisations. Following the NRTD approach (Bergmann et al., 2016; Tashman, 2011), the assumption of this study is that "not only human beings, but indeed all organisations, depend directly or indirectly on air, clean water, energy, a suitable climate, and other natural resources, because natural capital or the resulting ecosystems are the sources of raw materials for all physical assets" (Winn & Pogutz, 2013).

Table 7.1 Key findings for NSFs sustainable and climate adaptation strategies

Themes	Sub-themes	Key findings
Sustainability approach	NSFs awareness	• Increasing awareness and knowledge about environmental issues due to reputation, corporate image benefits and ethical perspective. • Developing sustainability strategies continuously (beyond compliance), engaging different stakeholders' groups.
Organisational climate capacity	Infrastructure	• High level of climate-dependent facilities. • Supporting the sports associations in developing a climate adaptation in their operational management of sport venues and their related facilities (e.g. green energy and maintenance of the turf grass).
	Human resources	• Creating specific team or internal unit (sustainability team), dedicated to environmental sustainability. • Organising educational and training sustainability programmes addressed to internal (staff federation) and external resources (staff sports associations and others).
	Financial resources	• Main objectives of the finances dimension for NSFs: (a) stable revenues, (b) stable expenses, (c) different sources of revenue. • Impacts of climate change negatively affect organisational turnover and profits of sport associations in the short term.
	Networks and external relationships	• Developing strong partnerships and networks founded on shared principles and values in order to respond to the institutional pressures.

Even if federations made some progress in terms of proactive strategy, naturally, much remains to be done. For instance, golf sport practice has long suffered from a reputation of being harmful to the environment.

While this perception is not entirely unfounded, golf federations at national and international levels have made great strides in becoming more environmentally responsible in recent years. Today, golf organisations offer numerous opportunities to improve the water quality of on-site and surrounding lakes, streams and rivers; support a variety of plants and wildlife; and respect and improve biodiversity (IUCN, 2018).

Climate change presents a significant and growing challenge to the sport industry, especially outdoor sports (Orr & Inoue, 2019) and sports federations could offer a significant contribution in enhancing environmental concern within the community.

Limitations for this research should be acknowledged, and addressing these limitations may represent avenues for future research. First, the sample size is relatively small if compared with other qualitative environment sport studies (e.g. Trendafilova et al., 2013). Nevertheless, the innovative feature of the study is the unit of analysis represented by the national federations, and its essential role in developing environmental awareness in sport system. The second limitation encompasses the measurement of the organisational climate change. This study was exploratory in nature and represents initial qualitative assessment of climate adaptive capacity of sports federations. While the conceptualisation was based on previous studies (Orr & Inoue, 2019; Judge & Douglas, 1998), the measurement introduced a number of challenges. Such challenges have also been identified in previous studies on organisational climate capacity (Orr & Inoue, 2019). Future research should extend this preliminary conceptualisation and measure organisational climate change and climate adaptive capacity using a larger sample of national federations. Quantitative data collection via surveys with presidents, managers, as well as surveys with related club managers, would be helpful to further investigate the level or awareness of environmental sustainability and the strategic resources needed in sports sector.

The potential impacts of climate change are such that all National Sports Federations and other sport governing bodies collectively need to examine the risks posed to their sports alongside the wellbeing issues for all the people involved.

Even if the sport sector alone cannot turn back the flow of climate change, it represents an essential player in this issue, with the competence of showcasing solutions to a great audience, including not only general public but business leaders and decision makers too. Consequently, the actions taken by large and small sport bodies will collectively make a positive difference that will reverberate across the whole sector and beyond.

References

Babiak, K., & Trendafilova, S. (2011). CSR and environmental responsibility: Motives and pressures to adopt sustainable management practices. *Corporate Social Responsibility and Environmental Management, 18*(1), 11–24.

Barney, J. B. (1991). Firm resources and sustained competitive advantage. *Journal of Management, 17*(1), 99–120.

Bergmann, A., Stechemesser, K., & Guenther, E. (2016). Natural resource dependence theory: Impacts of extreme weather events on organizations. *Journal of Business Research, 69*(4), 1361–1366.

Boulding, K. E. (1956). General systems theory: The skeleton of science. *Management Science, 2*(3), 197–208.

Brocherie, F., Girard, O., & Millet, G. P. (2015). Review emerging environmental and weather challenges in outdoor sports. *Climate, 3*(3), 492–521.

CONI Servizi – Centro Studi. (2017). *Monitoraggio CONI-FSN-DSA 2017* [CONI-FSN-DSA 2017 Monitoring]. www.coni.it

Daily, B., & Huang, S. (2001). Achieving sustainability through attention to human resource factors in environmental management. *International Journal of Operations & Production Management, 21*(12), 1539–1552.

DeChano-Cook, L. M., & Shelley, F. M. (2018). Climate change and the future of international events: A case of the Olympic and Paralympic Games. In B. P. McCullough & T. B. Kellison (Eds.), *Routledge handbook of sport and the environment*. Routledge.

Denison, D., Hart, S., & Kahn, J. (1996). From chimney to cross-functional teams: Developing and validating a diagnostic model. *Academy of Management Journal, 39*(4), 1005–1023.

Dingle, G., & Mallen, C. (2020). *Sport and environmental sustainability: Research and strategic management*. Routledge.

Dingle, G., & Stewart, B. (2018). Playing the climate game: Climate change impacts, resilience and adaptation in the climate-dependent sport sector. *Managing Sport and Leisure, 23*(4–6), 293–314.

Dodson, R. G. (2005). *Sustainable golf courses: A guide to environmental stewardship*. J. Wiley & Sons.

Doherty, A., Misener, K., & Cuskelly, G. (2014). Toward a multidimensional framework of capacity in community sport clubs. *Nonprofit and Voluntary Sector Quarterly, 43*, 124S–142S.

European Environment Agency. (2011). *The European environment – State and outlook 2010: Assessment of global megatrends*. European Environment Agency.

Gobikas, M., & Čingienė, V. (2019). Role of capacity in understanding organizational change in national sports federations. *Management of Organizations: Systematic Research, 82*, 13–23.

Gond, J. P., Grubnic, S., Herzig, C., & Moon, J. (2012). Configuring management control systems: Theorizing the integration of strategy and sustainability. *Management Accounting Research, 23*(3), 205–223.

Guo, H., Zhang, Q. Y., Shi, Y., & Wang, D. H. (2007). Evaluation of the international vehicle emission (IVE) model with on-road remote sensing measurements. *Journal of Environmental Sciences, 19*(7), 818–826.

Hillman, A.J., Withers, M.C, & Collins, B.J. (2009). Resource Dependence theory: A review. *Journal of Management*, 35(6), 1404-1427.

Intergovernmental Pannell on Climate Change (IPCC). (2001). *TAR Climate change 2001: The scientific basis*. Cambridge University Press.

International Olympic Committee (IOC). (2018). *Sustainability essentials, sports for climate action*. International Olympic Committee.

International Union for Conservation of Nature (IUCN). (2018). *Sport and biodiversity*. IUCN. viii+24pp.

Istituto Superiore per la Protezione e la Ricerca Ambientale (ISPRA). (2015). *Il clima futuro in Italia: analisi delle proiezioni dei modelli regionali* [The future climate in Italy: analysis' projections of the regional models]. Rome, Italy.

Judge, W. Q., & Douglas, T. J. (1998). Performance implications of incorporating natural environmental issues into the strategic planning process: An empirical assessment. *Journal of Management Studies, 35*(2), 241–262.

Judge, W. Q., & Elenkov, D. (2005). Organizational capacity for change and environmental performance: An empirical assessment of Bulgarian firms. *Journal of Business Research, 58*, 893–901.

Kitazawa, S., & Sarkis, J. (2000). The relationship between ISO 14001 and continuous source reduction programs. *International Journal of Operations & Production Management, 20*(2), 225–248.

Madella, A. (2002). Performance organizzativa delle Associazioni e delle Federazioni sportive: un modello di valutazione. *Atleticastudi, 3*, 47–58.

Mallen, C., & Dingle, G. (2017). Climate change and the Canadian community grass – Based sport fields. *The International Journal of Environmental Sustainability, 13*(2), 45–59.

Mallen, C., Stevens, J., Adams, L., & McRoberts, S. (2010). The assessment of the environmental performance of an international multi-sport event. *European Sport Management Quarterly, 10*(1), 97–122.

McCullough, B. P. (2013). Identifying the influences on sport spectator recycling behaviors using the theory of planned behavior. *International journal of Sport Management and Marketing, 14*, 146–168.

McDonald, K., Stewart, B., & Dingle, G. (2011). In the deep end: A study of responses to climate change by multi-purpose leisure facilities in Melbourne. In M. Burke, C. Hanlon, & C. Thomen (Eds.), *Culture and society approaches, methods and perspectives* (pp. 89–106). Maribyrnong Press.

Ministry of the Environment, Land and Sea (MATTM). (2015). *Strategia Nazionale di Adattamento ai Cambiamenti Climatici (SNAC)* [National Strategy for Climate Change Adaptation]. https://www.minambiente.it

Misener, K., & Doherty, A. (2009). A case study of organizational capacity in nonprofit community sport. *Journal of Sport Management, 23*(4), 457–482.

Orr, M., & Inoue, Y. (2019). Sport versus climate: Introducing the Climate Vulnerability of Sport Organizations framework. *Sport Management Review, 22*(4), 452–463.

Patton, M. (2002). *Qualitative evaluation and research methods.* Sage Pubblications, Inc.

Pfahl, M. E. (2010). Strategic issues associated with the development of internal sustainability teams in sport and recreation organizations: A framework for action and sustainable environmental performance. *International Journal of Sport Management Recreation and Tourism, 6*(C), 37–61.

Pfeffer, J., & Salancik, G. R. (1978). *The external control of organizations: A resource dependence perspective.* Harper and How.

Pratt, M. G. (2009). For the lack of a boilerplate: Tips on writing up (and reviewing) qualitative research. *Academy of Management Review, 52*(5), 856–862.

Ripple, W. J., Wolf, C., Newsome, T. M., Barnard, P., & Moomaw, W. R. (2019). World scientists' warning of a climate emergency. *BioScience, 70*(1), 8–12.

Robinson, L., & Minikin, B. (2011). Developing strategic capacity in Olympic sport organisations. *Sport, Business and Management: An International Journal, 1*(3), 219–233.

Russo, M. V., & Fouts, P. A. (1997). A resource-based perspective on corporate environmental performance and profitability. *Academy of Management Journal, 40*(3), 534–559.

Scott, D., & McBoyle, G. (2007). Climate change adaptation in the ski industry. *Mitigation and Adaptation Strategies for Global Change, 12*(8), 1411–1431.

Scott, D., & Jones, B. (2007). A regional comparison of the implications of climate change for the golf club industry in Canada. *The Canadian Geographer/ Le Geographe Canadien, 51*(2), 219–232.

Scott, D., Steiger, R., Rutty, M., & Johnson, P. (2015). The future of the Olympic Winter Games in an era of climate change. *Current Issues in Tourism, 18*(10), 913–930.

Shrivastava, P. (1995). Ecocentric management for a risk society. *Academy of Management Journal, 20*, 118–137.

Simons, R. (1995). *Levers of control: How managers use innovative control systems to drive strategic renewal.* Harvard Business School Press.

Spano, D., Mereu, V., Bacciu, V., Marras, S., Trabucco, A., Adinolfi, M., Barbato, G., Bosello, F., Breil, M., Chiriacò, M. V., Coppini, G., Essenfelder, A., Galluccio, G., Lovato, T., Marzi, S., Masina, S., Mercogliano, P., Mysiak, J., Noce, S., Pal, J., Reder, A., Rianna, G., Rizzo, A., Santini, M., Sini, E., Staccione, A., Villani, V., & Zavatarelli, M. (2020). *Analisi del rischio. I cambiamenti climatici in Italia* [Risk analysis. Climate change in Italy]. Lecce, Italy.

Tashman, P. (2011). *Corporate climate change adaptation, vulnerability and environmental performance in the United Stetes ski resort industry.* Unpublished doctoral dissertation, The George Washington University, Washington, DC.

Trendafilova, S., Babiak, K., & Heinze, K. (2013). Corporate social responsibility and environmental sustainability: Why professional sport is greening the playing field. *Sport Management Review, 16*(3), 298–313.

Tschirhart, M. (2006). Nonprofit membership associations. *The Nonprofit Sector: A Research Handbook, 2*, 523–541.

United Nations (UN). (2019). *The Climate Crisis – A race we can win.* The Climate Crisis – A Race We Can Win | United Nations.

Wheeler, K., & Nauright, J. (2006). A global perspective on the environmental impact of golf. *Sport in Society, 9*, 427–443.

Whiteman, G., Walker, B., & Perego, P. (2013). Planetary boundaries: Ecological foundations for corporate sustainability. *Journal of Management Studies, 50*(2), 307–336.

Winn, M., & Pogutz, S. (2013). Business, ecosystems, and biodiversity: New horizons for management research. *Organization & Environment, 26*(2), 203–229.

Yin, R. K. (2003). *Case study research design and methods* (3rd ed.). Sage.

8

The Impact of COVID-19 on the Mega Sport Events: The Case of the Postponement of Olympic Games "Tokyo 2020"

Mario Nicoliello

8.1 Introduction

For the *first time* in history, because of the COVID-19 pandemic, the Olympic Games were postponed for a year, from July 2020 to July 2021. In the past, three editions of Olympic Games were cancelled because of the First (1916) and Second World Wars (1940 and 1944), but never the Games were postponed by a year (Guttmann, 2002).

The unprecedented decision was made by the *International Olympic Committee* and the Japanese organisers in March 2020, when the epidemic was slowly spreading across the globe. The health emergency therefore also had an impact on the sports industry, generating a crisis on the organisation of the largest planetary event.

M. Nicoliello (✉)
University of Genoa, Genova, Italy
e-mail: mario.nicoliello@unige.it

D. Vrontis et al. (eds.), *Business Under Crisis Volume I*, Palgrave Studies in Cross-disciplinary Business Research, In Association with EuroMed Academy of Business, https://doi.org/10.1007/978-3-030-76567-5_8

This chapter aims at analysing how the crisis has made an impact on the business model of the Olympic Games and what opportunities the crisis has given to the organisers to rethink the Olympics in a more sustainable way.

Using the *Stakeholder Theory Framework*, the chapter will illustrate the consequences of the postponement on, for example the main actors involved in the Games: the Local Organising Committee, the International Olympic Committee, the athletes, the National Olympic Committees, the International Sports Federations, the sponsors, the journalists, the Organising Committees of the next editions of the Olympic Games, and so on.

This research would like to demonstrate how the crisis, initially considered a negative event, can instead prove to be an opportunity to formulate a new and more inclusive business model.

In particular, this chapter aims to take a cue from the Tokyo 2021 experience to extend the lesson learned from COVID-19 in the future, analysing how the postponement of the Games has contributed to redesigning a more sustainable event.

The chapter will continue as follows. The second section will contain the methodology of the analysis, while the third section will present the theory at the basis of the research, that is, the theory of stakeholders, and previous works on the field. The heart of the analysis will be the fourth section, which will first present the stakeholders of the Olympic Games, then the impact of the postponement of the Tokyo 2020 Olympic Games on the categories of stakeholders. Finally, the fifth section will contain some concluding remarks.

8.2 Methodology

The methodology of this study is a conceptual development based on a narrative research that derives from the participation or the author at three online conferences. The research was based on the analysis of information about the stakeholders of the Olympic Games collected from the statements made by senior IOC managers and by the heads of the Organising Committee. In particular, after the crucial decision made in March (we collected all the information and quotes on the *IOC Website*), the writer participated in three online events in which the testimonies reported in the analysis were collected.

The first event was a teleconference organised by IOC in April 2020, in which four IOC managers addressed questions about the complex challenges resulting from the decision to postpone the Olympic Games. The IOC directors joining the conference were Christophe Dubi (Olympic Games executive director), James Macleod (National Olympic Committees Relations and Olympic Solidarity director), Kit McConnell (sports director), and Timo Lumme (television and marketing services managing director).

The second event was an online session organised in April 2020 by the International Academy of Sports Science and Technology (AISTS) with the key-speaker Christophe Dubi, Olympic Games executive director, who talked about the work being done by the IOC, the Organising Committee and the entire Olympic Community to reorganise for next year.

The third event was an online session organised in July 2020 by the Japanese organisers of the Games, precisely one year before the new opening ceremony.

The three conferences were public and freely accessible online, upon registration for the event. The text of the interventions in all three cases was published in English and French on the IOC website. For the purposes of drafting this chapter, we have chosen to use the English text on the Olympic family portal (www.olympic.org) (International Olympic Committee 2020a, 2020b, 2020c, 2020d, 2020e, 2020f, 2020g, 2020h, 2020i, 2020j, 2020k).

The collected material allowed us to carry out our analysis, using the Stakeholder Theory as a conceptual reference. In this way, in fact, it is possible to analyse the business model of the Olympic Games, highlighting the individual stakeholders. Therefore, in the rest of the chapter there will first be a paragraph dedicated to the Framework, then a section dedicated to the stakeholders of the Olympic Games, then the analysis of the impact of the postponement and finally some concluding considerations.

8.3 Conceptual Framework

This chapter proposes to build a theoretical stakeholder framework, which identifies the stakeholders of the Olympic Games, drawing on the Stakeholder Theory (Freeman, 1994; Freeman et al., 2004; Mitchell et al., 1997) and on the Stakeholder Theory and Sport Management Framework (Friedman & Miles, 2002).

The stakeholder concept was introduced by Freeman in the 1984, to analyse the "Principle of Who or What Really Counts" in the organisational life. Freeman argued that: "A stakeholder is any group or individual who can affect or is affected by the achievement of the organisation's objectives" (Freeman, 1984, p. 46). Freeman (1984), in his book, points out that shareholders or stockholders, who are the owner of the companies, are not the only subject to be interested to organisational behaviour and life. For Stakeholder Theory, there are other parties involved, including governmental bodies, political groups, trade associations, trade unions, communities, associated corporations, prospective employees, prospective customers, and the public at large. Sometimes even competitors are counted as stakeholders (Freeman, 1984).

However, as Mitchell et al. (1997) argued there exist in the literature differences between broad and narrow views of stakeholders. In the narrow views, stakeholders are defined in terms of their necessity for the firm's survival (Bowie, 1988; Freeman & Reed, 1983) or in terms of those who have placed something at risk in relationship with the firm (Clarkson, 1995; Cornell & Shapiro, 1987; Freeman & Evan, 1990). Also, narrow definitions are related to participation in creating and sustaining moral relationships (Freeman, 1994) and fair distribution of the harms and benefits between stakeholders. Instead, as Mitchell et al. argued, "the broad view of stakeholders is based on the empirical reality that companies can indeed be vitally affected by, or they can vitally affect, almost anyone" (Mitchell et al., 1997, p. 857).

Also, the Stakeholder Theory being an instrumental theory (Freeman, 1994; Mitchell et al., 1997) uses several others theories to analyse several managerial issues. In particular, power, legitimacy, and urgency, which are the three attributes recognised by Mitchell et al. (1997) to identify stakeholders, are analysed by others theories like agency theory, resource dependence theory, transaction cost theory, and institutional theories. Donaldson and Preston (1995) argue that the core of the theory is the identification of the normative model. Furthermore, they point out that also moral or philosophical guidelines for the operation and management should be involved in the identification.

Mitchell et al. (1997) define a typology of stakeholders based on three attributes. The first one, power, is the ability of an organisations to involve other in its activities. The second one, legitimacy, is the socially accepted and expected structures or behaviours. Finally, urgency is related to the time sensitivity or criticality of the stakeholder's claims. Mitchell et al. (1997) identify eight types of stakeholders, by combining the three attributes in a binary manner. Their modality of identification, also, analyses the organisational implications that could exist by the combination of the attributes. Furthermore, the organisational implications of contentious relationships between stakeholders were explored, also, by Friedman and Miles (2002). They analyse this relationship by adding to the attributes of Mitchell et al. (1997) the compatible/incompatible interests and necessary/contingent connections to examine the configuration of these relationships.

However, this is a theoretical study in which, drawing on the Friedman et al. and on the Mitchell framework, we identify the Olympic Games stakeholders.

This chapter is about sustainability and inclusion, so we will put it into previous literature at the intersection between Stakeholder Theory and Sustainability. In this field we can find previous contributions by Schnitzer and Haizinger (2019) about 2026 Olympic Winter Games Bids, by Leopkey and Parent (2011) about the Olympic Legacy, and by Geeraert and Gauthier (2017) about the environmental issues.

To bring together stakeholders with the Olympic Games concept, it is possible to exploit the extensive literature on the management of sporting events. In this context we can obtain numerous works that have dealt one by one with the individual stakeholders analysed in this chapter. According to Bose (2012), "sport is simultaneously a global phenomenon and a local and personal one. It is simultaneously a gigantic commercial business and a gigantic voluntary enterprise. Sport fulfils all of these conflicting roles in global society through a multi-layered and mutually dependent relationship with the media and other commercial interests. There is no simple definition of what modern sport stands for and therefore no simple solutions to its many problems". For our aims, it is interested to underline the work of Tamir et al. (2014). According to them, modern-day sports are not just entertainment for the masses. They are also a "religion" with hundreds of millions of believers throughout the world (Price, 2001); they are fertile ground for political activity on both the international and national levels (Riordan & Kruger, 1999; Strenk, 1980). Sport is also a giant industry, encompassing countries and nations, shifting enormous sums of money annually. In short sport is both international and a part of everyday life. It shapes relationship at every level: diplomatic, cultural, economic, organisational, community, and interpersonal (Le'tang, 2006, p. 386). Who are the target audiences to which public relations mechanisms are directed, and what are their modes of operation? The list of target audiences can be long and varied and include the general public, customers and consumers, the organisation's employees, shareholders and investors, suppliers and service providers, donors and volunteers. Essentially, the different target audiences can often be defined as "sphericules". The accepted definition of a "sphericule", a term coined by media researcher Todd Gitlin (1998), is "a public sphere of a social minority or community with a unique way of life" (Limor et al., 2007, p. 367). If we broaden the definition to include common issues or areas of interest, the ramifications are that a person may simultaneously be a member of several public sphericules.

Finally, as regards the previous works on COVID-19 and sport, some authors analysed the impacts on athletes (Stambulova et al., 2020), others on the organisers (Hoang et al., 2020), and others on the entrepreneurial profile of the events (Ratten, 2020). The effort of this work is to put the points of view of the different actors together and analyse them contextually.

8.4 Analysis

The Stakeholders of the Olympic Games

The Olympic Games are configured as a mix of products and services that must be well coordinated to achieve the set objectives. To ensure an effective combination of these tangible and intangible factors, the contribution of multiple operators, both public and private, is almost always necessary, so as to constitute a project network, given the temporally limited nature of the event, which must be well selected and organised. It follows the importance of a careful identification of the necessary contributions and, therefore, of the design of the network as well as a subsequent ability to coordinate, formally and informally, the team that has been formed.

The task that should concern the event manager is precisely that of ensuring that the event system is able to interact in a functional way with the elements of the external environment, while ensuring the pursuit of those purposes and objectives deemed to be priority, and guaranteeing finally, a respect for the social climate and the community in which the event is organised and inserted.

Today the Olympic Games must be considered as an economic and social system, in which a multiplicity of players take part and in which an equally large number of interlocutors are interested. It is on this principle that the Stakeholder Theory is based, according to which the social dimension of the company or organising body joins the more properly entrepreneurial one, and consequently it is appropriate that the effects of the event guarantee a fair balance between the objectives: strictly economic, and the other repercussions including those of a social nature.

By accepting this vision of the event as a social system with multiple purposes, it follows a series of indications that are connected to each other: in addition to the traditional bearers of capital shares, there may be other categories (the stakeholders) that can also affect the management of the event favouring the creation of positive or negative situations to the activity of the event itself. Stakeholders are interested not only in economic results but also in the social value that the organisation or the events it organises are able to generate.

The stakeholders of an event are those groups or people who can influence or be influenced by the existence of an event (Freeman, 1983; Reed, 1983; Clarkson, 1991). In particular, the primary stakeholders are those individuals or groups without whose support the event would cease to exist, while the secondary ones are those actors which, although not directly involved in the event, can seriously influence or even prevent the success of the event.

Taking the view of who has to organise the Olympic Games, the primary stakeholders are as follows:

- **Athletes**: These people have an active role in the event, producing the most important part of the Games from the sport side. They participate in the Games with the aim of winning medals and prizes.
- **Organising Committee**: They create the Games, setting up the conditions for athletes to compete. The organisers bear the expenses and collect the revenues from local sponsors and spectators.
- **International Olympic Committee** (IOC): It is the body that supervises the Games, choosing the host city and managing TV rights and global sponsorships.
- **National Olympic Committees**: These are the national bodies that guarantee the participation of athletes in the Games, supporting travel and preparation expenses.
- **International Sports Federations**: They are the bodies that manage the sports included in the Olympic programme. Thanks to the revenues obtained from the IOC they manage to survive.
- **Employees**: They are the human resources who are involved in various capacities in the entire event management process, from the realisation of the idea to the operational development of the event. Generally, their activity is remunerated.
- **Volunteers**: They do not receive any monetary compensation, but they can equally play an important role in the process of carrying out the event.

- **Sponsor**: Sponsors are the organisations which collaborate in various capacities in the organisation of the event, providing material, intangible and economic resources for carrying out the event itself.
- **Suppliers**: They provide resources of a different nature in return for a payment.
- **Media**: They have the potential to promote the knowledge and image of the Games towards the general public.

The secondary stakeholders include:

- **Spectators**: They sometimes play an active role becoming protagonists through their participation in the event. They buy tickets, contributing to the turnover of the event, and add a touch of colour that increases the media value of the Games.
- **Local Institutions**: They may affect the performance of the event by defining the policies and procedures to be respected.
- **Host Community**: It is included among the stakeholders as a result of the fact that generally the events are held in a limited geographical area where citizens and businesses live and work.
- **Economic and Productive System of the Gost Territory**: It includes all those companies that offer various types of services to participants and visitors, also in terms of marketing and sponsorship.

The Postponement of Tokyo 2020

In March 2020, based on the information provided by the World Health Organization (WHO), the IOC president and the prime minister of Japan have concluded that the Games of the XXXII Olympiad in Tokyo must be rescheduled to a date beyond 2020, in order to safeguard the health of the athletes, everybody involved in the Olympic Games and the international community. The leaders agreed that the Olympic Games in Tokyo could stand as a beacon of hope to the world during these troubled times. The day after this announcement, IOC and Local organisers decided that the Games have been moved to 2021, as a result of an informed, albeit difficult, decision arrived at with the full consensus of all parties involved. During his speech, IOC President Thomas Bach emphasised that "the coming months will require flexibility and creativity from everyone involved as the Tokyo organisers deliver Games fit for a post-corona world". In doing so, the IOC president offered his gratitude "to all stakeholders, who are fully aligned with the measures being envisaged".

Since the decision to postpone the Games, the issue of stakeholders has become central. A new edition of the Games can only be built by balancing the needs of all the players involved.

After the new dates chosen, the practicalities of moving the event can begin in earnest, in partnership with everyone involved. Outlining what needs to be done, Pierre Ducrey, Olympic Games operations director, explained: "It's a very complex jigsaw puzzle of negotiations with private and public parties and a number of stakeholders in the Olympic Movement, to ensure that we have everything that we need".

The most important point was to maintain the unity of stakeholders, even at a time when the health crisis was having the upper hand. Christophe Dubi, the IOC's Olympic Games Executive Director, explained: "We were fortunate to be working with a very good Organising Committee and were able to navigate through complicated discussions because everyone was speaking with one voice: the IOC, the Organising Committee, the City of Tokyo and the government of Japan. This alignment between all parties really helped us to make the right decision at the same time".

In order to create the new Games, a task force called "Here We Go" was formed. The first decision was to consider strengths and weaknesses, threats and opportunities for all Stakeholders.

The New Idea of Games

In this paragraph we analysed the work done to secure the Tokyo 2021 Games, from the perspective of the stakeholders. Category by category, the elements considered will then be analysed, using the statements issued by the IOC managers and the Japanese organisers.

Athletes

First of all there are the athletes. In fact, concerns about their health and well-being were a major motivation factor for the postponement decision. Dubi said: "Some 11,000 athletes from 206 National Olympic Committees (NOCs) are hoping to compete at the Olympic Games. They have known for several years where and when the Games were due to take place and have trained, hoping to peak in the 2020 summer. Although 57 per cent had already qualified for the Games and have now received assurances that their qualifications will be valid next year, 43 per cent have yet to do so. But all will now have to re-plan their training programmes for the 2021. This is currently further complicated by containment measures in place in many countries, which have made training, particularly for team sports, hugely challenging".

In order to adapt the qualification systems for the remaining places to the new timing of the Olympic Games, the qualification system principles were updated with a number of changes, such as an extended qualification period and new deadlines. In particular: the new qualification deadline is 29 June 2021; the revised final entries deadline is 5 July 2021; if a qualification system specified age eligibility criteria, the criteria has extended to cover the new dates, allowing athletes who were eligible in July 2020 to remain eligible in 2021; athletes who will meet the age limits in 2021 but did not in 2020 can participate in the Games and, at the same time, athletes who would have been within the age limit in 2020 but no longer in 2021 can still participate in the Games.

There are many athletes who would be great for promoting the Games, who were planning their retirement after Tokyo 2020. Kit McConnell said: "We are in touch with a number of athletes. There are athletes at different stages of their careers and there are athletes to whom this gives opportunities. The main thing is now they have the certainty about when the Games are, and it also maximises their ability to prepare on the field of play next year. For others, it may give opportunities if they are recovering from injuries, if they have not had the chance to prepare properly this year because of the impact of the virus on their country and their own sports".

The International Olympic Committee and Organising Committee

There are 33 sports on the programme for the Olympic Games. Within these sports, there are 339 separate events taking place in 42 competition venues. "Making sure the venues are still available will be a first priority for the IOC. Every effort will be made to ensure that the schedule of sporting events can be replicated, in the same venues if possible", Thomas Bach said.

Regarding the situation with venues Christophe Dubi added: "On the venues, there are three different situations. Firstly, there are venues that are fully dedicated to sport on a day-to-day basis. Secondly, there are fully temporary venues, and then thirdly there are other buildings, in particular convention centres, especially the Chiba situation where a convention centre is being transformed into venues for the Olympic and Paralympic Games: these venues have a calendar of events and some events are already scheduled for 2021. All in all, we are not yet into contingency planning. The great thing with sport now is that it is an industry that has evolved tremendously, and you can do miracles, including with temporary settings. All of the 41 venues were incredibly proud to have the Games because it is a game-changer for any building to have hosted the events. We had a fabulous master plan in place, so hopefully we can reconduct it". In fact on July 2020, the Tokyo 2020 Organising Committee announced that "all the venues intended for the Games in 2020 have been secured for next year, and confirmed the sports competition schedule".

The second problem was to secure the Olympic Village, the beating heart of any Olympic Games. Dubi said: "The Village is home to the athletes and their entourage during the full period of the Games. In addition to 18,000 beds, it also houses medical facilities and an 18,500m^2, two-storey dining hall, along with recreational amenities and a gym. Built on the waterfront in Tokyo, this 5000-apartment complex was planned to fulfil a long-term housing need for the city after the Games. It is a consortium that is building this Olympic Village, which was to come back to the developers at the end of this year. In 2021 and 2022 transformations were planned, with the addition of schools, living spaces, recreation areas for citizens, who should move into the apartments in early 2023. The desire of everyone, and I also imagine on the part of the consortium, is to be able to make this Village available, because to have a community going into a place that will be mythical at that time since it is the home of the athletes at the time of the Games, obviously it is a very special dimension".

Tokyo 2020 President Yoshiro Mori commented in July 2020: "Our staff have been working tirelessly around the clock on these preparations, and it is my pleasure to announce that we have successfully secured all venues, even the Olympic Village, and confirmed the competition schedule for next year's Games".

International Sport Federations and National Olympic Committees

After the athletes there is the sports calendar. Dubi said: "The sporting landscape is very crowded, with many events serving as training and qualification opportunities for the Olympic Games. The International Federations, and indeed the professional leagues, were already facing difficult choices as a result of the health crisis. The decision to postpone the Games means that sports federations are now able to adjust their own calendars too, but will need to fit in with the new dates for the Games. The sports world has shown solidarity, with some federations already deciding to shift their own world championships to 2022. This nonetheless represents a logistical and financial challenge for them, as well as further uncertainty for the athletes, who were almost certainly training for these events too".

Regarding the International Federations' (Ifs) financial planning, Kit McConnell said: "Firstly, we are very conscious of the impact of the coronavirus across the world of sport, and sport is not operating in isolation of wider society. We know that the Federations have lost a number of events this season and the revenues, not only from this season, but potentially the next calendar year will be impacted as well. Similar to the work being done with the Organising Committee in Tokyo, we have heard that and had that discussion with the Federations already".

It is not only the IFs but also the National Federations, their event operators, and everyone else. McConnell added: "We acknowledge the challenges that a lot of them they face, and the fact that they are assessing that themselves at the moment. We will continue to discuss that with them, to assess and see what role we can play with them in addressing that".

Regarding, National Olympic Committees, James Macleod said: "In the discussions that we have had with the NOCs, we have seen a very strong solidarity between them and the countries to help each other get through this whole process. We have seen this in exchanges of information on best practices, how their athletes are preparing in these difficult circumstances, etc. NOCs are already looking at how they are going to be working and operating in the future, but what we have managed to do immediately is to reassure them with some of the key programmes we are preparing for the Olympic Games".

Obviously, the postponement has potential impacts at the NOC level regarding sponsorships and particularly sponsorships that were expiring at the end of 2020. IOC provided guidance to the NOCs regarding how to handle potential sponsorship extensions. Timo Lumme stated: "We are in the process of drawing up guidelines which will cover globally the principles that we are proposing to apply, but in general, what we will be coming up with is that NOCs will, in the main, be free to take the decision whether they want to extend a local partnership or partnerships that have been in place, in general".

The payment schedule for the broadcasters is usually quite close to the Games. So for IFs and NOCs a lot of problems could rise from the financial point of view. Timo Lummee explained: "The broadcasters' obligations were targeted towards this summer and now we are going a year later. Just having announced the new dates at this moment, we are only getting into all of this now, but we will be talking to all the broadcasters to make sure that we come up with an equitable solution. You can imagine it is a little bit early on and all these arrangements are always subject to contract, but we will be looking to find fair solutions with all the broadcasters to make sure that we are supporting them as they continue to plan for coverage of the Games in 2021. IOC has both the supply side from the broadcasters and the demand side from our constituents".

Sponsors and Suppliers

According to Dubi, "The IOC's 14 Worldwide "TOP" Partners alongside with the host country's 67 domestic partners were all gearing up to provide vital goods and services to ensure the smooth running of the Games. Technology, vehicles, financial and logistical services, food and beverage suppliers—these partners have planned their operations and supply chains well in advance and were preparing to deliver this summer".

Broadcast and Media

One of the features that makes the Olympic Games so special is that they are beamed around the world in real-time, and one half of the world's population tunes in to watch the competitions on digital or linear platforms. This is made possible thanks to the work of Olympic Broadcasting Services (OBS) and the Rights-Holding Broadcasters (RHBs). According to Dubi: "For Tokyo 2020, there are currently 26 RHBs, alongside the Olympic Channel. By Games time, there may be more than 300 sub-licensees. The broadcasters plan their schedules years in advance, often around the global sporting and entertainment calendars. They will need to re-visit their schedules, along with those of their advertisers. Furthermore, many of them grow their workforce at Games time (camera operators, sound technicians, signal coordinators, etc.) using contract staff and equipment. While there is every chance these staff will still be available on the new dates, it may have knock-on effects on other operations and suppliers".

To house the broadcast operations and staff, alongside members of the traditional print media—upwards of 25,000 accredited persons—Tokyo 2020 had planned to use the Tokyo Big Site. Japan's largest convention and exhibition centre, spanning 265,700 m^2, was meant to serve as the International Broadcast Centre (IBC)/Main Press Centre (MPC). This had the important advantage of avoiding the organisers having to build a dedicated facility, thereby representing savings in terms of cost and infrastructure.

Workforce and Volunteers

Any Olympic Games cannot take place without the dedication and enthusiasm of the workforce and volunteers. According to Dubi: "Tokyo 2020 had planned a workforce of 150,000 staff, volunteers and contractors, most of whom had already been recruited. This close to the Games, many had begun or were ready to begin work. Although the Organising Committee is going to make every effort to retain the volunteers who had already signed up, it may nonetheless find itself having to recruit a new volunteer force, while some may face disappointment at not being able to rearrange their own schedules to attend".

Spectators

Millions of people have already bought tickets, some for what was promising to be a once-in-a-lifetime experience. Others had already made travel arrangements and planned excursions and additional activities to coincide with the experience. According to Dubi, "For instance, some 4.48 million tickets have already been sold in Japan, in addition to tickets sold around the world by Authorised Ticket Re-sellers (ATRs). Although the Organising Committee plans to make every effort to ensure that tickets already sold remain valid in 2021, some spectators who were planning the trip may no longer be able to go. The logistics behind ticket reimbursements and a re-sale will offer an added layer of challenge to the operation".

The Organising Committee of Next Olympic Games

After the new positioning on the agenda, in the summer of 2021, the Tokyo Summer Games will precede the Beijing Winter Games by just six months, scheduled for February 2022.

Christophe Dubi said: "This is above all a new opportunity, especially with the possibility of actually having two Olympic Games editions in the space of six months, which is without precedent. Before 1994, we were in a configuration with two Olympic Games per year, but over two decades have passed, and it is the first time that we again have the possibility of hosting Games that are close to each other. Discussions are underway, in particular with the Beijing Games organisers and all the partners involved, to take advantage of this opportunity to generate interest in the Olympic Games. It will undoubtedly be absolutely wonderful: for Tokyo, the expectations are huge, and a few months later we will have a new peak of activity with Beijing 2022. It is an opportunity to do something extraordinary and to take advantage of the time we have left for the two events to work in this direction".

8.5 The Stakeholders Analysis and the Savings in Costs

The challenge for all parties now will be to realign all these one year from now. Commenting on the complexity of the operation, Dubi explained: "Clearly there is no way you can do something like this unless all stakeholders are on board. The Olympic Movement has walked in unison through this crisis, and the support we got was remarkable. It was understood by everybody that this was the best thing to do in this context. I think it shows that the unity of the Olympic Movement is very strong". He continued: "when we combine the capabilities and the commitments at the highest level, including of the IOC and the entire Olympic family, we can be confident. A postponement is never ideal, but at least we have all the conditions in place to deliver the best event possible, so we have a lot of confidence that we are going to deliver great Games next year".

At this point it is possible to highlight for the individual categories of stakeholders how the postponement of the Games has gone from being a threat to becoming an opportunity.

In any case, the athletes were given the opportunity to maintain their qualification path unchanged and to continue competing even if beyond their age. In any case, the proceeds deriving from television rights were guaranteed to the National Olympic Committees and to the International Federations, as well as the relations with sponsors and television stations. For the first time, the fact that the Games have been moved has led to consider the needs of all the players, and in doing so, we have also tried to work on the cost reduction front.

IOC and Organising Committee discussed the estimated USD 280 million (JPY 30 billion) in cost savings that will be achieved by initial simplification and optimisation measures developed to deliver Games fit for a post-corona world. Developed in response to the postponement of this year's Games, over 50 measures have been designed to maximise cost savings and increase efficiencies in Games delivery, splitting into four main categories: stakeholders, infrastructure, promotion, and other areas of interest.

According to the president of Coordination Commission, John Coates, "Examples of the initial measures include the reduction of stakeholder personnel attending the Games, streamlining transport services, adjusting spectator activities at competition venues and hosting a number of pre-Games meetings online. Examples of some of the key measures being implemented include: the review of specifications for temporary overlay and other equipment at venues; the reduction of service levels and the Look of the Games in venues and in the Olympic and the Paralympic Village; the optimisation of the Tokyo 2020 Olympic Torch Relay operations; encouraging stakeholders to optimise their delegation working in Tokyo; and also staffing plans for the Organising Committee".

The results of these efforts will now allow Tokyo 2020 to estimate the total additional costs associated with the postponement, including the approximate costs for COVID-19 countermeasures. According to Christophe Dubi: "There will be some additional costs for the Tokyo Organising Committee. There will be additional costs for the IOC and the Olympic family. And we are looking into those in great detail. We have this commitment to help and assist to find the right solution. Also, you have to remember that Tokyo 2020 was in a great financial position prior to the crisis hitting. They also had some contingencies, and that has to be factored in to everything that we need to do for the remainder of the organisation. So, it is many moving pieces, but one thing we can say is that the fantastic marketing campaign—the ticketing, the hospitality—is truly helpful because the revenues are incredibly high and that is something we can rely on".

Summarising our analysis, Table 8.1 shows the interests of individual stakeholders and how they were managed in the new Olympic Games model.

Table 8.1 Stakeholders in the new model of the games

Stakeholders	Their stake	How they fit in the new model
Athletes	Winning medals	Changes in the qualification system
IOC	Managing TV rights and global sponsorships	Reinforced Games Image and savings in costs
Organising Committee	Bearing the expenses and collecting revenues	More flexibility in the management of Venues and Village
International Sport Federations	Obtaining money from IOC	Revenues guaranteed and flexibility in the International Calendars
National Olympic Committees	Supporting preparation of athletes	Assistance in the phase of preparation
Sponsors	Increasing their image	New agreements with new long deadlines
Suppliers	Obtaining revenues providing resources	More flexibility in the supply chain
Broadcasters	Wide spreading the Games around the world	Games scheduled in the high season for the audience
Other media	Promoting the knowledge of the Games	Presence on the field with the same numbers
Workforce	Creating the event	New more massive and inclusive involvement
Volunteers	Creating the event	New more massive and inclusive involvement
Spectators	Playing an active role during competitions	Enhancement of their role at a distance
Organisers of next Olympic Games	Learning from the past to improve the future	Shortened the time of their commitment and savings in costs

Source: Elaboration by the author

8.6 Conclusion

This chapter has highlighted how the analysis of stakeholders and their needs can represent the starting point for transforming the postponement of the Olympic Games from a threat to an opportunity. The case of Tokyo 2020 demonstrates that the willingness of the parties concerned to involve all the relevant actors in the recalendarisation project of the exhibition has allowed not only to secure the 2021 edition, but also to design a new business model for the future.

Compared to previous works, this research aimed to bring together all the stakeholders of the Olympic Games and try to analyse the postponement of the Tokyo Games as an opportunity to make the Olympics more sustainable. In the literature on sustainability, the research results confirm that sporting events can be more inclusive if the needs of all actors are put at the centre, while on the level of event management, the work confirms how an exceptional event can become an opportunity to create new value.

Tokyo 2020 Coordination Commission Chair John Coates said: "The unique task of reorganising an Olympic Games has called for the Olympic Movement to be stronger together—this milestone illustrates our collective commitment. The 'Tokyo Model' will not only deliver a Games fit for a post-corona world, it will become a blueprint that will benefit future Organising Committees for many years to come".

Starting from a problem to redesign the Games of the future. The Tokyo Games can therefore represent an example of how the coronavirus pandemic can change the organisation of major sporting events for the better, allowing to reconcile the needs of the actors and to redesign a more inclusive model.

Compare to the previous literature, the work demonstrated that sustainability can be sought by bringing together the needs of different stakeholders, and that the total inclusion of actors in decisions can bring benefits for the whole system. Therefore, in the sports field, a greater application of Freeman's model (1984) could be the starting point for a more detailed analysis of events, so as to understand strengths and weaknesses but also to increase the potential for success in the future.

Finally, we can conclude with the words of IOC President Thomas Bach and the new Japanese Prime Minister, Yoshihide Suga, during their meeting in Tokyo on Monday 16th November 2020: both leaders announced their determination to stage safe and secure Olympic Games next year.

Prime Minister Suga assured: "Our determination is to realise successful and secure Tokyo Games next summer as proof that humanity has defeated the virus".

President Bach added: "We share the great commitment of the Prime Minister that the Olympic Games Tokyo 2020 will happen next year. We are determined that safe Olympic Games will be a symbol of solidarity and unity".

In December 2020, the Tokyo Organising Committee unveiled the version five budget for the Olympic and Paralympic Games, which included long-term investments for the city and country that will benefit future generations for decades to come by helping to create a more inclusive society—a key legacy of these Games. The version five budget reflected the reduction of expenses arising from these simplification measures. This version constituted an update of the OCOG budget version four announced in December 2019, based on the agreed allocation of additional costs due to the COVID-19 pandemic. Compared with the version four OCOG budget, total expenses have increased by USD 0.9 billion to a total of USD 6.7 billion. According to organisers, "The OCOG budget, which already includes a significant contribution from the IOC, foresees revenues increasing by USD 0.7 billion, which will help cover the additional expenditures arising from the postponement of the Games. A further USD 0.1 billion of additional expenditures, if they cannot be covered by Tokyo 2020, will be met by the Tokyo Metropolitan Government. The OCOG budget includes USD 1.2 billion of temporary and overlay facility expenditures, an increase of USD 0.3 billion over the version four budget, operational expenditures of USD 1.6 billion, an increase of USD 0.4 billion, and general affairs and communication expenditures of USD 0.8 billion, an increase of USD 0.2 billion" (Aips, 2020).

Concluding our work, we can just wish that these Games will be a light at the end of the dark tunnel in which the world found itself during 2020.

References

Aips. (2020). Tokyo 2020 unveils OCOG budget version five. https://www.aipsmedia.com/index.html?page=artdetail&art=28978

Bose, M. (2012). *The Spirit of the Game: How sport made the modern world*. Constable and Robinson Ltd.

Bowie, N. (1988). The moral obligations of multinational corporations. In S. Luper-Foy (Ed.), *Problems of international justice* (pp. 97–113).

Clarkson, M. B. E. (1995). A stakeholder framework for analyzing and evaluating corporate social performance. *Academy of Management Review, 20*, 92–117.

Cornell, B., & Shapiro, A. C. (1987). Corporate stakeholders and corporate finance. *Financial Management, 16*(1987), 5–14.

Donaldson, T., & Preston, L. E. (1995). The stakeholder theory of the corporation: Concepts, evidence, and implications. *Academy of Management Review, 20*, 65–91.

Freeman, R. E. (1984). *Strategic Management: A stakeholder approach*. Pitman.

Freeman, R. E. (1994). The politics of stakeholder theory: Some future directions. *Business Ethics Quarterly, 4*, 409–421.

Freeman, R. E., Andrew, C. W., & Bidhan, P. (2004). Stakeholder theory and "the corporate objective revisited". *Organisation Science, 3*, 364–369.

Freeman, R. E., & Evan, W. M. (1990). Corporate governance: A stakeholder interpretation. *Journal of Behavioral Economics, 19*, 337–359.

Freeman, R. E., & Reed, D. L. (1983). Stockholders and stakeholders: A new perspective on corporate governance. *California Management Review, 25*, 88–106.

Friedman, A. L., & Miles, S. (2002). Developing stakeholder theory. *Journal of Management Studies, 39*, 1–21.

Geeraert, A., & Gauthier, R. (2017). Out-of-control Olympics: Why the IOC is unable to ensure an environmentally sustainable Olympic Games. *J. Environ. Policy Plan, 20*, 16–30.

Gitlin, T. (1998). Public sphere or public sphericules? In T. Liebes & J. Curran (Eds.), *Media, ritual, identity* (pp. 168–175). Routledge.

Guttmann, A. (2002). *The Olympics. A history of the modern games*. University of Illinois Press.

Hoang, V. T., Al-Tawfiq, J. A., & Gautret, P. (2020). The Tokyo Olympic games and the risk of COVID-19. *Current Tropical Medicine Reports, 7*, 126–132. https://doi.org/10.1007/s40475-020-00217-y

International Olympic Committe. (2020a). Ioc and Tokyo 2020 joint statement – Framework for preparation of the Olympic and paralympic games Tokyo 2020 following their postponement to 2021. https://www.olympic.org/news/ioc-and-tokyo-2020-joint-statement-framework-for-preparation-of-the-olympic-and-paralympic-games-tokyo-2020-following-their-postponement-to-2021

International Olympic Committe. (2020b). Ioc releases revised Olympic Games Tokyo 2020 qualification principles. https://www.olympic.org/news/ioc-releases-revised-olympic-games-tokyo-2020-qualification-principles

International Olympic Committe. (2020c). Joint statement from The International Olympic Committee and The Tokyo 2020 organising committee. https://www.olympic.org/news/joint-statement-from-the-international-olympic-committee-and-the-tokyo-2020-organising-committee

International Olympic Committe. (2020d). Tokyo 2020, here we go: New dates, same commitment. https://www.olympic.org/news/tokyo-2020-here-we-go-new-dates-same-commitment

International Olympic Committe. (2020e). What goes into postponing the Olympic games?. https://www.olympic.org/news/what-goes-into-postponing-the-olympic-games

International Olympic Committee. (2020f). Frequently asked questions about the Olympic Games Tokyo 2020. NonProportional. https://www.olympic.org/news/ioc/tokyo-2020-q-a

International Olympic Committee. (2020g). Ioc announces adapted Tokyo 2020 qualification systems for each sport. NonProportional. https://www.olympic.org/news/ioc-announces-adapted-tokyo-2020-qualification-systems-for-each-sport

International Olympic Committee. (2020h). Ioc executive board and Tokyo 2020 discuss USD 280 million in savings from measures developed to deliver games fit for post-Corona world. NonProportional. https://www.olympic.org/news/ioc-executive-board-and-tokyo-2020-discuss-usd-280-million-in-savings-from-measures-developed-to-deliver-games-fit-for-post-corona-world

International Olympic Committee. (2020i). Ioc President and New Japanese Prime Minister Suga "determined" to deliver safe Olympic Games Tokyo 2020. NonProportional. https://www.olympic.org/news/ioc-president-and-new-japanese-prime-minister-suga-determined-to-deliver-safe-olympic-games-tokyo-2020

International Olympic Committee. (2020j). Olympic movement #Strongertogether to mark one year until Tokyo 2020 games. NonProportional. https://www.olympic.org/news/olympic-movement-strongertogether-to-mark-one-year-until-tokyo-2020-games

International Olympic Committee. (2020k). With one year to go, Tokyo 2020 confirms all venues and competition schedule for the games in 2021. NonProportional. https://www.olympic.org/news/with-one-year-to-go-tokyo-2020-confirms-all-venues-and-competition-schedule-for-the-games-in-2021

Le'tang, J. (2006). Public relations and sport in promotional. *Public Relations Review, 32*(4), 386–394.

Leopkey, B., & Parent, M. M. (2011). Olympic games legacy: From general benefits to sustainable long-term legacy. *The International Journal of the History of Sport, 29*, 924–943.

Limor, Y., Adoni, H., & Mann, R. (2007). *Media and communiaction lexicón*. Yedioth Aharonot.

Mitchell, R. K., Agle, B. R., & Wood, D. J. (1997). Toward a theory of stakeholder identification and salience: Defining the principle of who and what really counts. *Academy of Management Review, 22*, 853–886.

Price, J. L. (2001). *From season to season: Sports as American religion*. Mercer University Press.

Ratten, V. (2020). Coronavirus disease (COVID-19) and sport entrepreneurship. *International Journal of Entrepreneurial Behavior & Research, Emerald Publishing Limited, DOI.* https://doi.org/10.1108/IJEBR-06-2020-0387

Riordan and Kruger. (1999). *The international politics of sport in the twentieth century*. Routledge.

Schnitzer, M., & Haizinger, L. (2019). Does the Olympic Agenda 2020 have the power to create a new Olympic Heritage? An analysis for the 2026 Winter Olympic games bid. *Sustainability, 11*, 442. https://doi.org/10.3390/su11020442

Stambulova, N. B., Schinkeb, R. J., Lavalleec, D., & Wyllemand, P. (2020). The COVID-19 pandemic and Olympic/Paralympic athletes' developmental challenges and possibilities in times of a global crisis-transition. *International Journal of Sport and Exercise Psychology*. https://doi.org/10.1080/1612197X.2020.1810865

Strenk, A. (1980). Diplomats in track suits: The role of sports in the foreign of the German democratic republic. *Journal of Sport & Social Issues, 4*(1), 34–45.

Tamir, I., Limor, Y., & Galily, Y. (2014). Sports: Faster, higher, stronger, and public relations. *Human Affairs, 25*(1), 93–109.

9

Business Under Crisis: Digital Transformation of Learning and Development

Janhavee Ravindra Walvadkar
and Hans Rudiger Kaufmann

Abbreviations

CDIO	Chief Digital Information Officer
CEO	Chief Executive Officer
CIO	Chief Information Officer
CSCW	Computer-Supported Co-operative Work
HR	Human Resources
IT	Information Technology
L&D	Learning & Development

J. R. Walvadkar • H. R. Kaufmann (✉)
University of Applied Management Studies, Mannheim, Germany
e-mail: hans-ruediger.kaufmann@hdwm.org

D. Vrontis et al. (eds.), *Business Under Crisis Volume I*, Palgrave Studies in Cross-disciplinary Business Research, In Association with EuroMed Academy of Business, https://doi.org/10.1007/978-3-030-76567-5_9

9.1 Introduction

At the workplace, digital transformation is much more than just a phrase: it is an indispensable process of change involving the entire organisation or business exemplified by the operations of L&D of employees and their training. This is confirmed by Wade (2015, p.4) holding that "*organisational change is the foundation of digital business transformation*". Moreover, considering the current situation of crises, there is a huge potential for digital transformation to add value, not only to organisations, but also to the society; "*a successful digital transformation will involve empowering people in new ways, including reskilling and upskilling*". (World Economic Forum, 2020)

9.2 Background

> *When digital transformation is done correctly, it is like a caterpillar turning into a butterfly, but when done wrong, all you have is a really fast caterpillar.* (Westerman, in Euchner, 2019, p.13)

The aforementioned statement by Westerman describes the challenge of digital transformation using technology to fundamentally improve corporate performance and widen the reach of an organisation. Moreover, Westerman emphasised the fact that the concept of digital transformation is an opportunity towards success (MIT Sloan Executive Education Blog, 2014).

There is little or no doubt that digital software and tools are heavily influencing the functioning of the businesses and various departments within an organisation. As per a recent study, HR departments spend close to 60% of their time and resources on transactional and operational HR activities to be standardised by digitalisation. In addition, 80% of the HR employees relate HR technologies with improved employee attitude and engagement towards the company (Canon Europe Ltd, 2020).

Hence, digital transformation is necessary for a business to survive. Businesses with strong transformation abilities not only enable an expansion into new markets but also gain a competitive advantage by easier adapting to new environments; further, digitalisation competences open a new set of opportunities for businesses to support them in becoming more agile (Lucas & Goh, 2009; Karimi & Walter, 2015; Sambamurthy et al., 2003; O'Connell, 2015).

9.3 Research Gap

The key gap or problem according to the reviewed literature on the topic of digital transformation exists regarding a wrong focus within the process. Digital transformation should not only be concerned with technology issues, but also with people-related ones. Organisations fail to recognise that one of the biggest obstacles is people and not technology; in order to overcome this, the management needs to re-evaluate the choice of change tools (Parviainen et al., 2017; Bonnet & Nandan, 2011).

The core challenge is to connect digital transformation with the human side of the process. Such a change is not easy to handle (d'Amour, 2016; Ancarani & Mauro, 2018). Many organisations do not apply the right approach, or they lack the necessary skills to design a successful transformation. Before the right approach is imbibed by the organisation, it is regarded paramount to agree on common standards, understanding, and objectives throughout the organisation in order to achieve improvements in the field of digital transformation (Bel, 2018).

Furthermore, it was observed during a study that the biggest challenges to all digital transformation processes are the people and proper leadership and management of them (Fitzgerald et al., 2013). Such a transformation requires a continuous alignment of organisational structures, cultures, technologies, and the people (Parviainen et al., 2017; Bonnet & Nandan, 2011).

9.4 Research Objective

The main research objective of the study is to concentrate on and transform the method of working, as far as L&D is concerned, into digitalised methods and to facilitate the global approach in order to offer access to all employees to the L&D measures.

9.5 Literature Review

This section will concentrate on the strategic questions and challenges which an international company may face when it is on the verge of digitally transforming its processes of L&D.

International Organisations

A global corporation, also known as a global company, is coined by the base term 'global', which means all around the world: it means that a global company is a company that does business all over the world, has its business interests present in every major country of the globe (LaMarco, 2018).

International organisations are not pre-defined and do not follow a restricted meaning and description; thus, due to the heterogeneity, the definition of an 'international organisation' is not straightforward and easy (Dijkstra et al., 2019).

A detailed research on international organisations and the views of well-established authors from different journals, articles, books and web sources as mentioned earlier led us to one question which helps understand the current position of the various affiliates of an international organisation—'What is the affiliate's current approach as far as L&D measures are concerned?'

Digital Transformation

Wade (2015, p.4) defines digital transformation as the "*organisational change through the use of digital technologies and business models to improve performance*".

Digital transformation is much more than just an IT project or a marketing programme—it is a company-wide transformation that requires an all-embracing corporate strategy. The goal of digital transformation is the constant optimisation in order to sense the market trends and shifts and to respond and adapt quickly to them (Gobble, 2018).

Further, as studies show, digital transformation requires five core components, namely, Strategy, Engagement, Innovation, Technology, and Data & Analytics. If any of these pieces are missing, it can lead to penalties to international organisations; latter do refer not only to monetary terms but also to the entire functioning of the organisation possibly resulting in immobility and dissatisfaction (Rajeck, 2017).

One research question derived from the literature is: 'What are the basic requirements for a digitalised transformation to function smoothly and successfully?

Significance of Human Resources in Digital Transformation

According to Cummings, CEO of Peoplewave and Econsultancy's Entrepreneur-in-residence, a department in the company, to help lead the change, should have flexible budgets, a well-resourced team and existing relationships throughout the organisation; one department which fulfils all of these criteria is the HR Department (Peoplewave, 2018; Perkin, 2017; Kotter, 2020; Matt et al., 2015).

> *For the digital transformation to succeed, HR must not only be on-board since the very beginning in order to keep the momentum up, but also should ensure that all the bits and pieces required for the digital transformation, as mentioned above, become a part of the culture and are well-represented and fully-understood by the employees by carrying out proper training and workshops to adapt to the digital change.* (Rajeck, 2017)

In contrast, authors have argued that digital transformation in a company or organisation is driven by the chief information officer (CIO or CDIO or the IT director) who works closely with IT and computer systems (Schneider Digital in Collet, 2019).

Getting to know more about the role of HR in digital transformation coupled with the diverging views guided us to another question; 'Who should take up the responsibility of the digital transformation of processes in an organisation?'

Computer-Supported Co-operative Work (CSCW)

When co-operation and co-ordination is emphasised, one of the tools adopted is CSCW. CSCW covers collaboration in the same venue as well as across distances (Shirky & Ito, 2010; Grudin, 1994; Findley, 1987; Schmidt & Carstensen, 1999).

One popular and general method of conceptualising the notion of CSCW is the CSCW Matrix, also known as Groupware Matrix or Place-Time Matrix. The matrix considers working along two dimensions:

1. Whether collaboration is located in the same location or geographically distributed.
2. Whether individuals are located synchronously, that is in the same time zone or asynchronously, different time zones (Baecker et al., 1995).

Relevance of CSCW in International Organisations and L&D

Figure 9.1 reflects that an international organisation is quite a complex model including three distinct levels, namely:

- Level 1—The members associated with the organisation, that is the employees
- Level 2—The groups located at a global level, that is the different affiliates
- Level 3—The entire organisation

A secondary research on CSCW and Groupware Matrix led us to the next research question: 'how will digital transformation, here in the field of L&D, benefit the entire organisation, different affiliates (global group across distances) and lastly, an individual employee (member)?'

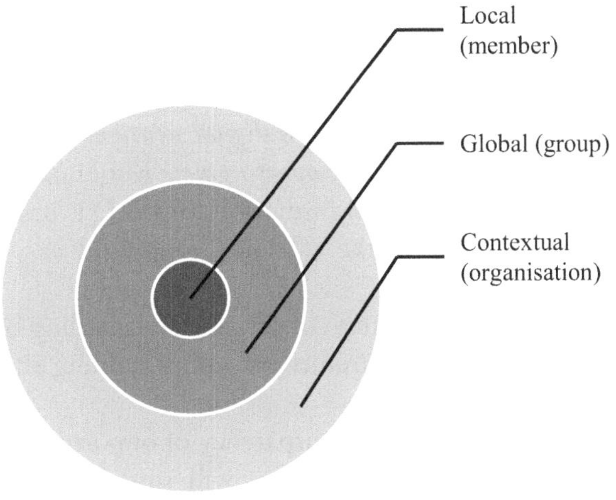

Fig. 9.1 Framework of analysing complexity in international groups (own representation)

Importance of Digital Transformation in an International Organisation

Within the past years, digital transformation has gained utmost value as an enhanced canvas, which has reached a level that directly correlates with the development and survival of an organisation (Kotarba, 2018).

As per an exclusive research, just 7% of the companies have already implemented their digital transformation approaches and are in the maintenance phase. When these organisations were asked, 50% conveyed that digital transformation improves employee productivity. Around 43% said that digital business drives revenue growth (IDG Communications, Inc., 2018).

Furthermore, according to a global study of digital business, digital transformation is important in order to attract and retain the best talents. Moreover, what is equally important to bear in mind is that digital transformation is becoming a cultural norm as more and more companies and organisations are seeking new levels of competitive advantages by pursuing digital transformation for various processes (Kane et al., 2015; O'Reilly et al., 2017; Bharadwaj et al., 2013).

Significance of Digital Transformation in L&D

Relevant contributions to the HR function of L&D are mentioned by Lambda Solutions (2018): "*Relying on digital solutions for training makes learning content more accessible and opens up new possibilities for learners*".

The significance of digital transformation for L&D is indicated by the following factors suggested by the Valamis Group (2020):

- Firstly, this change will create a common understanding by setting up regular and transparent communication about training offerings across the organisation.
- Subsequently, it will improve transparency of opportunities.
- Further, digitalised training offerings will support the competency development.
- Moreover, digital transformation of L&D will help plan and administer trainings professionally as well as control and monitor development progress for each individual employee.
- Setting up a trainer data base, a training catalogue and a training location list will increase transparency, overview, and accessibility within the departments.
- Furthermore, evaluating digital training and development programmes will ensure high standards of quality and effectiveness.

Researching on the importance of digital transformation in L&D leads us to the next research question: 'How will the digital transformation of trainings affect the upcoming/future setup or structure of L&D in the respective affiliate?'

Potential Challenges in Digital Transformation

According to a survey conducted, organisations say that the biggest obstacles that they faced in achieving success with digital business initiatives include lack of sufficient budget (39%), lack of staff and/or correct skill sets (36%), the need to replace legacy systems—that is, most companies have invested considerable time and money in their legacy programming and are not willing to waste those in order to adapt to new technologies (34%)—and cultural issues (33%). Moreover, another perceived challenge is managing the risks: each digital transformation within an organisation escalates to risks, and this might add confusion leading to a risk in the management process (IDG Communications, Inc., 2018; Mehndiratta, 2019).

At this stage, our next research question arose: 'What are the potential risks or challenges when initiating the digital transformation of L&D in a multinational company?'

Dealing with Digital Transformation Challenges

Irrespective of the size of the organisation, challenges faced by any organisation due to digital transformation processes seem to be the same. So, the question appears as to how organisations confront and deal with these challenges?

- Firstly, handling Employee Pushback: We, humans tend to like routines as they are our comfort zones; this can lead to discomfort by changing them. However, it is important to notice that these changes are vital to the organisation to mitigate risks in future.
- Further, making your organisational structure fluid and not rigid.
- Next, managing budget is utmost important whilst dealing with digital transformation obstacles.
- Lastly, developing a company-wide strategy: It is necessary for the whole company to work towards a common goal with purpose and strategy (Jabil Inc., 2020; Manzoor, 2019).

The aforementioned steps on dealing with digital transformations bring about the next research question: 'How could the company overcome the challenges or obstacles faced during digital transformations?'

9.6 Research Methodology

This section describes the used research methodology in the study.

Research Design

The study will use a qualitative research design to answer the research questions and achieve the objectives of the research to reduce or close the research problem/research gap. A qualitative study is regarded the most apt design method for the study as it involves a very sensitive and complex issue that requires high standards of dependability, reliability, and satisfaction to the user; it will also create openness by encouraging the interviewees to expand their responses to better understand their requirements and expectations in order to overcome the discrepancy associated with digital transformation of L&D. Further, finding potential participants were looked for, who have experience with the aspect and are willing to share their thoughts on the proposed study; this was carried out through interviews and focus group discussion. The analytical method is content analysis. The method of categorisation is an inductive qualitative analysis according to Marshall and Rossman (2016). The data were collected through interviews and were analysed, recorded, and transcribed (Marshall & Rossman, 2016).

Data Collection

The secondary data for the study is collected from journal articles, books, websites, and other online sources, and the primary data via focus group and interviews. The type of qualitative sampling used is purposive sampling. All the sources are divided in a systematic manner according to the topics of the sub sections. Further, based on the literature review, semi-structured interviews were carried out as to offer a high level of comparability (Creswell, 2002). In order to transcribe the interviews, all of them were recorded with prior approvals. This is also necessary and helpful to make deeper analysis of the interview (Collis & Husset, 2013).

Sampling

The data analysis will help in the investigation with the necessary information on the processes and roll out of digitalised processes of L&D.

The research will be carried out through Focus groups (R1-R6) and Interviews (R7-R12).

The overall goal is to understand the topic of digital transformation of L&D in detail and in as much depth as possible through the views and opinions of the interviewees (Blackstone, 2012). Further, the interviews consist of a diverse range in order to obtain the most from people's perspective (Crossman, 2020). Due to the situation of global pandemic, COVID-19 and different locations between the interviewer and interviewees, all the interviews as well as Focus group discussion were conducted online.

Testing of Research Questions

The research questions were derived from continuous progress of the literature review. As the research evolves and progresses and information and findings start coming in, adjustments need to be made in the questions to make them more comprehensive and understandable to the resources/target interviewees. The adjustments test whether a research question is good or not (Brand, 2018; Hall, 2018; Solar, 2016; Salkind, 2012).The pre-test brought important feedback on how to adapt the questions in order to have a successful interview with valuable data.

9.7 Presentation of Findings

This section presents the results of the collected empirical data from the focus group discussions and interviews.

Digital Transformation

Talking to 12 employees from different departments and cultural and educational backgrounds from a multinational company helps understand how employees create meaning on digital transformation in a professional environment. Three categories emerged to summarise the findings.

Starting with the first sub-category, most of the respondents are of the opinion that digital transformation is "*transforming manual processes into digitalised methods*" (R1; R3; R5; R7; R10; R11). R7 stated that "*digital transformation certainly requires a plan or a strategy and constant optimisation in order to keep up with the digital world*". This means that digital transformation is the need of the hour and with the view and aim to survive in the competition. Latter is confirmed that a company needs to constantly adapt by connecting people, processes, and technology and think more digital than ever before and focus at being efficient (R5; R10; R11). Exemplarily R4 mentions in this context: "We need to move away from long standing business processes we are used to for years or a lot of people are used to for years, but we need to try out new processes which are flexible, self-driven, social and sustainable; define new processes and also change with that or how business and people operate in daily life". Digital transformation is moving from paper-based processes to electronic processes (R1; R2; R3; R4; R5).

The second sub-category is the 'centralisation of process'. A central, global approach of processes has a great importance for every fourth respondent when it comes to digital transformation. R2 emphasised in this respect: "*it is to find the right and proper tool to make the offering accessible for all employees worldwide, so that everyone is working with the same tool*". Centralisation of processes will ensure a great co-ordination of work, further making sure that every piece of information is available at one common platform (R8; R12).

The third sub-category is named 'processes to solve problems'. However, only two of the respondents represent the view that evolving digital technology helps solve problems or issues (R4; R9). As mentioned by R9: "*The new, fast and frequently changing digital technology helps us solve specific problems in different departments as well as the entire organisation and it is really important to integrate digital technology into all and different areas of business*".

L&D

The analysis of the 12 responses specifically on L&D led to two categories. First, "*professional and personal growth and development*". More than half of the respondents hold that L&D is about personal and professional development (R1; R2; R3; R4; R7; R8; R9; R11). Exemplarily, R2 stresses that "*L&D is the area in an organisation where employees receive training and education with the aim to grow employees in their positions and to take over a future responsibility*". This refers to using L&D to identify individual strengths and weaknesses and skill gaps through appropriate training measures, like on-the-job training and external training (R1; R4).

One-fourth of the respondents agree with the statement that "*L&D is a life-long process*" (R5; R6; R10), which is the second category. Correspondingly, R10 underlines that "*L&D is any training which provides a continuous learning opportunity*". Moreover, an on-going process leads to increased engagement of employees and thus, increased productivity (R5).

Digital Synchronisation of L&D

The goal is to elicit advantages of the digital synchronisation of L&D. It is regarded important to understand the reasons as to why digital transformation is necessary in an international organisation.

The biggest reason according to most of the interviewees is 'Standardisation' (R2; R4; R6; R7; R9; R10; R11; R12). According to R7, "*one of the major benefits of digital transformation is that it will create a common understanding for everyone*". Further, a common system and a universal, global approach is necessary, wherein all necessary information will be received by all simultaneously (R2; R10; R11). For example, R9 emphasised the "*similarity in the way things work and are done*" to be important to ensure success.

The second biggest reason mentioned by the interviewees is 'Flexibility' (R3; R4; R6; R7; R8; R9; R10). R10 explains in this context: "*When a company will grow in terms of transformation, it will become more flexible and the business will be more efficient*". Further, "*mobility experience*" is vital to increase the skill set of employees, bringing them to the next higher level (R9).

Further perceived advantages of digital synchronisation of L&D are 'Efficiency' (R1; R5; R8; R9; R10; R11) and '*Easier Access*' (R2; R6; R7; R8; R11; R12). Efficiency in terms of personal and organisational factors is an efficient process, which optimises the operations and enhances the working experience of employees increasing satisfaction and performance and, thus, creating a positive environment (R1; R5; R8; R9). Referring to 'Easier Access', respondents stress practicability, convenience, availability of various types of training, and overall, making the process easier. This is exemplified by the following statement of R2: "*to automatically install workflows, like the approval process for line managers, as well the cancellation process*".

Other advantages of implementing digital transformation are 'Wider Reach' (R1; R4; R7; R10), 'Transparency' (R2; R7; R8; R11), 'Cost Effectiveness' (R1; R6; R10) and 'Environment-friendly' (R1; R3; R6): "*Via the process of digital transformation, we can reach out to a greater audience and share knowledge with a vast group through a common platform, which will not only increase transparency among employees of one department but also, between different departments, but also prove to be cost effective. Moreover, digital transformation can also help protect the environment, due to lesser usage of paper*" (R3; R8; R11).

Prerequisites of Digital Transformation

Interviewing employees of a multinational organisation with diverse backgrounds clarified the prerequisites of a digital transformation process. The responses can be divided into three broad categories: 'Strategy and Innovation', 'Focus on employees' and 'Ease of usage'.

According to 3 respondents, an effective system and overall strategy should be in place (R7; R11; R12). The innovative system and plan need to be stable. R7 strongly points to the importance of innovation by saying: "*Without innovation, there is no idea, and if there is no idea or plan, there is no digital transformation or any kind of change in the organisation*".

The second category, 'Focus on employees', plays a significant role for almost half of the respondents (R7; R8; R9; R10; R11). A focus on employees refers to employee engagement and employee involvement, close collaboration with employees/users and training of the employees (R7; R8; R11) exemplified by the view of R7: "*if there is no employee engagement, the progress becomes stagnant, it might affect the performance. This can cause a gradual resistance to change*".

The next fundamental prerequisite, according to three respondents, is 'Ease of usage'. As per the opinions of the interviewees, the category refers to accessibility of the system or software and the user-friendliness of the platform (R9; R10; R11). This is underlined by the statement of R10: "*The most important requirement is the user friendliness of any platform, as, if the software is difficult to operate, people will start losing interest*".

Ownership

The result of the question on who should take the ownership of a digital transformation process is very one-sided because almost all respondents consider HR to be responsible for this change (R1; R2; R3; R5; R6; R7; R8; R9; R10; R11; R12). In order to specifically define the category relating to the HR department, the sub-categories 'L&D is HR's field' and 'Relations with workforce' were created.

Starting with 'L&D is HR's field', most of the respondents expressed the opinion that "*HR should be in the driving seat*" (R1; R2; R3; R5; R6; R9; R10; R12). R2, for example, stated that "*L&D is one of the areas of HR; in order to grow and educate employees in regards to L&D, for today's and future requirements and to strengthen their competencies, it is the HR department which can predict the changes and prepare the employees to effectively and efficiently adapt to the change*".

The second sub-category as to why HR should take the responsibility is 'Relations with workforce' (R7; R8; R11). The respondents emphasised that, to implement a successful process of digital transformation, a department which has close relationships and is tightly interwoven with employees, should take over the responsibility (R8; R11). "*We need a department which can pull together all the working staff and make sure that all employees are well-explained, and the process is understood by everyone*", R7 briefly explained his view.

A shared responsibility between HR and IT when taking the ownership role is preferred by R8. R8 suggests, along with HR, the IT department to be a crucial part of the process from the very outset: "*IT should have a joint stake in the process and should look into the fact that all the technical part, technology works well and without any troubles, ensuring integration with other technologies in the organisation*".

Lastly, a "*Management team*" is also regarded viable for taking over the processing of any digital transformation (R2; R3; R4). The view persists that it is always the top management which is responsible for releasing new initiatives in the organisation, and hence, no department can do without the top management (R2; R3). Moreover, R4 perceives that "*if top management is involved from the very beginning, then there is no danger of failure*".

Challenges of Digital Transformation and Solutions

This category intends to elicit the roadblocks or challenges of a digital transformation process from a functional point of view. After having analysed the challenges, it is even more important to tackle them correctly. The interviews helped in scarving out the best ways to deal with the challenges and how to successfully overcome them.

Challenges

Analysing the transcripts of the 12 interviews resulted in the main subcategory of "*Creating awareness, integration and employee engagement*". Almost two-thirds of the respondents were on the same track despite a few different opinions. Nevertheless, creating awareness, proper integration of the new digitalised process, employee engagement and proper understanding are considered to be the main challenges of digital transformation (R2; R5; R8; R9; R10; R11; R12). Furthermore, the respondents described that proper execution can only be done if the task is understood by the employees and "*with proper understanding, also comes proper training that needs to be provided*" (R5; R10; R11; R12). Moreover, proper integration of the process/tool is also considered as a challenge (R8; R10; R12): "*Accurate integration requires complete employee engagement, which is the key; employees do not tend to engage themselves to the extent to which their engagement is actually required to make a process successful*" was a statement from R10.

The next most important challenge related sub-category is 'Comfort zone' (R1; R2; R5; R7): "*There are always some humans who don't want to change anything, they want to stick to their behaviour, they want to stay in their comfort zone*" as R2 stated. As people love their own spaces, their comfort zone as they feel things are working fine and do not want to undergo and accept any changes, this will ultimately prove to be one of the challenges to digital transformation (R5; R7).

Another barrier to digital transformation is "*Alignment towards company goals and company culture*". Keeping the company values and adhering to the organisation's goals and objectives is of utmost importance to ensure a successful digital transformation process (R5; R8; R9; R12). R12 emphasised in this respect that, "*if any change in a company is not in alignment with the overall company goals, it could be considered as an obstacle and unnecessary*".

Also, the aspect of Budget (R7) and Power Outage (R3; R6) are regarded major challenges while implementing digital transformation.

Figure 9.2 summarises the sub-categories of 'Challenges of Digitalisation'.

Solutions

After having identified the main challenges of digital transformation, it is important to address the possible solutions. Interviewing the respondents led to three approaches for implementing a successful digital transformation process. The sub-categories are 'Communication and Training', 'Lead by Example' and 'Managing Budget'.

'Communication and Training' are the key potential solutions. Any process or tool, for being successful, needs to be understood well by the

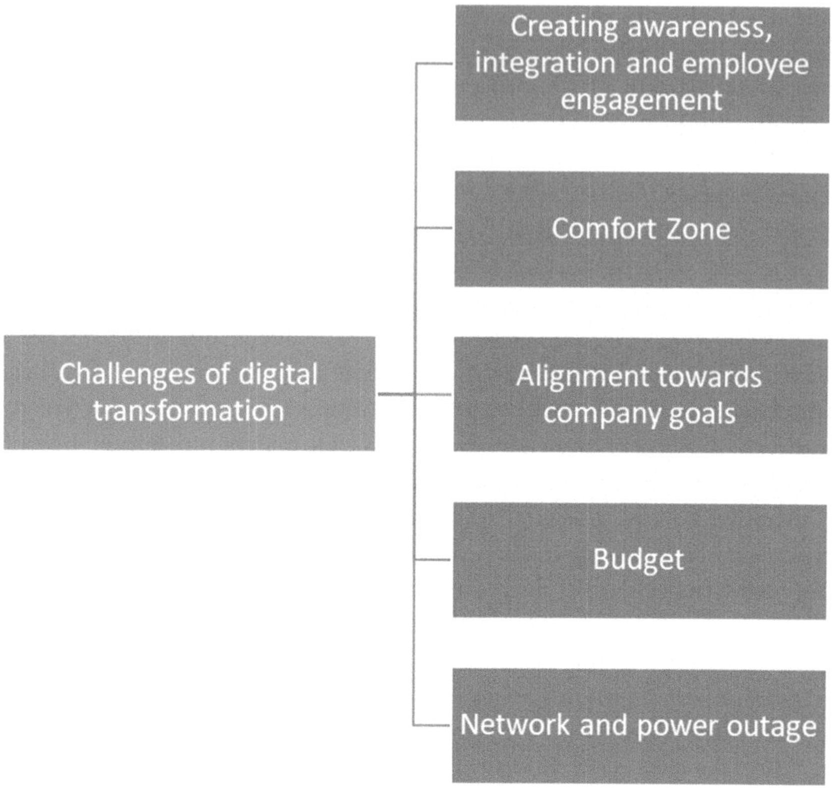

Fig. 9.2 Representation of category 'Challenges of digital transformation'

users (R2; R5; R9; R10; R11; R12). For better understanding, proper communication between the top management, line managers, and employees is required to raise awareness (R2; R5; R12). Further, once implemented, proper training needs to be imparted, ensuring clear understanding and "*user enablement*" (R9; R10; R11).

For one-third of the respondents, 'Lead by Example' plays a very important role. As a leader, it is important to create a mindset for digital transformation; this means they must live the change (R2). In line with R2, R7 stated: "*You need to understand the change, advantages of the change, relate yourself and your team or department with the new situation*". It is necessary for managers/leaders to understand the change and then work together along with the team to make it better for the organisation; this is essential in order to build up a good relationship and a good team spirit (R7; R8). Moreover, as explained by R10, line managers or supervisors need to have a regular check on the employees using the software, in order to ensure everyone is in the same direction and is benefitting from the software/tool.

In order to successfully deal with the challenges of digital transformation, 2 out of 12 respondents emphasised on 'Managing Budget'. Budget should be properly dealt with and planned for to avoid any obstacles in changes and digital transformation (R7; R8): "*Without budget, no change is possible*" was a concise statement by R7.

Summary of Presentation of Findings

Based on the empirical data collected from the interviews, it can clearly and distinctly be evidenced that digital transformation represents a radical change for businesses. In order to survive in the digitally ever-developing world, a transformation from the *analog world to a digital world* has to come to the fore. Moreover, in accordance with the responses, it is evident that a digital transformation process should be a globally *standardised* procedure, which means that all employees in the organisation are working with the same platform/tool. This new tool should help solve specific problems and, most importantly, *integrate technology into the business*. Moreover, digital transformation of L&D should ensure that the platform is *flexible*, *easy to use*, and *enhance the working experience*. All of this should be carried out with *HR* having the ownership, and of course, through support and backing from *IT* and the *Management team*. Further, *alignment towards the company' goals and culture* are of utmost importance for any process to be successful. Also, *creating awareness through training the employees* on the new tool is essential.

Based on the responses of the interviewees and the literature review, Fig. 9.3, the Input-Process-Output model has been portrayed, emphasising the digital transformation process in an international organisation.

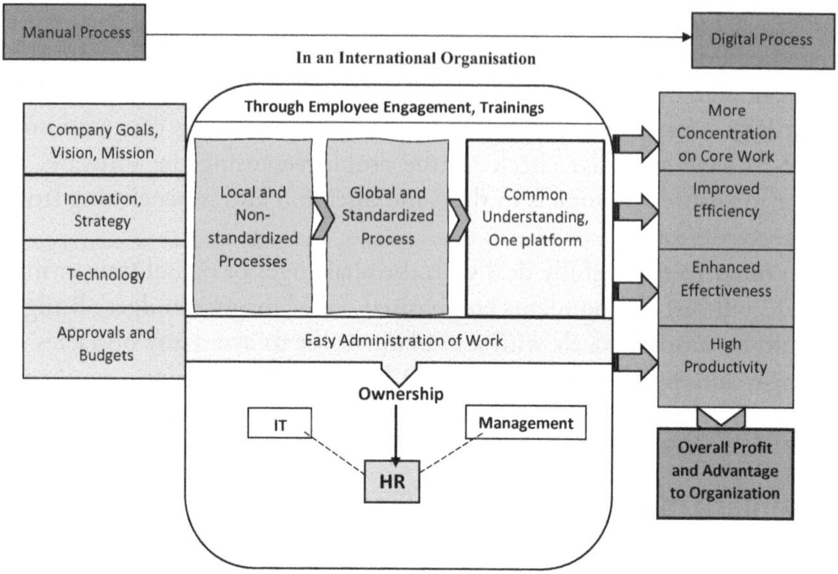

Fig. 9.3 Model depicting 'Digital transformation in an international organisation'

9.8 Discussion of Findings and Literature Review

This section aims at comparing the findings of the literature review with those of the empirical work on similarities and differences.

The literature review initially discussed provides the information that digital transformation is much more than just an IT project and requires constant optimisation in order to respond and adapt quickly (Wade, 2015; Gobble, 2018). This was validated by interviews with 12 employees from a multinational organisation. Literature review and interviewees agree that a digital transformation process requires a plan or strategy to be in alignment with the digitally growing business world and society.

As explained in the literature review, digital transformation revolves around five main prerequisites (Rajeck, 2017). Almost all of the respondents relate to at least one of these prerequisites.

Concluding from the literature review, the department which should lead the digital transformation process is the HR department. Contradicting this view, the literature review also mentions that IT should take the lead role (Collett, 2019). Most of the respondents opinionated that it is solely the HR department which needs to take the responsibility. Only a few respondents recommend IT to take this ownership, along with HR or a management team.

From the potential challenges mentioned in the literature review (IDG Communications, Inc., 2018; Mehndiratta, 2019), most have been confirmed by the respondents: comfort zone, budget, employee integration, and engagement. New findings related to challenges of digital transformation which are not stated in the literature review are alignment towards company goals and network, and power outage.

Where there are challenges, there must be solutions. According to the literature review, handling employee pushback, making an organisational structure fluid, managing budget, and developing a strategy form the pillars on dealing with digital transformations (Jabil Inc., 2020; Manzoor, 2019). All of these ideas are similar to what the employees suggest being done in practice. The findings of the interviewees also refer to 'Lead by example', which requires leaders and managers to live the change they would like to see implemented by their teams.

9.9 Conclusion

As presented in the introduction, digital transformation is crucial for an organisation or business to survive and grow; therefore, digital transformation can be perceived as not only an opportunity for companies but also the urgent need of the hour. Every company, irrespective of the field they function in, should be prepared to face, and be fully dedicated to the process of digital transformation, if they want to obtain competitive advantage and expand into new markets successfully. Moreover, moving from manual ways of working to digital methods would be an insurmountable barrier for many organisations if the employees are not involved in decision making and operationalisation. This might lead to concerns and resistance to change. It is, therefore, important to be much more empathetic, to understand the requirements of the employees, to communicate individually with every employee to prepare them for the upcoming changes and, to maintain a feedback environment. If organisations succeed in understanding the situation from the employees' perspective, it will avoid resistance and the success rate of the digital transformation process will be much higher.

Considering that this study is focused on the area of L&D, HR definitely plays an important role, as we observed throughout the study. Of course, with continuous assistance from IT and the management team, the process must be propelled in terms of technology and approvals, respectively. Moreover, if L&D processes are digitally transformed, it will not only benefit the HR department, but also the employees and ultimately, the entire organisation. It will create a common understanding, one common platform for all which ensures flexibility and easy access. It will further guarantee a wider reach, which will prove to be cost-effective to the organisation. When processes are more flexible and there are improvements in terms of personal and administrative aspects, the business will grow more efficiently, improving functions and the working atmosphere.

In order to carry out a successful digital transformation, organisations need to identify the issues or barriers and should be able to deal with them in an effective and efficient manner. Also, it is highly recommended to involve the people in the implementation rather than just prioritising technology.

In conclusion, the first and foremost prerequisite is *Strategy and Innovation*, as we have seen in the findings of the research. As one respondent mentioned, without innovative thinking, no new idea or plan will be in place, consequently, no growth and development will materialise. Hence, it is important for organisations to start the planning process and gear up to adapt to the digital environment and online world.

9.10 Research Limitations and Recommendations

The research is subject to several limitations, which need be taken into consideration and disclosed whilst evaluating validity and reliability of the findings and results.

The interviewees are part of culturally diverse countries; however, some of them are from the same countries and same departments and have shown similar thinking processes and, thus, resulting to the same arguments, as a consequence of similar cultural backgrounds and perspectives. This can affect the study's reliability.

Moreover, in order to get a better result out of the empirical work, it would be advisable to carry out more than 12 interviews with people belonging to different departments and backgrounds.

Also, the interviews and focus group discussion were carried out online and under great time limitations. If the interviews could have been conducted with more time and in a face-to-face manner, the results would have been more valuable.

Additionally, it would be recommended to test the results and functioning of the software solution under live conditions wholly to ensure usability of the software.

For further research, it would also be interesting to conduct quantitative research or perform mixed methods instead of exclusively qualitative research. This would contribute to triangulating the results and further enhancing the chapter's validity.

References

Ancarani, A., & Mauro, C. D. (2018). *Successful digital transformations need a focus on the individual* (pp. 11–26). Springer Gabler.

Baecker, R. M., Grudin, J., Buxtin, W. A., & Greenberg, S. (1995). *Human-computer interaction: Toward the year 2000* (2nd ed.). Morgan Kaufmann.

Bel, M. v. d. (2018). *Digital culture: Your competitive advantage.* [Online]. Retrieved May 13, 2020, from https://news.microsoft.com/uploads/2018/02/EEE-Insights-Report.pdf

Bharadwaj, A., Sawy, O. A. E., Pavlou, P. A., & Venkatraman, N. (2013). Digital business strategy: Toward a next generation of insights. *MIS Quarterly, 37*(2), 471–482.

Blackstone, A. (2012). *Methods, principles of sociological inquiry: Qualitative and Quantitative*. Orono: s.n.

Bonnet, D., & Nandan, P. (2011). *Transform to power of digital – Digital transformation as a driver of corporate performance*. [Online]. Retrieved May 13, 2020, from https://www.capgemini.com/resources/transform-to-the%2D%2Dpower-of-digital

Brand, D. (2018). *Why are research questions important? What makes them important?* University of Minnesota.

Canon Europe Ltd. (2020). *The digital transformation of HR*. Canon Europe Ltd.

Collett, S. (2019). *CIO feature*. [Online]. Retrieved May 20, 2020, from https://www.cio.com/article/3411916/who-should-really-be-driving-digital-transformation.html

Collis, J., & Husset, R. (2013). *Business research* (4th ed.). Palgrave Macmillan.

Creswell, J. W. (2002). Match between problem and approach. *Qualitative, Quantitative, and Mixed Methods Approaches*, 23–24.

Crossman, A. (2020). Understanding Purposive Sampling. [Online]. Retrieved May 26, 2020, from https://www.thoughtco.com/purposive-sampling-3026727

d'Amour, M. F. (2016). Change management for the transformation 3.0. *Sopra Steria – Direction Communication & Marketing*.

Dijkstra, H., Rittberger, V., Zangl, B., & Kruck, A. (2019). *International organisation* (3rd ed.). Red Globe Press.

Euchner, J. (2019). When physical meets digital. *Research-Technology Management, 62*(6), 13–15. https://doi.org/10.1080/08956308.2019.1661075

Findley, C. A. (1987). *Learning project – Digital equipment corporation*. Digital Equipment Corporation.

Fitzgerald, M., Kruschwitz, N., Bonnet, D., & Welch, M. (2013). *Embracing digital technology: A new strategic imperative*. [Online]. Retrieved May 13, 2020, from https://sloanreview.mit.edu/projects/embracing-digital-technology/

Gobble, M. M. (2018). Digital strategy and digital transformation. *Research-Technology Management, 61*(5), 64–70.

Grudin, J. (1994). Computer-supported cooperative work: History and focus. *Computer, 27*(5), 19–26.

Hall, A. (2018). *Why are research questions important? What makes them important?* s.n.

IDG Communications, Inc. (2018). *State of digital business transformation*. IDG.

Jabil Inc. (2020). *Top 5 digital transformation challenges (and how to overcome them)*. Jabil Inc.

Kane, G. C., et al. (2015). *Strategy, not technology, drives digital transformation*. Deloitte Consulting LLP.

Karimi, J., & Walter, Z. (2015). The role of dynamic capabilities in responding to digital disruption: A factor-based study of the newspaper industry. *Journal of Management Information Systems, 32*(1), 39–81.

Kotarba, M. (2018). Foundations of management. *Digital Transformation of Business Models, 10*(1), 124–127.

Kotter, J. (2020). *8-step process*. [Online]. Retrieved May 29, 2020, from https://www.kotterinc.com/8-steps-process-for-leading-change/

LaMarco, N. (2018). *Business models & organisational structure*. [Online]. Retrieved May 13, 2020, from https://smallbusiness.chron.com/global-corporation-63267.html

Lambda Solutions. (2018). *Digital transformation: The future of L&D*. [Online]. Retrieved May 17, 2020, from https://www.lambdasolutions.net/blog/digital-transformation-future-of-learning-and-development

Lucas, H., & Goh, J. (2009). How Kadak missed the digital photography revolution. *The Journal of Strategic Information Systems, 18*(1), 46–55.

Manzoor, K. (2019). *How to overcome digital challenges*. [Sound Recording]. Open Tech Talks – Technology Worth Talking.

Marshall, C., & Rossman, G. B. (2016). *Designing qualitaive research* (6th ed.). SAGE Publications, Inc.

Matt, C., Hess, T., & Benlian, A. (2015). Digital transformation strategies. *Business and Information Systems Engineering, 57*, 339–343.

Mehndiratta, M. (2019). *Overcoming the challenges of a digital transformation*. Forbes Councils, Sage IT Inc.

MIT Sloan Executive Education Blog. (2014). *The digital business transformation imperative*. MIT Sloan Executive Education.

O'Connell, K. (2015). *Digital business transformation: Disrupt to win*. Cisco Systems, Inc.

O'Reilly, P., Grace, A., & Morakanyane, R. (2017). *Conceptualising digital transformation in business organisations: A systematic review of literature*. s.n.

Parviainen, P., Tihinen, M., Kääriäinen, J., & Teppola, S. (2017). Tackling the digitalisation challenge: How to benefit from digitalisation in practice.

International Journal of Information Systems and Project Management, 5(1), 63–77.

Peoplewave. (2018). *Digital transformation.* [Online]. Retrieved April 17, 2020, from https://medium.com/@Peoplewave/meet-the-team-monday-damien-cummings-ceo-of-peoplewave-cb6aa8d1f7d4

Perkin, N. (2017). *Digital tranformation and the 'big opportunity'.* [Online]. Retrieved April 13, 2020, from https://agilebusinessmanifesto.com/agile-business/digital-transformation-and-the-big-opportunity/

Rajeck, J. (2017). *The essential first step toward digital transfomation.* Econsultancy Digital Intelligence Briefing.

Salkind, N. J. (2012). *100 questions (and answers) about research methods.* Sage Publications.

Sambamurthy, V., Bharadwaj, A. S., & Grover, V. (2003). Shaping agility through digital options: Reconceptualising the role of information technology in comptemporary firms. *MIS Quaterly, 27*(2), 237–263.

Schmidt, K., & Carstensen, P. (1999). *Computer supported co-operatice work: New challenges to systems design.* s.n.

Schneider Digital in Collett, S. (2019). *CIO Feature.* [Online]. Retrieved May 20, 2020, from https://www.cio.com/article/3411916/who-should-really-be-driving-digital-transformation.html.

Shirky, C., & Ito, M. (2010). *The 2010 ACM conference on computer supported co-operative work.* Savannah, Georgia, ACM.

Solar, R. G. d. (2016). *Why are research questions important? What makes them important?* University of Barcelona.

Valamis Group. (2020). *Competency model.* [Online]. Retrieved May 17, 2020, from https://www.valamis.com/hub/competency-model#what-is-competency-model

Wade, M. (2015). *Digital business transformation defined – Organisational change.* A Conceptual Framework for Digital Business Transformation, June, p. 4.

World Economic Forum. (2020). How digitisation and innovation can make the post-COVID world a better place. [Online]. Retrieved December 25, 2020, from https://www.weforum.org/agenda/2020/08/how-digitization-and-innovation-can-make-the-post-covid-world-a-better-place/

10

Business Under Crisis: Talent Management and Responsible Leadership in Luxembourg in Pandemic Times

Ursula Schinzel

10.1 Introduction

The objective of this research is to compare the link between talent management and responsible leadership in Coronavirus times in Luxembourg (1) before and (2) during/after the crisis. A total of 41 interviews were performed. Before the outbreak of the COVID-19 crisis, mainly in summer/autumn 2019, 26 semi-structured interviews were conducted. The method used was a combination of review of the extant literature and a qualitative study, with the objective to confirm the findings from the literature. It was planned that this would be a stand-alone study; however, the worldwide COVID-19 pandemic abruptly changed the situation. The first human cases of the new Coronavirus appeared in Wuhan City, Hubei Province, China, in early December. The first case in Luxembourg was confirmed by the Minister for Health, Paulette Lenert, on 29

U. Schinzel (✉)
Unicaf University, Larnaca, Cyprus

D. Vrontis et al. (eds.), *Business Under Crisis Volume I*, Palgrave Studies in Cross-disciplinary Business Research, In Association with EuroMed Academy of Business, https://doi.org/10.1007/978-3-030-76567-5_10

February 2020, followed by other cases and the first deaths in the ensuing days. This was then followed by the decision to implement a complete lockdown of the country starting on Friday 13 March 2020 with the closure of schools. On Sunday 15 March 2020 Prime Minister Xavier Bettel launched during a press conference a broad campaign: 'Bleift doheem—Stay at home'. This covered the mandatory closure of most restaurants, shops and playgrounds, the stopping of all bus and train services as well as flights. With most people remaining at home, almost all companies introduced remote home working for employees (Wikipedia) (today.rtl.lu).

The second part of the study, during the Coronavirus pandemic period in May/June 2020, consisted of 15 semi-structured interviews that were conducted mainly in May/June 2020 combined with a current literature and press review.

The objective is to compare the situation before and after the outbreak of the Coronavirus pandemic. In this context, before the crisis, respondents were mainly asked what responsible leadership in talent management is for them. After/during the outbreak of the COVID-19 crisis, they were asked how the Coronavirus crisis impacts the link between responsible leadership and talent management.

Cultural peculiarities following Geert Hofstede et al., (2010) in Luxembourg were under review. Excerpts of the interviews are reprinted and discussed. A discussion about business in times of crisis and implications concerning the link between talent management and responsible leadership follows with the Luxembourgish language as identifier.

For the 2019 study, the research questions in summer/autumn 2019 were as follows: (A) What is your company doing in the field of 'responsible leadership' and 'talent management' in Luxembourg? (B) What do you do to find the talent you are looking for? (C) Once found, what do you do to keep the people? (D) Please give some examples.

The author combines three existing theories, namely on culture following Geert Hofstede, who passed away on 12 February 2020 (Hofstede et al., 2010), on responsible leadership (Maccoby and Scudder, 2011), and on talent management (Lewis & Heckman, 2006). Convenience sampling is used in all sectors in Luxembourg, including the finance and banking sector, industry and the state, where most Luxembourg nationals work. As a single researcher, performing 26 and then 15 interviews is within the author's capabilities. More would have been difficult because of time restrictions and the effort required.

After this introduction, the chapter describes Luxembourg's linguistic and cultural peculiarities, followed by a literature review on responsible leadership, and on talent management, where the author offers a proposition. The method applied is as follows: review of the extant literature and 41 semi-structured interviews in summer/autumn 2019 and summer 2020. Results will be presented, reprinting parts of the interviews followed by implications, conclusions, discussion, research limitations and further research opportunities. References will conclude this chapter.

10.2 Luxembourg and Its Particularities

Luxembourg is a parliamentary democracy that is a constitutional monarchy and is the only remaining Grand Duchy in the world. With a total size of 2586 km^2, Luxembourg is one of the smallest countries in Europe at 82 km long and 57 km wide. It has 148 km of borders with Belgium, 138 km with Germany, and 73 km with France (The World Factbook, n.d.).

Located in the middle of Europe and also called 'the green heart of Europe', Luxembourg's specific cultural and linguistic context can be seen through its heterogeneous population composition. According to statec (2020), on 1 January 2020, Luxembourg's total population was 626,100 of which just more than half, 329,600 (52.6%), were Luxembourgers, speaking at least three languages—Luxembourgish, French, and German—and 296,500 (47.4%) were foreigners, speaking French, German, and many other languages. The different cultures and languages have a particular impact for the country as regards talent management and responsible leadership. Of the foreign population, 95,100 were Portuguese, speaking Portuguese, 47,800 French, speaking French, 23,000 Italians, speaking Italian, 19,800 Belgians, speaking French, Flemish or German, 12,800 Germans, speaking German, 49,300 from other EU countries, speaking the language of their country, and 48,700 were from other countries of the world, speaking the language of their country. Despite the compactness of the place, the entire world is present in this small country, covering a large part of the world's cultures and languages. Additionally, the impact of this mix of cultures and languages on employment is peculiar for the place. Domestic employment is at 443,900, but nearly half of these comprised 204,200 cross-borderers who commute to Luxembourg every day for work—107,600 from France, 48,000 from Belgium, and 48,500 from Germany—representing a huge challenge for traffic circulation, with enormous traffic jams at certain times of the day, particularly in the mornings and evenings. The unemployment rate was 5.5% in 2019 and 2.4% in 2000. Luxembourg has three official administrative languages: Luxembourgish, French, and German (statec, 2020), with Luxembourgish (Lëtzebuergesch) being the national language.

10.3 Literature Review

Responsible Leadership

> Machiavelli advocates that a leader who makes him- or herself 'responsible for the lives of others' has to place their welfare first. A Machiavellian leader must thus always choose pragmatic morals over idealistic or dogmatic ones. (Mahbubani, 2018)

According to Maccoby, "In times of great cultural change, such as the present, people need leaders to take them to a positive future" (Maccoby, 2007b, p. 1) and "There is only one irrefutable definition of a leader, and that is someone people follow". Three questions arise from this definition. Why do people follow somebody? How do people follow? Most importantly, who are the leaders we need? (Maccoby, 2007), especially in this time of crisis.

Maccoby (2007) states that we need different kind of leaders, depending on the situation. In times of crisis we need a leader who leads us to a positive future. Among other statements, Maccoby says that there are three types of leaders: the strategic leader, the operational leader and the network/bridge-building leader. However, they all need to understand that not everybody is like them, on the contrary, the key to success is understanding the diversity of people. Understanding people, combining head and heart, and education are central to Maccoby's idea of responsible leadership (pp. 14–15). Some educational mottos are as follows: "Work hard, be nice"; "The team always beats the individual"; and "Never give up". The advice "Never give up" is most important in these times. During the Coronavirus crisis, "Never give up" is the main motivator for those hardest hit. These include employees who have lost their jobs—unfortunately there are many of them—restaurant and hotel owners, who remained closed for several months, and independent workers whose income shrank to nearly zero.

> I believe that success comes from doing the best I can do, not from winning. (Maccoby, 2007, p. 137)

About 2500 years ago Lao Tzu described the ideal leader as one who helps people so that they finally no longer need him. Less ideal is the leader people love and admire, followed by the leader they fear, with the least ideal being the leader who pushes people around. People will not trust a leader who does not trust them. The best leaders say little, and people say "we did it ourselves" (p. 176).

According to Szekely and Knirsch (2005, pp. 628, 629), responsible leaders build sustainable relationships with all of their stakeholders: "Sustainability is about building a society in which a proper balance is created between economic, social and ecological aims".

Voegtlin, Patzer, and Scherer (2012, p. 6) state: "Leaders (and followers alike) are increasingly confronted with heterogeneous cultural contexts, devoid of shared moral orientations or legal frameworks".

Talent Management

There are different definitions of "talent management" and it is challenging to come up with one single definition. "It is difficult to identify the precise meaning of talent management" say Lewis and Heckman (2006, p. 139).

Talent management comprises in the first instance the variety of typical human resource management activities (Vrontis et al., 2020a), including candidate selection, recruiting, development, training, career planning, and succession planning. It also implies gender diversity (Vrontis et al., 2020). Secondly, talent management's focus is on talent pools and the management of the progression of employees through different positions in the company. Thirdly, talent management looks at talent in general, speaking about the 'war for talent' and 'highly competent performers', and the talent inherent in each person. (p. 141). Making talent management strategic is the objective of more recent authors (Kaufman, 2012; Chanda et al., 2007) and/or making it global (Minbaeva & Collings, 2013). There are four categories of employees, ranked according to their difficulty to be replaced and their value added: (1) difficult to replace, high value added; (2) difficult to replace, low value added; (3) easy to replace, low value added; and (4) easy to replace, high value added.

Social media, computer technology, cloud computing, and globalisation (Guo et al., 2016) imply a different approach to strategic talent management (Oracle, n.d.). This is in line with research by Vrontis et al. (2018) on the impact of innovation and change on an employee's performance, claiming the need for change and innovation as determinants for success in organisations.

Some ten years ago, Malaeb and Chanaron (2010, p. 1) said that "Talent is the only differentiator for a company's success in a global, complex, extremely competitive and dynamic environment".

The following proposition is offered: Luxembourg's talent management and its COVID-19 response depends on its linguistic and cultural particularities.

Talent Management During the Coronavirus Crisis: Literature and Press Review

In times of crisis, companies are laying off employees, often regardless of their value added or replaceability. They lay off thousands of people in one stroke. This is where others see the opportunity to recruit. This is exactly the right time to finally find the talent one had been looking for without ever succeeding.

The impact of the Coronavirus crisis on public finances is huge (Gantenbein, 2020), with debts rising to a never-before-seen 30% of Luxembourg GDP, disrupting the national stability and growth programme.

On the other hand, digitalisation has a transformative impact on companies, state Makrides et al. (2019), not only in marketing, but in all areas.

With the objective of business continuity, a mix of measures is the solution to the Coronavirus crisis for Romain Girst of BGL BNP Paribas. These cover (1) bank agency activities—in person banking, or physical presence banking; (2) telephone or mobile consulting; and (3) online or web banking (Leyers, 2020). He concludes that it is important to leave one's comfort zone. As consequence, it is essential to be learning for the future!

Coronavirus. Home office? Home office! The Coronavirus crisis has revealed that most employees enjoy working remotely, confirming that they do not want to return to their former offices, once the crisis is over, preferring to work from home, or from wherever they are (Bilo, 2020).

While employees confirmed their willingness to work remotely in April 2020 (Bilo, 2020), two months later their main concern was losing their job (Meng, 2020). Uncertainty about one's own job security is dramatic in a country such as Luxembourg with its high Uncertainty Avoidance Index (UAI).

10.4 Methodology

For the purpose of this study, a total of 41 semi-structured interviews were performed with the objective to allow a comparison between (1) before and (2) during/after the Coronavirus crisis. The method used in summer/autumn 2019, before the outbreak of the COVID-19 crisis, was firstly a review of the extant literature and secondly a qualitative study, where 26 semi-structured interviews were conducted mainly in summer/autumn 2019 with the objective to confirm the findings from the literature. This was followed, after/during the Coronavirus pandemic in May/June 2020, by the second part of the study, in which 15 semi-structured interviews were conducted mainly in May/June 2020 and was combined with a current literature and press review.

For the initial 26 semi-structured interviews before the crisis in summer/autumn 2019, respondents were mainly asked: (A) What is your company doing in the field of 'responsible leadership' and 'talent management' in Luxembourg? (B) What do you do to find the talent you are looking for? (C) Once found, what do you do to keep the people? (D) Please give some examples. After/during the COVID-19 crisis, in May/June 2020, they were asked: "How does the Coronavirus crisis impact/has impacted the link between responsible leadership and talent management?"

For confidentiality reasons, interviews were not recorded or filmed. In-depth notes were taken during the interviews. After the interviews, the respondents were presented with a summary of the interview and asked for their consent. Interviews were in Luxembourgish, French, German, Italian, or Spanish and translated into English.

10.5 Results from the Interviews

This study contributes to the discussion on talent management in the field of leadership theory. It is the combination of research about talent management and responsible leadership in Luxembourg before and during/after the worldwide Coronavirus crisis. The Luxembourgish language is used as an identifier, a guarantee of success.

Respondents in the summer/autumn 2019 study mentioned that if you want to be a responsible leader in Luxembourg, you need to (1) attract, (2) keep/hold/retain, and (3) train the talent the country needs. Despite numerous attempts by human resource management to attract talent to Luxembourg, many a candidate hesitates to take or stay in a job in the country.

In this regard, the director of an industrial firm stated: "The first priority in the long-term is the capacity to develop and attract the necessary talents and the qualified profiles in all sectors of the economy. Either these necessary talents have to innovate or they will envision serious regulatory constraints. The government needs to provide access to resources to ensure more innovation".

Respondents in the summer/autumn 2019 study also mentioned that what is needed is (4) to create motivators to make them come and stay, and (5) to install change.

An employee at a research institution said: "It is difficult to recruit talent for Luxembourg. Besides money, there is nothing interesting in Luxembourg that would attract talent. In addition, there is the bad weather. Furthermore, Luxembourgers are very slow. They are so much into their procedures, you would like to shake them to wake them up to get things done faster. They stick so much to their old habits, it is impossible to make them change or make them move".

Geert Hofstede's cultural dimension of Uncertainty Avoidance is very high in Luxembourg. This is illustrated by the following comment from a manager: "I know somebody who is a true Luxembourger, who is a manager. He has a company. He says that he has done his business for 30 years now and that he does his business the way he does and he will continue this way and he will not change. The young people he hires all leave, because they want change, innovation. But he doesn't want to change anything or innovate. He wants to stick with his procedures and his business connections that he has since the beginning".

A significant practical problem that respondents highlighted as needing to be solved is (6) the traffic issue. One respondent said: "The traffic situation is chaotic! There are road works everywhere. The entire town is in road works, traffic jams are so long, you take 1 hour or 2 hours to cross town, just 1 km. This is getting on our nerves, there are too many road works all over".

Another respondent put it this way: "The cross-borderer's biggest issue is the traffic. All day they reflect on how to get back home best, and how to come to work best the next morning. They arrive at 10 a.m., by the time they start working it is 10:30, because they are so exhausted from the traffic. In the afternoon, around 3 p.m. they get nervous and want to leave before the traffic starts. Others decide to stay later to leave after the traffic. But employees with children have to leave early. They will skip lunch and work through their lunch break".

Respondents also mentioned (7) the real estate prices being so high, a solution for the housing issue needs to be found. One working mother outlined her situation: "The real estate situation is discouraging newcomers. Housing, lodging, is horribly expensive in Luxembourg. Who can afford to buy an apartment here? If you want to live in town, and to avoid the traffic jams, then you need to go small. Small apartment, yes, my children even agreed on sharing a single room, just to stay living in town".

And most importantly, respondents spoke of (8) the need to learn the languages: Luxembourgish, German, French, as well as English and Portuguese.

Here is what one interviewee said: "The tri-lingual public education system is a challenge for all new entrants into the country. Luxembourgish, German and then French as instruction language in this order in school is demanding for children and their parents, mathematics in Luxembourgish, German and then in French is a real challenge, if you thought mathematics on its own was a challenge, then try it in these 3 languages, and add English and/or Portuguese to it!"

People like to reduce the effort, while talking, they prefer to speak in their mother tongue and not in a foreign language. The owner of a company noted: "Of course Luxembourgers prefer to hire Luxembourgers, this is because of the language. People all over the world prefer to reduce their efforts, therefore they prefer to speak their mother tongue. This is valid for the French working in Luxembourg who prefer to hire French speakers, and/or Germans hiring German speakers. The language is the identifier".

Another respondent said this about talent management: "Luxembourg lacks talent. There are not enough qualified people. There is no 'Knowledge Community', as the university only started 15 years ago. There is a top 1% that rules the country, inaccessible for the common citizen. Luxembourg seems to be an open society, but it is not. The language is the key issue. Either you speak it, then you are in the in-group, or you don't speak it, then you are out. The foreigners work hard, they bring the talent. In my opinion, the typical Luxembourger is dying, not only his language, but also the species".

A headhunter said: "When looking, for example, for an accountant in a country other than Luxembourg, you are looking for somebody with the technical skills of an accountant. The right person for the job. When looking in Luxembourg for an accountant, you add the language skills to the technical skills. This is where it gets tricky. Because technically-able accountants speaking Luxembourgish, French, English, German and so on are rare. Often, they have the technical skills, but don't speak all of the languages. Or they speak all of the languages but don't have the technical skills. The few 'cherries on the cake' are known all over the place (Luxembourg), and are highly paid, to make them stay in their position. Therefore, it is almost impossible to make such a highly paid, technically-able accountant who speaks Luxembourgish, French, English, and German move to another company. Money being one of the motivators, but not the only motivator, is not always the best argument for a job change".

One respondent said this about talent management in Luxembourg: "Besides, I do not work with Luxembourgers. I am the founder and manager of my own business. Not one single Luxembourger wants to work in our business, or in other businesses. It's too hard work. They all want to be employed by the State, which means earning a lot of money for little work. Most Luxembourgers study at a University, they come back with their diplomas and claim a highly paid position, instead of starting in a private business and learning from a boss, like me. They do not want to do that. We employ only French and Belgians. They work well, they are happy with the good work, to learn, to be treated well, and to contribute to a small private business".

In summary, a company owner noted: "We have to clarify what we are looking at. In Luxembourg, Luxembourg Nationals are a minority, those who are Luxembourgers by birth representing less than 30% of the population. Adding 189,000 cross-border workers to the 71% foreigners living in Luxembourg. The real Luxembourg National has his origins in farming. Nearly all Luxembourg Nationals work for the State as civil servants. There are hardly any Luxembourg Nationals working in the private sector, where foreigners and cross-borderers work. This is a dilemma, as Geert Hofstede excluded civil servants from his cultural study; here in Luxembourg, you will hardly find any Luxembourg Nationals in the private sector. What counts in Luxembourg is the social class to which you are born, not whether you are foreigner or not".

Finally, other minor points mentioned by respondents were: if possible you need to get used to (9) the smallness of the place, only 100,000 inhabitants in the city of Luxembourg and (10) the weather conditions. Some people never get used to the weather.

The various points raised in the interviews around the themes of talent management and responsible leadership are summarised in Table 10.1.

Respondents stated that combinations of these typical peculiarities such as the trilingual education system, sticking to old traditions,

Table 10.1 The link between talent management and responsible leadership

If you want to be a responsible leader in Luxembourg, you need to attract and keep/hold/retain and train the talent the country needs. You need to create motivators to make them come and stay, you need to install change. You need to solve the traffic issue. You need to solve the housing issue. You need to learn the languages: Luxembourgish, German, French, in addition to English and Portuguese. You need to get used to the smallness of the place, and to the weather conditions, if possible.
• **The need for new talents**: We urgently need new talents. Luxembourg does not have enough suitable talents.
• **The need for new motivators**: We urgently need new motivators, attractive reasons for people to come to work to Luxembourg. Besides money, there is nothing interesting in Luxembourg that would attract talent.
• **The need for change**: We urgently need change. Luxembourgers are very slow. They stick so much to their old habits, it is impossible to make them change or make them move. Everything takes too much time here, procedures are followed to the letter; they are long lasting, and discourage new entrants.
The **Luxembourgish language** is the key issue. Either you speak it, then you are in the in-group, or you do not speak it, then you belong to the out-group.
Therefore:
The lack of talent, especially the lack of talent speaking Luxembourgish, is one of the biggest issues to be solved in the future. Luxembourgish, French, and/or German language courses are inherent components of expatriates' relocation packages.
Traffic
The cross-borderer's—and not only this group—biggest issue is the traffic. Cross-border workers consistently arrive late in the mornings. They will skip lunch and work through their lunch break. At around 3 in the afternoon they get nervous and want to leave before the traffic starts. There are horrendous traffic jams and there are road works everywhere.
Real Estate/Housing
The prices for housing, both buying and renting are very high.
The Trilingual Public Education System
Luxembourgish, then German and then French as instruction language in public school is a challenge for all children and parents.
Climate/Weather
The weather is difficult to live with. If you are not born in Luxembourg, it is difficult to stand the greyness.
The Smallness of the Place
Luxembourg is small in size and has less people. Everybody knows everybody and everything.

avoiding change, the expensive real estate prices, the traffic situation, the weather conditions, and the smallness of the place combined with a lack of attractions prevent many a person from accepting a job and/or from remaining in the job. On the other hand, Luxembourg often is and has been forerunner in promoting peace and tolerance in the European Union and the world, in start-up creation (Mercier, 2018), in satellite technology and many more innovative projects. The lack of talent, especially the lack of talent speaking Luxembourgish, is one of the biggest issues to be solved in the future. Luxembourgish, French, and/or German language courses are inherent components of expatriates' relocation packages.

10.6 Lessons Learned from Luxembourg During Times of Crisis

The primary impact on talent management is the acceleration of digitalisation with the effect that now, after/during the crisis, the cross-borderers do not want to commute any more. They mostly all want to work from home ('télé-travail'). Remote working, much requested by employees before the crisis, was all of a sudden possible more or less overnight. Everybody works from his/her computer, over Skype, Zoom, Webex, Microsoft Teams with email and WhatsApp calls, phone calls, and video calls. "The banking sector solved the social distancing issue by consulting via telephone or video conference", said one bank employee.

Employees see the advantages of working from home as follows: no more commuting, no waste of time in traffic jams, and working from your kitchen table means work whenever you want without time restrictions. Additionally, they say they do not need to get dressed in expensive clothes or buy such clothes, they eat when they want, and there is no need to see unfriendly colleagues.

The disadvantages that can be seen from the point of view of the employee are: no social contact, no coffee breaks with colleagues standing at the coffee machine, nor going for lunch together, eating together, no socialising, no laughter over a drink, no contact, need for a professional psychologist to solve one's problems, no common experiences, no outings, no meetings in person, no dancing, and no sharing of good vibes or good food.

The advantages that can be seen from the point of view of the employer are no infection possible and potentially cheaper office rents and lower costs for water, electricity, cleaning, and so on.

The disadvantages that can be seen from the point of view of the employer are: no real control of the work done, no control of working hours, breaks, absences, and whereabouts of the employee. There is also the possibility of social tensions, domestic violence, and disputes, with explosive family situations. In general, communication is not the same, collaboration is not the same, work is done differently, with errors because some work is not done at all while other work is done twice. Other disadvantages are the fact that employees "remain in their pyjamas all day long", they eat unhealthily, they gain weight, and they sit / lie on their couches. Communication is not the same, as employees suffer from 'cabin fever'.

Worldwide, we are facing a huge globalised economic crisis, including the laying off of thousands of people.

In general, this crisis spans three areas: (1) the economic crisis, (2) the social crisis, (3) the health crisis. One of the respondents from HR formulated it this way: "We can see there is less recruiting, there is no relocation, there are no longer overseas activities, and there is no hiring of interns/trainees. But what there are: the laying off of employees, including non-replacement of departing employees, retirements; and employees quitting jobs. There is a huge restructuring activity going on, including a social plan. Most people do not dare to change jobs as they are worried about their trial period, if they do not succeed in this period, then what next?" He continued: "The leadership in the Unites States of America is questioned. This implies an increase of social disasters: (1) increase in racism, (2) increase in crime, and (3) increase in job losses".

On the other hand, this is a period of great opportunities for innovation and change. One respondent said: "This Coronavirus pandemic gives the world the opportunity for much needed change and innovations. Something completely new will come out of this. Great inventions will be made now, during this crisis. This crisis is the opportunity for great inventions".

Some employers are hiring right now. One business owner stated: "This is the occasion for finding the right talent, at a lower cost. As so many people are laid off, the choice is larger and the price is low. This is the moment to recruit the talent we have been looking for so long without finding them. Now, they are at our disposal. We recruited someone just last week".

The points raised in the interviews concerning the pros and cons of remote working are summarised in Table 10.2.

10.7 Conclusions, Limitations, and Further Research

The objective of this research was to compare the link between talent management and responsible leadership in Coronavirus times in Luxembourg (1) before and (2) during/after the crisis.

In conclusion, and by confirming the extant literature about culture by Hofstede (2001) and Hofstede et al. (2010), about talent management by Lewis and Heckman (2006), about Luxembourg by Leyers (2020), and about responsible leadership by Maccoby (2007a, 2007b, 2015) and Maccoby and Scudder (2011), the link between talent management and responsible leadership is the following: if you want to be a responsible leader in Luxembourg, you need to attract and keep/hold/retain and train the talent the country needs. Is this one of the myths Minbaeva and Collings (2013) write about? Or how can companies find and retain the best people (Oracle Corporation, n.d.)? You need to create motivators to make them come and stay, you need to install change. The change would be to allow for flexible working possibilities, in time and place. You need to solve the traffic issue, which with the working from home will solve itself. You need to solve the housing issue, increased by working from home, home schooling, online education, and working in general. Employee performance will increase once these issues are solved (Vrontis et al., 2018). You need to learn the languages (Weber & Horner, 2008):

Table 10.2 Advantages and disadvantages of working from home seen by the employee and the employer, general views and opportunities

	Employees' viewpoint	Employers' viewpoint
Advantages	• No infection possible • No more commuting • No waste of time in traffic jams • Working from home means working whenever you want without time restrictions • No need to see unfriendly colleagues	• No infection possible • Cheaper office rents, water, electricity, cleaning, and so on
Disadvantages	• No social contact, no coffee breaks with colleagues standing at the coffee machine, nor going for lunch together, or eating together, or socialising • No laughter over a drink, no contact, but need for a professional psychologist to solve one's problems • No common experiences, no outings, no meetings in person, no dancing, no sharing of good vibes or good food.	• No real control of the work done, of working hours, of breaks, absence, whereabouts of the employee • Social tensions, domestic violence increases, disputes arise, family situations explode • Employees remain in their pyjamas all day long, they eat unhealthily, they gain weight, they sit/lie on their couches • Communication is not the same, collaboration is not the same, work is done differently, with errors because some work is not done at all while other work is done twice • Employees suffer from 'cabin fever'.

(*continued*)

Table 10.2 (continued)

	Employees' viewpoint	Employers' viewpoint
General views	• This crisis spans three areas: – Economic crisis – Social crisis – Health crisis • There is less recruiting • There is no relocation • There are no more overseas activities • There is no hiring of interns/trainees • Laying off of employees • Restructuring • Social plans for laid off employees • Most people do not dare to change jobs as they are worried about their trial period, if they do not pass it, what next? • Leadership in the United States is questioned • Possible increases of social disorder: • Increase in racism • Increase in crime • Increase of job losses	
Opportunities	• Digitalisation • Work from home/remotely • This is a period of great innovation and change. It gives the world the opportunity for great innovations. • Something completely new will come out of this. • This is the moment to find and hire the talent we were not finding until now.	

Luxembourgish, German, and French, in addition to English and Portuguese. You need to get used to the smallness of the place, the importance of the Luxembourgish language as identifier (Schinzel, 2013, 2014a, 2014b) and to the weather conditions, if possible.

While analysing and comparing values and behaviours in Luxembourg among Luxembourgers with Luxembourg Nationality, they are characterised by Hofstede's (2001) cultural dimensions: low Power Distance Index (PDI = 29), high Uncertainty Avoidance (UAI = 95), low Individualism (IDV = 34), high Collectivism, medium Masculinity versus Femininity Index (MAS = 54), high Long-Term Orientation (LTO = 65) versus Short-Term Orientation, medium Indulgence versus Restraint Index

(IVR = 55), and low Monumentalism Index (MON = 24), with a mix of at least three official languages: Luxembourgish, German, and French.

Due to the high level in the Uncertainty Avoidance Index (UAI), Luxembourgers tend to hold to traditions and to avoid any change or innovation. Firstly, the lack of talent and, secondly, the slowness in applying digital transformation combined with stagnating productivity have resulted in Luxembourg's loss of three places in the IMD World Competitiveness Yearbook (Klein, 2020) from 12th place in 2019 to 15th in 2020. In 2005, Luxembourg was sixth and in 2017 eighth.

As 'homework' the Swiss company IMD gave Luxembourg the task to draw up a reconstruction plan after the Coronavirus crisis in order to address the three aforementioned issues.

- Lack of talent, difficulty in finding the talent the country needs
- Slowness in applying digital transformation, due to high Uncertainty Avoidance
- Stagnating productivity

Future research could look into how this reconstruction plan in responsible leadership and talent management has been realised.

In this study, the primary research limitation was one of time. This research was carried out with the objective of conference presentation and publication. Secondly, there was a limitation in resources. The author is a lone researcher and cannot compete with huge groups of researchers, such as the GLOBE (House et al., 2004). Also, the author decided to concentrate on Geert Hofstede's research. This decision can be contested; however, Hofstede was the initiator of cultural dimension research, despite later criticism of his methods.

This being a combination of literature review, secondary data, and primary data from qualitative research, more sophisticated statistical methods could be used in the future with the objective to validate the results.

Many questions remain open:

- Will the right talent be found for Luxembourg as a result of digitalisation and working remotely?

- Will the language issue, in addition to the job qualification issues be solved through learning languages remotely?
- Will the housing and traffic issues be resolved through working remotely?

These questions constitute matter for future research.

References

Bilo, M. (2020). Vom Homeoffice zurück ins Büro. *Luxemburger Wort*, April 10, p. 12.

Chanda, A., Krishna, B. S., & Shen, J. (2007). *Strategic human resource technologies: Keys to managing people*. n.p.: Los Angeles: Response. Texas State – Alkek Library's Catalog. Web. 9 Mar. 2016.

Gantenbein, M. (2020). Gewaltiges Loch in der Staatskasse. *Luxemburger Wort*, June 16, p. 4.

Guo, Y., Rammal, H. G., & Dowling, P. J. (2016). *Global talent management and staffing in MNEs*. Emerald Books. https://opus.lib.uts.edu.au/handle/10453/66225

Hofstede, G. (2001). *Culture's consequences: Comparing values, behaviours, institutions and organizations across nations* (2nd ed.). Sage.

Hofstede, G., Hofstede, G. J., & Minkov, M. (2010). *Cultures and organizations. Software of the mind* (Intercultural cooperation and its importance for survival) (3rd ed.). McGraw Hill.

House, R. J., Hanges, P. J., Javidan, M., Dorfman, P. W., & Gupta, V. (2004). *Culture, leadership, and organizations: The GLOBE study of 62 societies*. Sage.

Kaufman, B. E. (2012). Strategic human resource management research in the United States: A failing grade after 30 years? *Academy of Management Perspectives, 26*(2), 12–36. Business Source Complete. Web. 9 Mar. 2016.

Klein, T. (2020). Luxemburg verliert an Boden. *Luxemburger Wort*, June 17, p. 15.

Lewis, R. E., & Heckman, R. J. (2006). Talent management: A critical review. *Human Resource Management Review, 16*(2), 139–154.

Leyers, P. (2020). Wir mussten unsere Komfortzone verlassen. *Luxemburger Wort*, June 16, p. 13.

Maccoby, M. (2007a). *Narcissistic leaders. Who succeeds and who fails*. Harvard Business School Press.

Maccoby, M. (2007b). *The leaders we need. And what makes us follow*. Harvard Business School Press.
Maccoby, M. (2015). *Strategic intelligence*. Oxford University Press.
Maccoby, M., & Scudder, T. (2011). Strategic intelligence: A conceptual system of leadership for change. *Performance Improvement*, March 2011.
Mahbubani, K. (2018). *Has the West lost it?* Penguin Books.
Makrides, A., Vrontis, D., & Christofi, M. (2019). The gold rush of digital marketing: Assessing prospects of building brand awareness overseas. *Business Perspectives and Research, 8*(1), 4–20.
Malaeb, R. C., & Chanaron, J.-J. (2010). Talent management DNA.
Meng, M. (2020). Angst vor Arbeitsplatzverlust. *Luxemburger Wort*, June 10, p. 13.
Mercier, J. (2018). Job today. *Paperjam*, Novembre 2018, pp. 56–97.
Minbaeva, D., & Collings, D. G. (2013). Seven myths of global talent management. *International Journal of Human Resource Management, 24*(9), 1762–1776.
Oracle Corporation. (n.d.). An innovative approach to strategic talent management in the cloud. Finding and retaining the best people. *Oracle Corporation*. http://www.oracle.com
Schinzel, U. (2013). Why are people in Luxembourg happy? An exploratory study of happiness and culture measured by the dimension of a language as identifier in the Grand Duchy. *Journal of Customer Behaviour, 12*(4), 315–340.
Schinzel, U. (2014a). Hofstede in Luxembourg. Intercultural comparison of Luxembourg-France-Germany. *Journal of Strategic and International Studies, IX*(6), 58–65.
Schinzel, U. (2014b). Multinational, multicultural, multilingual Luxembourg – A system of integration or a system of failure? *Journal of Strategic and International Studies, IX*(6), 5–13.
Spizzo, D. (1995). *La nation luxembourgeoise. Genèse et structure d'une identité*. L'Harmattan.
statec Luxembourg. (2020). *Luxembourg in figures*. Imprimerie Centrale.
Szekely, F., & Knirsch, M. (2005). Responsible leadership and corporate social responsibility: Metrics for sustainable performance. *European Management Journal, 23*(6), 628–647. https://doi.org/10.1016/j.emj.2005.10.009
The World Factbook. (n.d.). https://www.cia.gov/library/publications/the-world-factbook/geos/lu.html
Today.rtl.lu. https://today.rtl.lu/

Voegtlin, C., Patzer, M., & Scherer, A. G. (2012). Responsible leadership in global business: A new appraoch to leadership and its multi-level outcomes. *Journal of Business Ethics, 105*(1), 1–15. https://doi.org/10.1007/s10551-011-0952-4

Vrontis, D., El Nemar, S., Al Osta, B., & Azizi, J. R. (2018). Impact of innovation and change management on employees' performance. In D. Vrontis et al. (Eds.), *Innovation and capacity building* (Palgrave studies in cross-disciplinary business research, in association with EuroMed Academy of Busniess). Palgrave Macmillan.

Vrontis, D., Liu, Y., Visser, M., Stokes, P., Smith, S. M., Moore, N., Thrassou, A., & Astha, A. (2020a). Talent management and the HR function in cross-cultural mergers and acquisitions: The role and impact of bi-cultural identity. *Human Resource Management Review*. https://doi.org/10.1016/j.hrmr.2020.100744

Vrontis, D., Vacca, A., Iazzi, A., & Fait, M. (2020b). The role of gender diversity on tax aggressiveness and corporate social responsibility: Evidence from Italian listed companies. *Sustainability, 12*(5). https://doi.org/10.3390/su12052007.

Weber, J. J., & Horner, K. (2008). The language situation in Luxembourg. *Current Issues in Language Planning, 9*(1), 69–128. https://doi.org/10.2167/cilp130.0

Wikipedia: COVID-19 pandemic in Luxembourg. https://en.wikipedia.org/wiki/COVID-19_pandemic_in_Luxembourg

11

The Revealing Shades of the Pandemic Crisis in Romania

Larisa Mihoreanu and Laura Mariana Vlăducă

11.1 Introduction

For more than one year the SARS-CoV2 infections causing the COVID-19 pandemic crisis hold the humankind attention up with debates and disputes provoking both anxiety and hope. Commercial unforeseen illegal activities or actions have critically affected the market and the society at various levels—medical, social, political, financial, economic and technological—changing people's life (Costea, 1996). The economic drawbacks and the worries linked to are followed by social revendications caused by the increase daily life uncertainty.

The first documented cases of SARS-CoV-2 infection in Romania are dating from 24th of February 2020, therefore the government declared

L. Mihoreanu (✉)
Bucharest University of Economic Studies, Bucharest, Romania

L. M. Vlăducă
Hyperion University, Bucharest, Romania

D. Vrontis et al. (eds.), *Business Under Crisis Volume I*, Palgrave Studies in Cross-disciplinary Business Research, In Association with EuroMed Academy of Business, https://doi.org/10.1007/978-3-030-76567-5_11

an emergency state for two months starting mid-March, followed by a state of alert, frequently renewed, based on the pandemic statistics and continuous monitoring of COVID-19 cases (worldometers.info/coronavirus).

At the beginning of 2021 when WHO report showed over 90 million of cases worldwide including almost 2 million deaths (2.17%), Romanian Statistics showed 671,284 confirmed cases including 16,654 deaths (2.48%). From a political perspective, the severe acute respiratory syndrome coronavirus 2 (*SARS-CoV2*) pandemic appeared in Romania two months before the local elections of May 2020 under high needs for medical and administrative human resources, consequence of the labour massive emigration of the last 30 years.

The need to find solutions aligned the political forces into the synergy of increasing the institutional collaboration and modernising the public and local administration according to the European modern principles of *Legality, Ethics and Morality, Equality, Transparency, Proportionality Satisfaction the public interest, Impartiality, Continuity and Adaptability* (www.coe.int). However, the political organised groups, serving the caste interests, still suffocate the businesses and the administrative apparatus, blocking the adoption of the innovative technology implementation and country's digitisation. Meritocracy, performance, competencies are not yet the base of the Romanian public or local administration. This shows that corruption persists and weakens the health system fundamental, contributing to the regression of democracy amid the COVID-19 pandemic. In the last year, together with the political change, the liberals, temporary in power and now part of the government coalition, prove determination to bring such situations to light; they take both the advantage and the opportunities of the market conditions influenced by the SARS-CoV-2 pandemic and mandate the newly elected persons to make the necessary changes in the administration to sustain the long-term social transformation of the Romanian society towards a modern European one. The good liaisons with the European Commission and its Council made the Romanian decision-makers in force to consider and apply the 12 principles of good governance endorsed since 2008 and covering issues such as ethical conduct, rule of law, efficiency and effectiveness, transparency, sound financial management and accountability (https://www.coe.int):

- Fair Conduct of Elections, Representation and Participation
- Responsiveness
- Efficiency and Effectiveness
- Openness and Transparency
- Rule of Law
- Ethical conduct
- Competence and Capacity
- Innovation and Openness to Change
- Sustainability and Long-term Orientation
- Sound Financial Management
- Human rights, Cultural Diversity and Social Cohesion
- Accountability

The belief is that the effectiveness of the response to the COVID-19 emergency greatly depends on the level of coordination and cooperation between the different actors involved. Therefore, implementing the good governance principles at all levels is essential in the mission to increase resilience of public administration in coping with emergency situations such as COVID-19 pandemics together with raising the confidence of the public in the state institutions.

At present, the SARS-CoV-2 pandemics, a foregoing global challenge with no precise estimations about the magnitude of its socio-economic impact, provides an opportunity for specialists to accelerate reforms, increase exchanges of good practices between disciplines and implement new and ambitious societal solutions.

11.2 The Methodological Background and Its Approach

Despite the socio-economic challenges of the pandemics, 2020 enhanced the need for real and overall economic recovery, highlighting the long-term effects of the lack of competence and good management for public and private sectors. The research, in the broad sense, is a combined exploratory-descriptive type, based on objective and verified information obtained by observation, confirmed and processed in order to build scientific explanations of facts, phenomena and consequences on socio-economic processes and their impact assessment and consequences at national level.

Based on examples from life and the real market, we bring to light the scientific elements that make such acts of corruption possible. They reveal the economic affliction and social consequences of the hidden economic and informal financial movements, the long-term impact of the lack of a structural, resilient and evidence-based reform, together with the unexpected and underestimated influence of the current pandemic issue (Costea, 2000). The latest studies (Deloitte, 2020) highlight the direct link between the data provided by the Corruption Perceptions Index (CPI) and how countries can cope with the challenges of the actual COVID-19 pandemic. They show that states with a good CPI score invest more in the health system, provide quality healthcare support, promote the legal medical businesses development, and ensure compliance with democratic and institutional rules and the rule of law. The CPI report provides, yearly, snapshots of corruption by ranking and scoring countries at the world level. According to the 2020 data, Romania scores 44/100 and ranks 69/180 while the Global Corruption Barometer shows that in 2020 more than a fifth (18%) of the public service users paid bribes (Transparency International Report, 2020).

From this perspective we present here some of the hidden and informal economic sides of the Romanian medical sector, linked to unlawfully situations approved under the public sector umbrella abusing the official channels and exploiting highly public sector positions. We make distinction between formal/informal, legal and black market and economy showing that the most of cases of corruption develop there where the laws in force are neither doubled by regulation and standards of implementation nor linked to corrective procedures defining the finest legal details that might facilitate inappropriate operations and profits.

A legal system based on superficially elaborated laws with a dense quantity of information but very difficult to navigate through is opened to subjective implementation allowing similar situations to repeat. For the past 30 years, lacking of rigorous, conscientious, and compelling corrective, evidence based from the assessment and monitoring of responsible management activities measures and their implementation is causing accumulated shared public loss due to lack of transparency and accountability in the public administration with no individual repercussions for the authors.

The informal activities and services developed at the border of the law are amounting almost to 21% of GDP (insse.ro) and are allowing non-fiscalised activities, VAT return and money laundering with no origin justification; therefore the acknowledgement of their existence supports the idea of reforming the public administration and the healthcare system towards full digitisation, implementation of innovative tools and technologies, putting to use all principles of good governance to create transparent support for appointments, medical consultations, payments, acquisitions, trade and so on in order to limit and prevent future unlawful actions so that no further action of fraud or misappropriation of benefits happens (coe.int/en/web/good-governance).

The dynamics of the present crisis is directly related to (1) the scientific progress made in understanding the SARS-CoV-2 virus itself—origins, early reported genomics data, basic reproduction number, transmission type and speed, detailed epidemiological analytics; (2) the methods developed to maintain the increase of the number of cases—populational tracking systems, setting in place news social rules, quarantine; (3) the reaction time to contain the spread of the infection; (4) the investment made into the health care system in order to optimise constantly the resources for the long term; (5) the effort made in sharing knowledge, efforts and resources; (6) the run against the time to find the most efficacious and affordable treatments; and (7) the active participation of civil society as regards not only the respect of confinement measures but also the direct involvement in voluntary work aimed at sustaining the response effort. Only some of the things described are certain for the moment and the decision-makers all around the world are facing complex decisions bases on a lot of uncertainty.

The data on population gathered from 137 countries by the WHO show that from the total of COVID-19 cases reported, 49% are women and 51% are male. Number of deaths is also higher in the case of male patients (43% women and 57% for men). The number of cases correlated with the age groups shows the increase of the prevalence disease with age.

The over 65 years old group is seen as the more vulnerable with the highest mortality rate. All retrospective analysis is easy to prove and often use to tilt the scales between controversial issues supported by political groups for their own political benefit.

The magnitude of the present multilevel crises has long-term consequences over generations; it brings losses and risks but also opportunities. The *tipping point* could become a one-time opportunity pushing us to the next level, asking a fast adaptation of another world of achievements or total economic distress.

In Romania, the ignorance in managing the public assets, the frauds committed at all administrative levels blame the greedy politicians or charge the incompetent managers. But the informal movements still exist in the market and their consequences against companies and people, although ignored become stronger under pandemic times because of the systemic reforms.

The disruptive times of the COVID-19 pandemic fed the invisible economy and spread their tentacles in activities of production, distribution, services, transport, healthcare, social assistance, police and politics allowing illegalities to easily pass unnoticed since they were promoted by officials politically nominated in the state apparatus used for their own interest the exceptional pathways set up to protect lives and livelihoods, and to redress the economy. These channels are hijacked to use resources and carry operations unlawfully and illicitly out. Often, no records or correct registrations are kept, so their traceability deleted or lost between multiple accounts.

The existence of such practices distorts the lawfully allocation of contracts, resources, funds, time on meritorious bases with the main scope to reward and enrich a small, selected group and impoverish those who act honestly with respect for work, fellows and laws.

This kind of economy includes acts or facts carried out in the dark side of society, known as unseen, unofficial, parallel, informal, illegal, grey or shadow economy. These activities, out of the taxation system, are neither recorded in national accounts nor produced revenues and profits for the society or its citizens.

In a crisis situation, the speed of action increases, the number of actors involved also increases, attention span is shrinking, the focus is fragmented, the decisions time is constricting and all these details together create the perfect setting for a "mistake", an innocent or a premeditated type of action. Often the border between the two is very thin.

The pandemic times unexpectedly brought to light plenty of such situations. In the recent months, the extensive use of technology and digitisation pushed some areas for development, and on this occasion some obscure circumstances were brought to light.

As science deals with the observation of realities, the treatment of facts and the research of their origin by analysing causal links (Miron, 2020), multidisciplinary scientists trained and anchored in set already out world realities decided to identify the state of affairs in pandemic, to capture the correlatives and the causalities defining the current economic and social landscape, to anticipate developments by substantiating simplistic assumptions and providing to the executive decision-makers' judgement and guidance for transformation. We will join them and consider here, descriptively, the Romanian reality in times of pandemic and provide few ideas and resilient solutions.

11.3 The State of Crisis in Romania and Its Misty Facets

In a rigorous approach, the crisis appears after a flourishing period of glory in the cyclical evolution of human society and a continuous expectations and demand for economic growth, creating even more discrepancy between developed countries rising even higher and the rest of the world left even more behind. The course of the crisis is defined (Keen, 2001), in terms of development, by (a) scientific and technical innovations; (b) creation of gaps between the ability to bring competitive products to market and people's ability to buy them; (c) boom of economic activities and the immeasurable increase of stocks of goods and products; (d) overvaluation of some assets and actions, especially in the real estate field; (e) flourishing activity of the stock exchange as a possibility to obtain "*easy money*" in the absence of clear regulations in the field; (f) banks' strategy to extend the policy of profits and to use various loans types to fuel the psychosis of consumption; and (g) the need for transformational behaviour.

The crisis has many facets, potentially linked to all sectors: resources, production, investment, labour and unemployment, jobs, consumption, public finances and debts, monetary and currency, health system, confidence, law and morality and, more recently, the SARS-CoV2 pandemic.

Beyond a strict social distance and individual hygiene, the two pandemic waves of coronavirus disease COVID-19 put authorities and strategists in the position to decide severe restrictions at all levels: (1) close the schools, fairs and markets, (2) reduce the economic activity, (3) restrict the local travels and international traffic, (4) quarantine different towns and cities, all with dramatic consequences at national economic and social level, bringing changes with irreversible alterations of the working schedule and interpersonal communication and behaviour. This new virus is wrongly to be considered the planet's only enemy. Vicious organisational behaviours residing in the unnoticeable economy at the borders of regulations or in non-regulated sectors are sources of much bigger societal evil. Studies show that there are other things to consider than competition that determines the best results in business (Suhail & Tsoukatos, 2019) and consumption as the core of profit and satisfaction (Mihoreanu, 2020b). Experiments conducted at different interdisciplinary centres for policy and strategy in countries like Israel, Hungary and Romania show that no matter the assets or the parameters, the human resources' complex quality and intelligence link market, executive authorities and society for their own better. Not worrying about past mistakes or current political stress and disregarding possible negative outcomes, together with the lack of action at general level, will never really improve the lives of the citizens. Therefore, unemployment is also a time bomb, in the midst of a coronavirus pandemic. At the end of 2019, unemployment in Romania was 3.9%. For 2020, the forecast shows an unemployment rate of 8%; the number of people returning home from Diaspora or that one of suspended contracts does not count here. Analysing the concrete data, it can be estimated that, in reality, Romania faces a real unemployment of approximately 10% in the conditions in which there are many sectors of activity that are in great labour deficit.

Coronavirus shows the germs of a debt crisis too. The pandemic costs many lives treatment and economic losses which so far amount to 110.8 trillion euros and the situation to come will generate a massive increase in debt. As the IMF warns, no country will get rid of it. Regarding the euro/RON exchange rate, in the next 12 months, it is anticipated the continuation of the depreciation of the leu from 4.8603 lei /euro to 5.0102 lei /euro. The anticipated inflation rate for the 12-month horizon (November 2021/November 2020) predicts an average value of 2.68%.

But good news also arises under the crisis: despite the IMF's calculations to reduce the performance of the global economy in the worst recession since the global economic crisis about 90 years ago (Repousis et al., 2018; Gita Gopinath, 2021), even though all countries are affected by the pandemic, the financial sector has a special look. Currently, the trade in financial products is experiencing a real boom, attested by the record values of stock market indices. Investors often direct their money to financial markets because, from their perspective, it is more profitable to multiply them with financial instruments than to invest them in the real economy. The derivatives market (futures, options, futures, swaps) exceeds the performance of the global economy several times.

The real economy suffers more under the influence of the crisis, as a result of the amounts of money in circulation, to compensate for deflationary trends or the desire to reduce the danger of a recession. Romania faces great challenges during these times too. Beyond a turbulent and versatile geopolitics, the COVID-19 pandemic opens unexpected opportunities and solutions to reflect, reimage and reset the situation. For country, government, companies and society, it is the high time to act and make the change.

The regulatory/deregulatory activities with direct potential on the economy and the society shake from the foundations the edifice of our world; sometimes even dynamite it, in parallel with the appearance of the first global social consequences of the pandemic. Here, the supreme verification and audit bodies should have a special role. In the situation where financial, ethical and behavioural slippages (Profiroiu et al., 1999) on the labour market appear daily, the question that always comes back refers to the superficial, subjective involvement of the national auditing authorities in verifying the elaboration of labour and collaboration contracts, the analysis of expenses from public institutions and of the way in which the procurement plan is realised, the way in which the Police does its duty to ensure the observance and application of the law. The very raison d'être of these institutions consists in verifying the way of spending the public resources, having at the same time the power conferred by law to recover any amount spent in violation of the legal provisions. The involvement of the national authorities of control and audit, although commendable, is not convincing as long as this institution is not endowed by law with the coercive means necessary to verify the preparation of documentation and, where appropriate, to recover damages from the real culprits. The non-existence or non-observance of the norms of the laws in force generates abusive behaviours that result in economic and social losses.

The healthcare and medical sector crisis was added globally to the ones already existing, but previously ignored or constantly postponed. Growing like an oil spill, the present crisis generates mass behaviours that allow irreversible derailments in all key sectors: economic, social and institutional. Other types of crises are folding into the notorious economic and financial ones; it appears the crisis of the health insurance system, the crisis of generations coming with another one, of attitude and moral nature.

The new types of crises, present in the health market become notorious from economic and financial point of view too. We bring here the health insurance system, that of generations coming with the crises of attitude, behaviour and moral nature. These new types of crises, sustained within the super-networks of powers, become stronger through the political manipulation. Thus, the moral crisis is inherently triggered and inflamed by the rising political crisis, the fractures of understanding the current situation, the inability to correctly predict the future or understand the operational and technological advantages of innovation, robotics and artificial intelligence.

New movements influence the entire social networks, create imbalances that feed people—employers, employees, teenagers and students of which enthusiasm degenerates, sometimes, into rallies to muster for different purposes linked to school, health system, political approach of executive decisions and freedom move.

The informal economy is present in the medical sector through deficient legislation, the lack of transparency, the perpetuation of practices at the laws' periphery without correct norms of interpretation and standards of application, and the lack of ethical behaviour generalised among administrative and medical staffs (Profiroiu et al., 1999). The lack of medical preventive education, the cloudy solutions with regard at the personnel problems, the incapacity in organisation ended with unethical management, lack in taking decisions or in assuming responsibility, the superficiality and infatuation of the audit apparatus experimenting self-sufficient and abusive behaviour in monitoring and control institutions are other reasons of delays in increasing profit and satisfaction. All these come together with the economic and budget limits, in parallel with the societal real shortcomings, the acute lack of quality identified in the medical acts development too, with lasting influence and continuous dissatisfaction for patients, employees, decision-makers and institutions. In order to improve and professionalise the workforce, mentality, attitude and behaviour must get streamlined; the proactive attitude accepted as part of the daily life within partnerships in favour for digitisation, the administrative simplification and de-bureaucratisation sustain the peoples' rights, the partnering values, the reality of climatic changes, to build up a new employee-employer relationship and institutional qualitative dialogue between citizens, stakeholders and policy-makers. Thus, there will be a great chance to eliminate inequities in the market and society: black (hidden) or grey (informal) work discrepancies between public and private institutions, differences between the same types of work paid differently depending on the contract. These times of illness make commerce, hospitality industry and transportation sick as well. When informal economy is accepted as existing, the analytical and empirical knowledge about the size, the growth, the components, the causes and consequences of it in the direction of the society development is necessary, to calculate influences against society, profit, companies and people (Repousis et al., 2018).

The knowledge of behaviours generate specific processes related to the underground /informal economy (tax fraud, grey labour, inert decision-makers and economic operators, money laundering by offshore companies) and their understanding may lead to their causes elimination. Therefore it is important to adhere to economic-legislative frameworks and support the development of a legal, efficient entrepreneurial system.

A competent diagnosis of the phenomenon of informal economy involving different categories of specialists helps identifying and configures this type of activity and by implementing standards and parameterised solutions based on monitoring and control indicators. Likewise, smart and appropriate strategies and policies may be identified to combat lawful tax evasion.

11.4 About the Romanian Health System Under the Pandemic Crisis

Romania is known in Europe as an ageing nation with a precarious health system, inefficient in terms of services and funding, unable to meet the health needs of the population. Life expectancy is among the lowest in Europe (73.5 /81.0 yo), 27th place out of 29 European countries. Healthy life expectancy *measures the number of years people can expect to live without disabilities at different ages* (European Commission, 2019). The country faces challenges in combating infectious diseases that are major concerns for the public health. Romania has the highest number of tuberculosis and measles cases in the European Union (EU) with several measles outbreaks in recent years, also due to dramatically declining immunisation rates (European Commission, 2019). Since 2017, a project of vaccination law was presented to the public to debate on regulating the organisation and financing of immunisation, but has not yet been passed, despite the SARS-CoV-2 pandemics. Cardiovascular disease is the leading cause of death, but cancer deaths are on the rise. Chronic diseases or disabilities after retirement affect more and more women over the age of 65. Other major issues related to primary health care and the health status include the high prevalence of unhealthy diet and diabetes, low physical activity, smoking, obesity and the consumption of alcohol and drugs from earlier ages.

The health system in Romania is based on a model of social health insurance with a share of publicly financed health spending (79.5%) in line with the EU average (79.3%), but the overall spending, per capita (1029 € vs. 2884 € the EU average) and per GDP ratio (5% vs. 9.8% EU average), is the lowest in the European Union. Before the SARS-CoV-2 pandemic, data showed that Romania has 7.2 nurses and 3.1 doctors per 1000 population in 2018, less than the EU 27 average of 8.2 nurses and 3.8 doctors, although Romania is preparing the highest number of medical students, future doctors and nurses in the EU. The integrated community healthcare is hampered because of a reduced number of general practitioners and operational overuse of hospitals to the detriment of family physician offices (European Commission, 2019).

Subject to three-decades of reform, the Romanian health system is known to be inadequate, incoherent and unstable showing people that regardless the budgets allocated for modernisation, all funds allocated are still not sufficient. Long-lasting hospital services and a direct and unregulated access straight to secondary and tertiary medical care contribute to the creation of an ineffective and unsustainable health system. The primary health care constantly misses resources, but trying to obtain more from reallocation of resources. When rigorous assessment of health system performance is missing, it is difficult to make improvements.

One of the conditions for Romania to join the EU was to increase the quality of its public health services. Because of the magnitude of the political implications, this task registered delays and only two years after Romania joined the EU, in 2009 a new entity was created to drive the setting of quality management within the public health system. Since then, the respective institution was reformed and transformed into an authority of quality management, but only in 2015, public hospitals initiated, on a voluntary basis, the first round of the newly accreditation process to help them first assess their services.

By law, only accredited care units are able to have contracts with the National Insurance Fund, but since it is hardly difficult for a public hospital to function on their own funds, exceptions are often made, allowing extensions of the deadlines to find solutions to improve under pressure. The SARS-CoV-2 pandemic delayed by one year the cycle of the accreditation process because of the challenges that the hospitals had to overcome in 2020, but unfortunately this change of focus allowed few dramatic incidents to occur when lives were lost. At present, the management and performance of the public hospitals in Romania is under question because of the strong political connections revelled in far too many cases.

The COVID-19 pandemic has generated dramatic and disruptive behaviours in health business, market, production and services: high political interference in hospitals' management and their system of procurement, breaks in the auction rounds, unauthorised operations with medical products like quality medical masks and adequate personal protective equipment and necessary medical devices, tests, vaccines, medicines, biocides and other disinfectants, close to severe behaviours and disruptions in the interpretation of laws. The increase of the health insurance quotas, twice as high as 20 years ago, did not succeed to reveal any competitive advantages in this field.

The health crisis, amplified by the present pandemic is deepening the financial consequences fed by: (1) the differences between understanding and accepting the private medical sector rather the public one, (2) the employers financial indiscipline, (3) the lack of competences or administrative experience, (4) the medical staffs proper training or incompatibility perceived in the medical services' market, (5) the public and private medical false competition and the mobility of staff between the two, (6) the corporate needs and the informal behaviour linked to the medicine and medical devices industry.

The last report of the Organisation for Economic Co-operation and Development stipulates that citizens and authorities understand that the world faces the most severe health since past 90 years, with unprecedented impact on the labour and health market and welfare (OECD, 2020).

The situation is even more sensitive there where health problems have been either ignored or postponed. In Romania, the share of out-of the pocket expenditure is estimated at 20% (more than the EU average of 15.8%) mostly for medicines (13.2%), dental care (3.2%), ambulatory visits (1.8%) posing some financial challenges for the patients, especially vulnerable ones. Unfortunately, this estimate is not realistic because of the magnitude and widespread of informal payments also included in this category (mainly in hospital care) and because private providers under-report income (OECD - C/MIN(2020)7/FINAL). Until the phenomenon was publicly recognised, the medical act had become a luxury for many Romanians paying health insurances. A pragmatic approach of tax evasion is needed to stop the degradation of the physician-patient relationship. Every month, at least one medical specialist is prosecuted because of tax evasion through bribery.

In this phase of the pandemic dynamics, beyond applauding at open scene those who fight every day in emergency, anaesthesia, infectious diseases services and intensive care units in the absence of a real health reform, many public hospitals are left in the rear or completely closed to avoid transmitting the virus. Such situations put the chronic patients waiting for hours in the cold, for a scheduled consultation to get their current treatment. In the meantime, the family doctors were thrown into the anti-COVID frontline, without adequate equipment and security measures. Using digital ICT tools, they overcome themselves and, through huge efforts, they obtain special results with patients having mild or moderate forms of disease under home monitoring, using the m-health's tools and contributing to hospitalisation cost reduction, more room in the hospitals for the most serious cases.

The public health policies, weak in corroborating the Executive's decisions with the healthcare and medical services development, split the patients when is about setting up a smart approach in medical regulation implementation. The measures taken by the executive were often late or timid, leaving room for interpretations and subjective behaviour especially from the young people or those who are still refusing to accept and assume the civic obligations established by the government norms (quarantine, social distance, behaviour, correct and permanent protection by wearing permanently masks of protection, rigorous personal hygiene).

During the first half of 2020, Romania imported masks worth 272 million euros at an average value of 14 euros/person (Eurostat) for its 19 million inhabitants. The main exporter was China, an EU-recognised partner. Together with Hong Kong and Vietnam, China delivered 92% of the total quantity contracted by unverified documents, drawn up with many undercuts and deficiencies. Many of these masks did not comply with European medical standards of protection. The consumer protection authorities checked 35,180,666 masks with a value of 19,763,739 lei and 59% of them did not comply with the legal provisions in force. Thus, 22 millions of masks found in the market have been taken away from shops as inappropriate. According to their last published Report, the National Authority for

Consumers' Protection (ANPC report 2020) controlled all economic operators involved in medical masks selling and found out that 66% of them did not comply with the legal provisions in force, being sanctioned. Among the companies fined with more than 18 million lei (3.7 million euros), there are retailers with a solid experience in trading, contracting and marketing such as Lidl, Rewe, Kaufland, Mega Image, Auchan, Altex, Dedeman, Profi, DM and Lukoil Romania near pharmacies like Help Net and Sensiblue. The rush to supply the masks in the necessary quantities, to avoid panic and satisfy the population needs, made that over 16 Romanian state and private companies (among of which Romarm National Company, Techtex, Taparo, Inox SA, Coramed, Interbabis), ready for delivery their products, have been ignored from the major auctions and procurements procedures even if their prices, quality and quantity were more advantageous than the Chinese ones. Thus, a real criminal mechanism appeared and developed in our country that transformed the Romanian economy and society, with the ignorant involvement of the government, in a general business with influential traffickers, without any scruples who made black money from trade with state companies. During the emergency period, a large-scale criminal mechanism became a long-term profitable business of influential traffickers who managed even the indirect involvement of the government and unscrupulously obtained fabulous profits trading products highly necessary to survive the COVID-19 era, with public companies or on their behalf. An example is the contract without public auction, of UNIFARM, for 3 million medical masks and 250,000 coveralls, along with biocides, medical fans and COVID-19 tests. The general director of UNIFARM—a representative logo for the public pharmaceutical sector—requested and received favours of 780,000 euros. Neither masks were according to health standards nor has money been recuperated yet. Such financial engineering contributes to the economic imbalances close to the fiscal and procurement indiscipline of medical and non-medical staffs, but also to the fact that the current health system doesn't go in the right direction in a market economy.

The existing specifics gap between the private and public health and care networks are to the detriment of patients. On one side, in the private sector, the consequences of the increase of 6.75 times in the health insurance contributions corroborated with their reduced degree of collection and the insufficient medical staff per population caused by the medical outsourcing does not contribute to increase the quality of the medical act. On the other side, in the public sector, the existence of informal payments both substantial and widespread with subjective approaches in treating patients while waiting for personal favors is added to a generalized non-ethical conduct which is perpetuating at all levels through:

- suspicions of corruption and plagiarism for professional or scientific advantages (doctorates, academic titles, committees nominations),
- acquisition of undue personal benefits while using professional and/or political positions,
- misleading information maintaining outdated administrative hierarchies for access to public procurement purposes, and
- undeclared conflicts of interests of persons with multiple employment contracts within similar or different institutions

Surveys on the impact of the coronavirus crisis on the national economy reveal that 2021 will bring a higher economic impact, with substantial unfavourable influences on the budget deficit, GDP evolution and unemployment rate. However, as mentioned already, the current crisis also offers many opportunities: (1) capitalisation of work possibilities; (2) administration and archiving modernisation; (3) improvement of operational management systems in audit, monitoring, feedback, sustainable, resilient and inclusive economic recovery through the use of Green Deal and 5G technology in increasing connectivity, eliminating fraud; implementing the digital transformation and national decarbonisation; creating smart clutches and sectors in production and logistics; rural communities, traffic and green disposal and recycling; developing public services in favour of communities, all with a high direct impact on the health market too. In Romania, the clusters of intelligent rural communities, smart production and logistic chains, have the highest net benefits, of 2 billion euros and 1.5 billion euros, respectively, although their benefit-cost ratios are small compared to the smart cities sector. Benefits through public funding can also be obtained for health and hospitals, municipal buildings, education, tourism, agriculture and urban areas, including public transport. Studies and research show funding opportunities of over 50 billion euros that can be generated through public funding of less than 20 billion euros.

The recovery must be supported in an aggregate manner: joint actions, mutual decisions and united efforts, through continuously harmonised monetary and fiscal-foreign exchange policies, intelligently combined with the investment policy to get rid of the COVID-19 dramatic consequences. Then, it will be possible to create resonant connections, generalise the market and society digitisation and give space to e-health and m-health to evolve by supporting everybody's constructive efforts to adapt to the new environment and legislative requirements and create a modern employer-branding and a new working and living style.

Farther the facts that the crises periodicity generates continuous consolidation of the invisible businesses with potential impact on the medical market too and that the clinic of proximity (Mihoreanu, 2020a, b) is due to be the core of the sustainable and resilient health reform, we carefully corroborate the influences highlighting links and amplitude with the informal economy. The application of the Altman, Conan-Holder scoring models to assess the risks of unprofitability and potential bankruptcy of the medical clinic of proximity (Mihoreanu, 2020), by using financial-accounting data from the balance sheet and the profit and loss account provided as many tools of recovery as possible (Vlăducă, 2020). Based on the binary logistic regression analysis applied to the company's main components under the scoring model, the clinics' behaviour is brought to light and emphasised in terms of their tax evasion potential capacity and laws' subterfuges.

Based on the scores obtained, we identify three distinct classes, according to which proximity clinics can be classified. When the parameterisation coefficient (Z) is higher than 2 ($Z > 2$), the clinic is in a safe operating mode defined by legal activities and formal employed staffs. In the situation where $0.5 < Z < 2$, the clinic enters a risky area of temporary financial difficulties, which also indicates vulnerabilities caused by different kinds of informal activities. When $Z < 0.5$, than the clinic is in a high risk area eventually leading to bankruptcy, due to risky, informal or illegal actions and activities. Based on the results, a hierarchy of clinics with inclinations towards informal activities can be made. It is easier to take action against them before the damage reaches high levels and the losses are irrecoverable.

The informal sector remains an important part of the economy and the labour market in most of countries, especially in developing ones. Thus, measurements of the informal sector are important as long as they take into account the contribution to GDP. It is important to keep in mind that the analysis of the relationship between the real and the informal economy from the typology of the practices included in the scope of the underground economy are based on the conceptual differences between the formal, informal, registered and unregistered economy.

11.5 Conclusion

The coronavirus crisis has turned the world's economy upside down. Countries have taken unprecedented steps to revive their economies. Even if they do happen, there are voices arguing that a complete return to a normal life in the near future is impossible. The global coronavirus crisis has become a test of endurance for the resilience and determination with which the democratic system defends its fundamental principles of law and international respect for human rights.

The pressure in the context of the COVID-19 pandemic on core institutional practices established multilateral agreements, and the economic foundations underlying common prosperity is enormous. The governance democratically acts through the elected parliament, based on the principles of solidarity, fairness and justice.

The current pandemic has projected discourses sustaining that democracy does not handle the tools to deal with a health emergency system. Such ideas are erroneous, because democratic nations are already proving their capacity for cooperation to ensure that a health crisis, affiliated with an economic crisis, does not become a crisis of democracy.

During the pandemic times Romania has remained in the top three most corrupt countries in the European Union. The score of 44/100, similar to the 2019 one, shows Romania together with Bulgaria and Hungary on the last place in the European ranking. The perception of corruption in both public system and medical affairs environment in Romania is unchanged since 2012; this shows that the measures taken during the past decade have been neither constant nor changed the perception of the independent experts and the business environment. The lack of transparency in public procurement, the underfunding of the medical system and the lack of consistent measures to digitise administrative processes are problems intensified in the context of the COVID-19 pandemic. The reports of the audit bodies on the procurement carried out to combat the pandemic showed serious shortcomings in both local and central authorities. Corrupt practices in companies, which at the declarative level assume integrity policies, have been likely to affect the credibility of the business environment, and image beautification campaigns have had the effect of reducing public vigilance. For this reason, in order to truly sanction corruption and lack of integrity as a general scourge, Romanian society needs structural transformation coming up with long-term smart solutions.

The implementation of the clinic of proximity model as a relational nucleus between the actors on the medical scene, together with a permanent, correct and general application of laws, remains a handy tool for everybody—decision-makers, manufacturers, medical services providers, traders and distributors of products and equipment health as seen in the Fig. 11.1.

Now, the present situation could be an opportunity to rethink the administrative policies and implement a real reform of health recovery and resilience, having in mind major measures, as the following: (1) accelerate the fight against corruption; (2) recover damages from those guilty of damage and mismanagement; (3) tighten sanctions in case of inefficient spending of public money; (4) enhance transparency of budget expenditures through full digitisation, with permanent operational monitoring at European institutions' standards; (5) ensure unitary management through consolidated multiannual projects; (6) provide citizens access to a medical act and related quality services, and (7) set coherent, predictable and sustainable legislation accompanied by technical norms, specific implementation and coercive or punitive measures, as the case may be.

The priorities for the recovery of the healthcare sector are based on transparency and administrative simplification, increasing the quality of dialogue between citizens and the administration, between the business

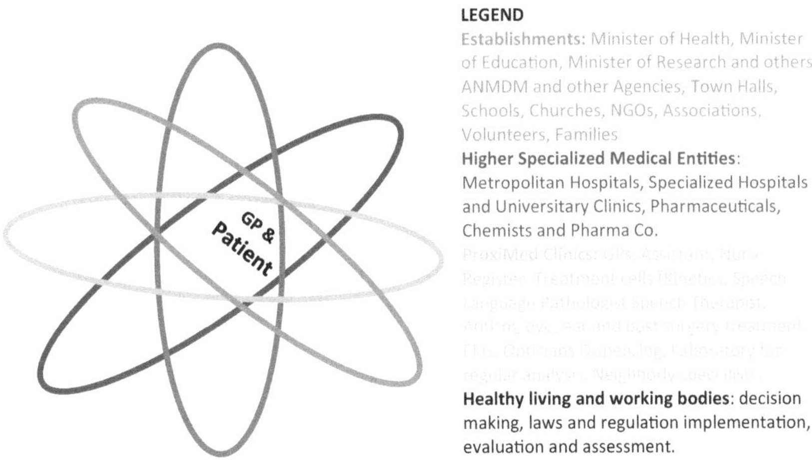

Fig. 11.1 The implementation of a healthcare model centred on the clinic of proximity and patient legal relation
Only the legal, concerted and simultaneous actions of all the operators in the market and the medical industry will be able to move away for good the corruptive processes that, for decades, generate hot money only for corrupted political clients, harming people, burdening institutions and businesses and damaging the society

environment and the administration, through digitisation and simplification. Stability, digitisation and fiscal consolidation are the priority pillars, achievable by maintaining the single quota of tax revenues, digitisation and modernisation of national authorities of fiscal administration, fiscal consolidation and operational fiscal facilities for research and development activities.

The next priority is the public-private investments, by encouraging, combining and harmonising public and private investment, as well as by designing a legal framework to accommodate large-scale investments. Improving all infrastructures, where Romania ranks 26th in the EU, as well as the reform of the central and local administration are the next priorities. European funds, economic support packages provided by the government, health education reform and harmonisation of issues related to labour market performance are not only important but also leading aspects for building a solid health system and we need to see who we go to fight with again. Looking at the managerial system its unprofessionalism and lack of power are highly visible because of the politic interference in the system of employment and hierarchical responsibility, far from the principles of value and meritocracy. Serious deficiencies are continuously identified in all communication segments in absence of digitisation. The public health departments reveal the lack of professionalised capacity of specialists without capital attributions in the present circuit in favour only of few types of approvals for medical offices or fitness rooms. Many hospitals are not yet accredited as they miss the necessary procedures, protocols or doctors. Disengaging the dialogue between managers and medical staff endangers the patient. The legislation is constantly changing: the health reform project alone has so far undergone more than 1000 alterations. The investment policies are incoherent while Romanian investments or those of producers on the Romanian market are discouraged as a result of an archaic authorisation system. The current drug policy discourages the Romanian production; therefore, both drug policy and claw back policy must change. The fact that doctors receive sponsorships from pharmaceutical companies is another sensitive issue that deserves legislative clarification to avoid incompatibilities. The use of the good practices system, generally appreciated, generated its politisation in the end. Therefore a Health Pact Patient Centric is needed if related to a versatile structure of clinics of proximity (Mihoreanu, 2020), engaging responsibly all operators and recognising their affiliation through funding, responsibilities, equipment and qualified staffs' infusion. Romania needs to take advantage of the new conditions generated by the COVID-19 pandemic and accelerate the digitization implementation, especially in the primary health services, to coherently persue both the multisectoral measures and major investments related to the entire system of health's reform. Efforts must be focused on both modernisation and computerisation of the health system as well as for the creation of the framework favourable to the effective use of digital technologies. Then, people will understand the value of our proposal and the importance of the clinic of proximity model implementation (Mihoreanu, 2020) together with the role of the general practitioners and will decide their endowment according to European standards and local needs.

The smart access to EU procurement mechanisms will pave the way for logistical integration into the European blockchain. The current moment, although sensitive, offers huge opportunities generating potential sustainable results through which recovery could become a success. Patient management, therapeutic alternatives, access to the vaccine all can be managed at the national level, beyond WHO oversight, to ensure credibility and build a climate of medical, healthy and profitable business.

References

Costea, C. (1996). *Piata de capital*. Revista de Statistică nr 4/1997.

Costea, C. (2000). *Protecția consumatorlului de produse financiar-bancare*. Ed Uranus.

Deloitte. (2020). Navigating with confidence Australia and New Zealand's bribery & corruption report 2020. March 2020. https://www2.deloitte.com/content/dam/Deloitte/nz/Documents/risk/Bribery%20and%20Corruption%20Survey%202020_WEB.pdf

European Commission – EC. (2019). *State of health in the EU*. România: Profilul de țară din 2019 în ceea ce privește sănătatea. https://ec.europa.eu/health/sites/health/files/state/docs/2019_chp_romania_romanian.pdf

Gita Gopinach. (2021). *IMF: How vaccine equity could help economic recovery*. WEF. https://www.weforum.org/agenda/2021/02/a-race-between-vaccines-and-the-virus-as-recoveries-diverge/

Keen, S. (2001). *Debunking economics*. ZED PH.

Mihoreanu, L. (2020a). *Empowering the health care reform*. PRO Universitaria.

Mihoreanu, L. (2020b). The medical clinic of proximity: Business controversies and medical challenges. In A. Thrassou, D. Vrontis, Y. Weber, S. M. R. Shams, & E. Tsoukatos (Eds.), *The changing role of SMEs in global business* (Palgrave studies in cross-disciplinary business research, in association with EuroMed Academy of Business). Palgrave Macmillan. https://doi.org/10.1007/978-3-030-45831-7_3

Miron, D. (2020). *Notes at the commemoration of the 80th anniversary of the assassination on November 27, 1940 of Virgil Madgearu, a prestigious professor at the Academy of Advanced Commercial and Industrial Studies in Bucharest*. www.ase.ro

OECD. (2020). Turnning hope into reality. Economic Outlook. December 2020. https://www.oecd.org/economic-outlook/december-2020/

Profiroiu, M., Parlogi, A., & Crai, E. (1999). *Etica și corupție în administrația publică*. Ed. Economica.
Repousis, S., et al. (2018). Innovation performance and development assistance and growth in four East European member states. In D. Vrontis, Y. Weber, A. Thrassou, S. M. R. Shams, & E. Tsoukatos (Eds.), *Innovation and capacity building: Cross-disciplinary management theories for practical applications* (Palgrave studies in cross-disciplinary business research, in association with EuroMed Academy of Business) (pp. 109–130). Palgrave Macmillan.
Suhail, S., & Tsoukatos, E. (2019). From theory to practice of formal and informal Palestinian small businesses. In A. Thrassou, D. Vrontis, Y. Weber, S. M. R. Shams, & E. Tsoukatos (Eds.), *The synergy of business theory and practice. Advancing the practical application of scholarly research* (pp. 39–58). Palgrave Macmillan.
Vlăducă, L. M. (2020). *Economia informală. Efecte asupra dezvoltării robuste a societății*. Ed. PRO Universitaria.

Web References

https://anpc.ro/galerie/file/544/2020/Raport_ANPC_2019.pdf
https://www.coe.int/en/web/good-governance
https://www.oecd.org/mcm/C-MIN-2020-7-FINAL.en.pdf
https://www.worldometers.info/coronavirus/

12

Transforming India's Logistic Industry During COVID-19 Crisis

Asha Bhatia, Komal Jain, Ravi Teja Boddapati, and Prashant Goyal

12.1 Introduction

Pandemic or epidemic outbreaks in the world recently or the past have a severe impact on society and even the economy (Loske, 2020). The first COVID-19 outbreak was reported in the last week of December 2019 in Wuhan City, China (LU et al., 2020). The pandemic outbreak has disrupted the lives of people of over 160 countries, posing an existential crisis of humanity. To slow down the spread of the highly contagious virus, governments worldwide imposed several temporary restrictions that have disrupted every activity on the earth, including food supply, healthcare, education, and employment. The underdeveloped regions and communities are more vulnerable to the crisis. Due to the novelty of the COVID-19 pandemic, it has thrown grim challenges to the

A. Bhatia (✉) • K. Jain • R. T. Boddapati • P. Goyal
Universal Business School, Karjat, Maharashtra, India
e-mail: asha.bhatia@ubs.org.in; komal.jain@ubs.org.in; raviteja.boddapati@ubs.org.in; prashant.goyal@ubs.org.in

D. Vrontis et al. (eds.), *Business Under Crisis Volume I*, Palgrave Studies in Cross-disciplinary Business Research, In Association with EuroMed Academy of Business, https://doi.org/10.1007/978-3-030-76567-5_12

governments across the world, not fully developed for the pandemic (Shen et al., 2020; Yu et al., 2020; Phan et al., 2020).

The official data released by WHO claims more than 2,327,308 deaths are globally reported on February 8, 2021. India's nationwide lockdown was implemented in four different phases, making 68 days, and then the unlock was started in different phases. COVID-19 pandemic has created havoc across the globe, which has impacted the developing and developed nations severely. The countries have been using all of their resources available to combat the impact of COVID-19. India too is facing the heat of COVID-19 severely.

The government has been proactive to curb the spread of infection and death, and various initiatives were taken to contain the spread of COVID-19: from strict lockdowns to establishment of health care infrastructure, procurement of essential pieces of equipment, providing food and shelter to millions of displaced and migrant workers. These measures taken by the government around the globe have a significant impact on the world's economy, and this disruption has a powerful impact on the supply chain (Ivanov, 2020). Therefore, understanding the impact of COVID-19 on the logistic industry is of central importance.

In this chapter, we investigate how COVID-19 impacts the logistic industry in India and the effect of the lockdown. The examination was done by including the interviews with the industry leader in the logistic industry to see how they have sustained crisis and gained new market share. This chapter will provide the growth rate in the lockdown period of different logistic service providers starting with the background of the logistics industry. They follow the logistic industry's transformational journey, key growth drivers, and future growth opportunities. A small case study is prepared on one of the leading logistic service providers in India.

The chapter is provided in ten sections. Section 12.1 talks about global COVID-19 situation. Section 12.2 briefly discusses the literature review available to date. Section 3 discusses research methodology. Sections 12.4, 12.5, and 12.6 talk about the effect of a pandemic on the Indian logistic sector. Section 12.7 discusses the key drivers of the logistic industry in India. Section 12.8 displays the case study undertaken during the study, and Sects. 12.9 and 12.10 state the managerial implication and concluding remarks.

12.2 Literature Review

This section highlights the major article on the impact of COVID-19 on the logistic industry of the world. Loske (2020) studied the impact of COVID-19 on German food retail logistics. The study highlights that the increase of freight volume of the dry product in retail logistic does not depend on the duration of the COVID 19 pandemic, but it depends upon the new infection per day. It indicates that transport volume does not depend on the duration of the COVID-19 pandemic but the individual strength.

Lina Guo (2020) has discussed modelling the demand for financial support for the logistics industry under the financial crisis. She stated that the company needs to continuously innovate its internal operating mechanism by reducing the inventory and material pressure. It will speed up the company's capital turnover and reduce the cost of capital occupied, thereby improving the company's fund financial management level to enhance market competitiveness.

Rastogi and Jean-Francois (2020) stated how a collaborative effort between government and logistic industry could help address the immediate crisis and draw out the sector's economic resilience path. Various policies increased e-services at ports, and green express lanes for truckers to be adopted. Border control and inspections should be streamlined and harmonized based on international standards.

Chakira et al. (2020) has done this research to solve decision-making problems encountered in information systems for supply chains in a crisis. The paper finds mathematical models, and inter-agent cooperation protocols, to minimize the risk of stock shortage in any supply chain area.

Agrawal et al. (2020) have discussed the effect of COVID-19 on India's economy and supply chains. They have found a total of 18 critical barriers that affected the supply chains in India. It expected that this study would be helpful for researchers to develop conceptual models to overcome this issue.

Zhu et al. (2020) have explored the connection between shortage and supply chain issues, such as the lack of supply chain transparency and resilience as unsustainable just-in-time manufacturing. Recommendations include nationalizing the medical supply chains, adopting a plus one diversification approach, and increasing safety stock given to mitigate the ongoing crisis's current consequences.

Singh et al. (2020) identified a simulation model of the public distribution system (PDS) developed in three scenarios to demonstrate the disruptions in the food supply chain to match the varying demand.

Liu et al. (2020) identified the reasons behind the gradual alleviation of the COVID-19 outbreak in China, and they observed factors that had impacted China's logistics industry within the pandemic period and when the pandemic sustained.

12.3 Research Methodology

To gain a better insight into the Indian logistic industry's problems during the COVID-19 crisis and how an entrepreneur can thrive in challenging times, we did primary and secondary research. The authors did secondary research for calculating the impact of lockdown on the supply chain industry. Trade figures were taken from the government database to see the trend in the supply chain industry. Interviews of many industry leaders available on the internet were analysed to see the impact of the crisis and the logistic sector's future. Primary research involves an interview of the co-founder of a Mumbai-based logistic company Seashell Logistics Pvt. Ltd. as they have a presence in 26 cities in India and two offices international. It will help us get a broader perspective and know the strategies they adopted to thrive in crisis times.

12.4 Background

Effect of the Pandemic on Indian Logistics

The Government of India and state governments have forced lockdown in the nation as a fearless measure to control the expected calamity. However, still, the economy needs to follow through on its cost. Logistics being a key area of India's Government will undoubtedly endure the financial emergency's results. Also, given its essential nature of managing transport, this area is relied upon to confront the extreme effect of states and international borders' lockdown.

The supply chain depends on labour, and it is the foundation of the logistics and shipping industry, and the unavailability of the same has brought the whole supply chain to a halt. The orders in the factories are pending; warehouses were also shut-in prompt. Lockdown has made a severe drop in business, which has additionally affected finance flow to this industry. The road transporters can't get the goods from the production units to the ports. The import shipments containers from different countries remain at the ports incurring daily rents and warehouse charges.

India's overall exports (Merchandise and Services consolidated) in April–September 2020–2021 are assessed to be USD 221.86 billion, showing a development of -16.66% over a similar period a year ago. Overall imports in April–September 2020–2021 are assessed to be USD 204.12 billion, displaying a development of -35.43% over a similar period a year ago.

Road Transport

According to the All-India Motor Transport Congress (AIMTC), trucks' daily movement has decreased to less than 10% of normal levels. According to the Ministry of Road Transport and Highways, road transport accounts for about 60% of freight traffic in India. The most grounded effect of COVID-19 has been seen on the second or third day of the lockdown when trucks' movement fell by 90–95%. The little movement saw was essential goods that had not gone under the domain of limitations forced because of the lockdown. There is a scarcity of human resources to drive a truck. The movement was strictly restricted, and they could not access food or shelter. The driver stopped the loaded truck on the road and highways aside. Many drivers left for their hometowns for personal safety. As a line, 30 million people are directly employed by the truck industry. More than 150 million people indirectly rely on this industry for their bread and butter, including roadside food stalls and mechanics.

The market share of rail rose forcefully over the five months finished June 2020 to around 25% (ordinary it is about 15%) because of the shortage of transporters. In any case, e-way bill collection and diesel utilization have just recovered to about 5% of their ordinary levels, showing that rail may have already conceded its market share.

Shipping Industry

World Trade Organization has anticipated the world trade to fall by up to 32% this year. CRISIL has cut the GDP development forecast for India for the 2021 fiscal to 3.5% from the last 5.2%. However, shipping and logistics are a lifesaver to worldwide consumers. According to orders from the Ministry of Shipping, Government of India, the port area has been announced only essential services, for keeping up of flexible link within the country.

There are some significant concerns concerning Indian shipping organizations' general income in the principal quarter of 2020. There has been a straight drop in the dry cargo load movements since the third week of January 2020. Indian port administrators encounter a drop-in payload volume, and nobody is sure about turnaround time. Cargo movements at ports saw a sharp drop of around 60% over the weeks due to a tremendous fall in the nation's productions. Ports across India are working at limits under 30%. The Central move to waive demurrage charges during the lockdown is a disincentive for merchants to sort out approaches to move the stagnated cargo. Unexpected declines in trade and production harm businesses and households. Aspects of International Trade Governments can find domestic production measures and reduce the country's ratio to the country. China has the most extensive foreign trade with India and is a significant market for many Indian products such as seafood, jewellery, and petrochemicals. According to UNCTAD, the impact on India's business is expected to be approximately 34,348 million. India has become one of the 15 most-affected economies, disrupting the entire world trading system due to China's declining production.

In the mid of the pandemic, there was also a shortage of labour, hence cargo cannot be emptied from vessels, and products can't be moved from ports to town because of deficiency of trucks. The CBIC (Central Board of Indirect Taxes and Customs) has given an order for nonstop custom clearance at ports. However, shipping lines have anchored their vessels, and the scarcity of containers arose.

Exports Recorded Negative Growth

Essential and significant commodities recorded negative development growth in September 2020 opposite September 2019 (see Table 12.1).

Imports

Imports in September 2020 as seen in Table 2 were $30.31 billion, which is a decrease of 19.60% over imports of $37.69 billion in September 2019.

Table 12.2 Significant commodities of import showing negative growth in September 2020 over the comparing month of last year

Table 12.1 Decline in exports of significant commodities (September 2020 vis-à-vis September 2019)

Particulars	Percentage (%)
Cashew	-44.25
Gems & jewellery	-24.67
Man-made yarn/fabs/made-ups	-9.12
Mica, coal and different metals, including minerals	-6.71
Marine items	-5.41
Leather	-3.36
Tea	-2.27
Fruits and Vegetables	-1.44

Source: Trade figures (2020), Ministry of Commerce and Industry

Table 12.2 Decline in Imports of significant commodities (September 2020 vis-à-vis September 2019)

Particulars	Percentage (%)
Transport equipment	-47.08
Machinery, electrical and non-electrical	-36.76
Petroleum, crude products	-35.88
Pearls, precious and semi-precious stones	-4.89
Organic and inorganic chemicals	-2.48

Source: Trade figures (2020), Ministry of Commerce and Industry

Logistics Service Providers

Logistics service providers (LSPs) are organizations, frequently going about as intermediaries, that embrace the execution of logistic-related work that has been generally kept in-house, additionally offering for the spread of precise and ideal data among flexibly chain accomplices. The most widely recognized sorts of LSPs are as follows:

- Transporters
- Third-Party Logistics Providers (3PLs)
- International Freight Forwarders (IFF) Non-vessel Owning Common Carrier (NVOCC)

Demand for global logistics services has grown dramatically and has become extraordinarily complex and dynamic as a result of a series of changes in manufacturing and industrial production. In response, the logistics industry changes in many ways, including integrated transportation service providers, outsourcing, and mergers to increase information technology use. This is an overview of developments and the most critical trends in the logistics service provider (LSP) industry.

The long-term economic and logistic trends generally form the progressions we have encountered in industrial production in the new economy. Markets have become more global, and organizations have outsourced. Out of the blue, these distribution models are changing the interest in transport methods, yet also offering administrations. Dispatchers are expanding the value on different properties.

Transportations refer to sea carriage, air/rail-shipments, and inland haulage. The services they typically give incorporate inbound and outbound transportation, entryway-to-entryway transportation, contract conveyance, transport organization, documentation measures, and shipment planning.

A wide range of logistics industry consists of players like exporters and importers, medium- and large-scale traders to MNCs. Traders with small shipments need to see how they can fit into the supply chain. It is essential to identify the target departments for which logistics solutions are designed. There is a clear gap in the capacity of LSPs to provide services throughout the supply chain. Expert expertise in the field is required to standardize processes, and soft issues such as skilled labour for logistics should be preferred. The contribution of the technically more agile, early-age contributors is significant.

There is a need to focus on more digital platforms in India that enable to take advantage of efficiency with transportation modes and between users and third-party service providers. Finally, logistics service providers need to evolve as a category of "logistics solution providers" and move beyond the status of "logistics service providers" to provide unified end-to-end solutions. To understand the potential of "end-to-end integrated logistics," they need to be trained to sell their service and provide the most efficient and personalized solutions, regardless of the merchant's shipment size.

12.5 On the Path of Transformation: Indian Logistics Industry

The presence of a robust logistics-related framework and a viable logistics framework encourages consistent development of merchandise from the point of origin to that of utilization. It helps an economy's growth to flourish. The logistics industry's advancement holds a tremendous incentive for the Indian economy also; as such promotion would expand exports, produce employment, and give the nation a considerable spot in the global supply chain.

Government Initiatives

The logistics policy proposed by the Government of India is a vital component of the COVID-19 recovery in the region. This policy aims to eliminate inefficiencies and reduce costs by removing barriers to the logistics value chain. Logistics costs associated with customs clearance and border customs clearance are expected to be reduced. The development of cold storage infrastructure and digital technology adoption will reduce the costs associated with warehousing operations. This policy is expected to streamline the trade and investment process in India and improve export competitiveness.

Collaborative efforts are underway to streamline domestic and import/export logistics' regulatory process in collaboration with central ministries and state governments. The Ministry of Commerce is developing an integrated logistics portal that acts as a transactional electronic marketplace by connecting buyers, logistics service providers, and relevant government agencies such as customs, community port systems, port terminals, shipping lines, and railways,. When it works, it reduces delays, promotes a transparent, informative, and convenient trading system. The ministry recently launched a new Logistics Facility Index to rank states for the support they provide to improve their logistics infrastructure within their respective jurisdictions.

Business convenience in trade is a crucial factor in simplifying procedures and reducing business barriers. In India, the Central Board of Indirect Taxes and Customs (CBIC) is at the forefront of the business to promote economic development through business transparency, harmony, flexibility, and automation. The idea was to save time and money in the export and import community. This will help them to be more competitive in the international arena. In recent years, India has demonstrated significant improvements in several independent global indicators that assess cross-border ecosystems' efficiency. It includes the World Bank's Logistics Performance Index and Business Evaluation (cross-border trading index) and the United Nations Global Survey on Digital and Sustainable Trade Facility.

The Indian Customs EDI System (ICES) and the Indian Customs Electronic Gateway (ICEGT) are now synonymous with the journey of the digital evolution of Indian customs, so the department is at the forefront of e-governance initiatives in the country. Recently, the opportunities offered by technologies for trade facilitation have expanded rapidly.

The combination of technology applications with modern trust-based processes has led to the realization that trade facilitation can be significantly improved without compromising national interests (including economic, social, and environmental). Furthermore, the recent uncertainty of COVID-19 has led to a move to a "new normal" based on the widespread use of technology.

One of the critical factors for the logistics industry recovery from COVID-19 is the logistics policy proposed by Indian government. The roadmap aims to eliminate inefficiencies and reduce costs by removing barriers in the logistic value chain. The logistics costs associated with customs and border clearing are expected to decrease. The expansion of cold store infrastructures and the introduction of digital technologies will reduce the costs associated with warehouse operations. Politicians are expected to streamline trade and investment processes in India, which will improve export competitiveness. "The combination of technology applications with modern trust-based processes has led to the realization that trade facilitation can be significantly improved without compromising national interests (including economic, social, and environmental). Furthermore, the recent uncertainty of COVID-19 has led to a move to a "new normal" based on the widespread use of technology.

One of the critical factors for the logistics industry recovery from COVID-19 is the logistics policy proposed by India's Government. The roadmap aims to eliminate inefficiencies and reduce costs by removing barriers in the logistic value chain. The logistics costs associated with customs and border clearing are expected to decrease. The expansion of cold store infrastructures and the introduction of digital technologies will reduce the costs associated with warehouse operations. "Politicians are expected to streamline trade and investment processes in India, which will improve export competitiveness."

Digitalization and robotics are expected to transform the value chain with digital platform-based freight solutions, the logistics process should be automatized, and last mile delivery solutions clearly identified. The integration of technology enables interoperability by linking people, processes, and data without any physical movement. Reducing human interference at different levels of the supply chain is a game-changer in the event of an epidemic or similar crisis. For example, the fear of the COVID-19 virus transfers when multiple parties handle the same large documents. So, it has been made mandatory for Indian customs to use a one-stop-shop system to share export documentation.

The micro, small and medium enterprises (MSMEs) contribute to one-third of the total economy, and to promote it further, the government is introducing measures under the "Atmanirbhar Bharat" and

"Made in India" campaigns. It helps by engaging stake holders involved in delivering essential services, e-commerce players in B2B, and abandoned purchasing domains. RBI announced a moratorium on loans, suspended interest payments on working capital facilities, and flexible working capital financing. While these measures are promising for the logistics industry, there are still other initiatives that the government must take to help ill-health logistics industries such as MSME loan repayment, GST exemption, subsidy warehouse or inventory delay, or extended tenure. Facilities, measures to reduce the MSME workforce's impact, increase access to credit, and cut utility and social security payments.

Atmanirbhar Bharat ideally is India being self-reliant and exist in the world in terms of its technologies and processes. High priced items are currently related to the shipping industry, and there are many ship building items that can be manufactured indigeneously in India. Being confident that once they start their production, will be a great way to attract FDI in India and provide a helpful environment. Having worked closely with the government to formulate national logistics policies, the investors and private companies are willing to invest in shipping to create an ecosystem. Another area we can work on is India's railway system, which at present cannot handle a large number of cargoes for short durations. We can invite private players to invest here to establish a final mile connection. "The stakes are not very high and will significantly help India's logistics."

12.6 Invigorating Logistic Industry Post Pandemic

Future of India's Trade, Challenges and Opportunities in the Post Pandemic World

India's supply chains are about to undergo a massive transformation in the next few years as the impact of COVID-19 threatens our supply and demand frameworks. As we begin to address current supply-side issues, we see a decline in demand in some industries, causing chaos.

Organizations have to accept this new reality and incorporate some of the following ideas to improve supply chain resilience.

During this crisis, many companies operate timely supply chains with limited pipeline stock and cannot provide products when needed due to the whole logistics industry being blocked. Risk management and prevention will gain prominence in supply chains, where companies will begin to build more safety stock in their distribution pipelines. It adds more warehousing space to the network. This practice of developing many more robust contingency plans will now be taken more seriously.

To reduce the virus's spread, it would be desirable to reduce the number of touchpoints that the product traverses the entire supply chain, from manufacturing to processing to corporate and home gateways. Automation of handling systems such as palletizing, conveyor systems, robotics, unscrewed aerial vehicles, and drop boxes tends to accelerate. With a massive shift in the supply chain, the digital transformation of the industry is accelerating. Every aspect of the logistics process is reconsidered, redesigned, and digitized, from project to execution.

We are experiencing one of the most significant global external shocks; almost every aspect of supply chain management will change significantly. In our country's case, some long-term transformations are being accelerated, and a generation of incremental improvements may be overlooked. Logistics and supply chains will strive to become more resilient and dynamic in this new world order.

Indian Logistics Industry Evolves over the Next Few Years with Multi-Dimensional Changes

The logistics industry in India is changing rapidly. The interaction of infrastructure, technology, and new service providers determines whether the sector can help its customers reduce their logistics costs and provide adequate services. Government policy on taxation and regulation of service providers plays an essential role in this process. Coordination between different government agencies requires multiple ministries' approval, which has hampered multimodal transportation in India. There is a managerial focus on reducing cycle time to provide additional value to customers at the company level.

Contract logistics will now be more serious, as the country seeks suppliers who can offer automated and mechanical solutions rather than manual options. In the future, the department will develop state-of-the-art facilities, material handling equipment, and state-of-the-art technology for highly secure and secure premises. Health, safety, and security will be paramount, including fire extinguishers, hydrants, and automatic recovery systems.

Ground transport in India will also expand significantly by removing the barrier, and more national actors will develop in this space with a combination of MNCs and local forces. The industry will become more efficient with the development of transport infrastructure across the country (expansion of roads, rail links, barge operations, coastal shipping etc.).

As the customer focuses on the ease of doing business across India, the freight space will evolve, and services will increase from end to end. Customers value the same partner for the shipment, but now they have five or six touchpoints before shipping. Service providers can offer end-to-end solutions with end-to-end visibility.

The Indian 3PL market is expected to grow by more than 11.5% during the forecast period of 2020–2025. The logistic industry market is expected to grow due to growth in manufacturing, FMCG, retail, and e-commerce industries. Indian companies seek new logistics capabilities and end-to-end solutions from 3PL service providers to help them successfully manage their supply chain processes, reduce the cost of traditional logistics, and face more complex challenges. Key areas include roads, railways, warehouses, cold chains, coastal transports, container freight stations, and inland container depots (CFS/ICD). Infrastructure development, such as dedicated freight corridors, free trade warehouse zones, logistics parks, and container freight stations, is expected to improve the Indian third-party logistics market's efficiency. The Indian logistics industry has a relatively high cost associated with transportation and storage. A significant proportion of the price can be attributed to the lack of efficient intermodal and multimodal transport systems due to the road's low infrastructure features, which are affected by any commercial vehicle and reduce the maximum distance on highways. Furthermore, higher warehouse costs are driven in India due to lack of warehouse capacity, standardization of warehouses in terms of IT application, and so forth.

12.7 Key Drivers for the Logistics Industry in India

People are already relying on e-commerce for their needs, and by 2020, the logistics industry will have a large online shopping market. The entry of several MNCs into the country's FMCG sector creates new growth opportunities for the Indian logistics industry. The development of these unique and promising sectors directly impacts inventory management's growth in India's logistics industry and the potential warehouse solutions for retail. Many companies of different industries rely heavily on the Indian logistics industry to help them meet their customer base's individual needs.

The warehouse system plays a vital role in the manufacturing industry in global buying and selling and distribution system. Improving existing technology by investing in recent research and development using indigenous and domestic technologies will boost the economy by forcing other industries such as tech to perform better. Constant changes and upgrades in the logistics companies' operation system will benefit consumers as it creates a healthy competitive environment while providing the best services.

Thoughts to improve India's logistics industry are currently focused on reducing logistics costs for consumers while providing first-class services on a budget. That is the challenge facing the Indian logistics industry. Increasing availability encourages corporations to invest heavily in logistics services through bargaining or outsourcing. Lack of proper storage and warehousing training is also found in the logistics industry. By establishing such training and development centres, the industry can create trained professionals dedicated to the logistics industry rather than employing a semi-skilled or skilled workforce.

Technology usage in the logistics industry illustrates the burden of operation and various system progress. Technologies such as artificial intelligence and machine learning aim to lay the groundwork for traditional logistics operations in the country. It may take some time, but it shows results that can be expected to be more productive than other methods when streamlining India's logistics industry. We are looking forward to big things when these latest technologies replace bug-prone systems. The economic backbone is healthy and, in turn, strengthens other sectors of the industry. While many may argue that it is costly to embrace this technological advancement, the logistics industry can integrate organizations before the current and future technology gap widens. It will be a maximum profit. This will backfire in your attempts to cut costs and increase them at least three times. Integrating such technology requires upfront investments such as installation, testing, and staff training in these programmes. Once fully configured, companies will enter a new world of streamlined processes that older technologies can never compete with. The technology will give the logistics industries a place to work with larger clients through powerful management tools.

Looking at the bigger picture, globally, logistics as an Indian industry has come a long way and is expected to see a significant increase in global platforms' operations. International companies and corporations will join the various Indian logistics companies to build a win-win relationship by reducing their logistics costs, increasing transportation capacity for customers, and generating much-needed revenue to make the logistics industry the largest. In the future, we can expect high demand for specialized operations for logistics and delivery from clients in all sectors. Whether it is technology spare parts, car equipment, or food delivery, they will focus on the efficiency of the logistics industry optimized to meet all industries' transportation, warehousing, and delivery requirements. The progress of e-commerce will soon reach new highs, resulting in more opportunities for the logistics industry to make a mark on classy express delivery and get clock services, in addition to the company's in-house logistics system.

12.8 Case Study

Rajesh Gujjarlapudi, the founder and director of Seashell Logistics Pvt Ltd, through his continuous Innovation, the relentless pursuit for excellence, efficiency, foresight, un-matched execution capabilities, and entrepreneurial spirit has been able to not only survive in the industry but gain some new opportunities. Seashell Group is a leading SINGLE WINDOW service provider in offering integrated and turnkey services in shipping, logistics, supply chain management, engineering projects, consultancy for DGFT/customs (own customs licence)/Central Excise/other Indirect Taxation matters and International Trade. Mr Rajesh shared his journey through this pandemic.

Challenges Faced During the Pandemic

The government announcement of lockdown was sudden and extremely useful in the sense that it stopped everything. All sectors were affected during the pandemic initially. The government slowly allowed essential services that included shipping and transport, but there was confusion among state government agencies on coordinating. It took time for the government to smooth out issues. All the essential services like medical, FMCG, and banking were able to operate in a week. For export/import services it took a month to normalize. In export/import, they have to deal with many government authorities. The government offices were allowed to open for a limited time every day, which created many operations problems. It was something that was beyond their control, so they kept their client regularly updated on this. Transportation between states was a significant problem. Every state had its set of rules and containment zones because transportation got halted, and it stopped exports and imports for a few days. Another factor was the unavailability of drivers who went to their native states. They faced a shortage of workforce in transportation for a month, and then they brought their drivers back from their hometown in a phased manner, following all the safety measures. There was a shortage of labour in Container Freight Stations (CFS), and it took two months to normalize.

Response to the Crisis

The management of the Seashell Group anticipated this move by the government and was ready with all possible solutions to minimize the impact on their work. Export and Import services were given essential services category and were allowed to open office with bare minimum staff. All the directions regarding lockdown were instated by the Central government and were applied by the respective state government. They have to talk to local authorities for passes for their key employees to run their operation smoothly. Confusion among leaders made it very difficult to take permission initially and slowly it improved.

Communication Is the Key

While handling clients, they made sure that there is no communication gap. They keep updating their client regarding government authorities' decisions so that their shipment would not get stuck. It was not allowed to go outside in a pandemic, so there was no question of meeting clients. One of the important things to provide the services to their customer is to be online and communicate through the mail. They emphasized tele-calling and regularly checked if their client needs urgent assistance.

Employee Safety and Work Continuation

Apart from this, the management made sure that people must avoid coming to the office unless necessary. It is the best way to ensure the safety of their employees. If anybody was coming to the office, they had to follow all the safety protocols like wearing a face mask and using sanitizers regularly. COVID-19 insurance was provided to all of their employees and their families. To ensure smooth operations, they provided their employees with a laptop and arranged for an internet connection to work from home. In some cases, they have to offer other facilities like printers/scanners at their home. They were keeping in mind a good work culture; they haven't lay off employees during this period. They have started hiring new employees after the anticipation of profitable business in the future and the availability of the right talent post-pandemic.

Opportunities in the Crisis

This pandemic has brought many challenges as well as opportunities. Companies that were prepared and well organized were able to increase their market share because others could not operate and provide services. Seashell Group was able to increase its revenue despite the pandemic. Their salespeople kept their effort all the time. This pandemic provided them with the opportunity to convert some clients whose service providers could not do work properly.

Financial Planning

Financially prudent companies survived the pandemic, others went bankrupt. In the logistic industry, credit is a significant issue. They do provide credit to their clients, but all service providers start asking for advance payment during the lockdown. They were sure that they would not do business with a client who seems risky during this period. They profiled all the customers and found risky ones and decided to either do business with them or ask for the advance payment. Moreover, they have provided an extended credit facility to their esteemed clients for their previous debts.

Changes in the Work Culture

One significant change that happened during this pandemic in all organizations is the validation of work from home culture. Seashell Logistics' management has tested this concept successfully and has made sure to include this in their HR policies. They further stated that they might see this as a permanent change in their working culture.

12.9 Managerial Implications of the Research

This is the first of its kind detailed analysis of the Indian logistic Industry. In this chapter, the authors provide a perspective on the critical challenges through secondary research using information available in the public domain and describe some exciting initiatives that some firms and industries are taking to compete through excellence in managing their logistics during the COVID-19 pandemic. The authors have provided a case study that will help academia and corporate organizations gain insight into what steps can be taken to thrive the time of crisis and how entrepreneurial spirit helps find opportunity in crisis. A detailed analysis was provided of the government's actions and how collaborative efforts between the logistic industry and government can lead to stability and recovering the losses faced by the industry during this challenging time. It will also help corporates and the government analyse the gap and plan accordingly so that India's logistic industry can be reinvigorated.

12.10 Conclusion

In the present study, the effect of COVID-19 on India's economy, logistic industry, and supply chain has been analysed. This study also suggests a road to a overcome and impact. COVID-19 is affecting our supply chains and manufacturing operations daily. The peak of the COVID-19 virus has impacted the global logistic industry and supply chain and forced thousands of companies to throttle down or shut down their operations in the U.S and Europe and now in developing nations like India.

However, this change may still be nipped in the bud if the government makes an effort and its associated regulatory mechanism to provide an enabling environment to facilitate a paradigm shift in how the logistics industry can grow unfettered. It is well recognized that the government is making improvements to correct the infrastructure deficit—whether it is in physical transport, warehousing, and port terminal infrastructure. However, while physical capacity creation is being facilitated slowly, other changes must be made along with the capacity creation drive to realize the full impact of such changes. Given the bigger picture, globally, Indian logistics has come a long way as an industry and is expected to maintain significant performance improvements on the global platform. Businesses and international corporations that partner with various Indian logistics companies will build mutually beneficial relationships while reducing their logistics costs, increasing consumer transportation capabilities. It will lead to increased income in terms of revenue to the country's largest industry. In the future, we can expect specialized logistics and delivery operations to be in high demand by customers from all walks of life. Whether it is technical spare parts, automotive equipment, or the whole trade, everyone will soon rely on a formal logistics industry's performance to meet all transportation, warehousing, and delivery needs.

In this chapter, the authors provide an overview of these issues and use secondary information to outline some of the significant challenges in India's logistics industry affected by the COVID-19 pandemic. Also outlined are some exciting initiatives that the government, logistic service providers, and other authorized authorities supporting this industry have taken to transform India's logistic industry.

References

Agrawal, S., Jamwal, A., & Gupta, S. (2020). Effect of COVID-19 on the Indian economy and supply chain. *Preprint, 2020*, 2020050148. https://doi.org/10.20944/preprints202005.0148.v1

Chakira, I., Khailia, M. E., & Mestaria, M. (2020). Logistics flow optimization for advanced management of the crisis situation. *Procedia Computer Science, 175*, 419–426.

Guo, L. (2020). Modelling the demand for financial support for the development of port logistics industry under the financial crisis. *Journal of Coastal Research, 103*, 605–608.

Ivanov. (2020). Predicting the impacts of epidemic outbreaks on global supply chains: A simulation-based analysis on the coronavirus outbreak (COVID-19/SARS-CoV-2) case. *Transportation Research Part E-Logistics & Transportation Review, 136*, 101922. https://doi.org/10.1016/j.tre.2020.101922

Liu, W., Liang, Y., Qin, X. B., & Lim, M. K. (2020). China's logistics development trends in the post COVID-19 era. *International Journal of Logistics Research and Management*. https://doi.org/10.1080/13675567.2020.1837760

Loske, D. (2020). The impact of COVID-19 on transport volume and freight capacity dynamics: An empirical analysis in German food retail logistics. *Transportation Research Interdisciplinary Perspectives, 6*, 100165.

Lu, H., Stratton, C. W., & Tang, Y. W. (2020). Outbreak of Pneumonia of unknown etiology in Wuhan China: The mystery and the miracle. *Journal of Medical Virology*.

Phan, L. T., Nguyen, T. V., Luong, Q. C., Nguyen, T. V., Nguyen, H. T., Le, H. Q., … Pham, Q. D. (2020). Importation and human-to-human transmission of a novel coronavirus in Vietnam. *New England Journal of Medicine, 382*(9), 872–874.

Rastogi, C., & Jean-Francois, A. (2020). Logistics and freight services: Policies to facilitate trade. In *Trade and COVID-19 guidance note*. World Bank.

Shen, M., Peng, Z., Guo, Y., Xiao, Y., & Zhang, L. (2020). Lockdown may partially halt the spread of 2019 novel coronavirus in Hubei province, China. medRxiv.

Singh, S., Kumar, R., Panchal, R., & Tiwari, R. K. (2020). Impact of COVID-19 on logistics systems and disruptions in food supply chain. *International Journal of Production Research, 2020*, 1–16. https://doi.org/10.1080/00207543.2020.1792000

Yu, H., Sun, X., Solvang, W. D., & Zhao, X. (2020). Reverse logistics network design for effective management of medical waste in epidemic outbreaks: Insights from the coronavirus disease 2019 (COVID-19) outbreak in Wuhan (China). *International Journal of Environmental Research and Public Health, 17*(5), 1770.

Zhu, G., Chou, M. C., & Tsai, C. W. (2020). Lessons learned from the COVID-19 pandemic exposing the shortcomings of current supply chain operations: A long-term prescriptive offering. *Sustainability, 12*(14), 5858.

Index

D. Vrontis et al. (eds.), *Business Under Crisis Volume I*, Palgrave Studies in Cross-disciplinary Business Research, In Association with EuroMed Academy of Business, https://doi.org/10.1007/978-3-030-76567-5

The manufacturer's authorised representative in the EU is Springer Nature Customer Service Centre GmbH, Europaplatz 3, 69115 Heidelberg, Germany. If you have any concerns regarding our products, please contact ProductSafety@springernature.com

Printed and bound by CPI Group (UK) Ltd, Croydon, CR0 4YY

22/09/2026

02221054-0014